HANDLING OF CRIMINAL PROCEEDINGS

Before Trial Begins

Walter Mahlangu

LLB, LLM [UP]

Senior State Advocate

Advocate of the High Court of South Africa

⸻ ★ ⸻

This publication was subjected to an independent double-blind peer evaluation by UCTPress.

DEDICATION

It is written for legal practitioners who refuse complacency before trial—who understand that preparation is not routine, but responsibility; that every affidavit, every decision, and even every silence leaves a psychological and human imprint; and that justice is never accidental, but shaped through conscious and ethical choice.

It is dedicated to all officers of the court who choose discipline over haste, courage over convenience, and humanity over indifference; who enter the courtroom not merely to process files, but to protect dignity, restore balance, and recognise the lives behind the case numbers.

Ultimately, this work is for all who believe that the courtroom must be more than a place of procedure—it must be a space where justice is deliberately, consciously, and courageously made real.

ACKNOWLEDGEMENTS

"If you want to go fast, go alone. If you want to go far, go together." — African Proverb.

This work is the product of many hands, open hearts, and guiding minds.

I am deeply grateful to the blind reviewers for their constructive criticism and thoughtful insights, which helped shape this manuscript into a more rigorous and meaningful contribution.

To my family: you have been the ground beneath my feet and the wind at my back. To my beloved wife and friend, Mahlatse Magoro, and to our children, Botlhale, Nasisipho, and Ntombizandile—your patience, love, and unwavering faith in me have been my greatest treasures.

To my departed best friend, Advocate H. J. Mthimunye—the first person to whom I entrusted this vision—your words of encouragement continue to echo in my heart. Though you are no longer here to witness its completion, your influence is woven into these pages. May your soul rest in peace.

Above all, I give thanks to the Creator and to my ancestors, whose guidance, sustenance, and grace have carried me through every step of this journey.

Borrowing from the motto of my alma mater:

Ad Destinatum Persequor — With zeal and perseverance, I strive toward the goal.

Asante sana (Thank you very much).

Pretoria
January 2026

PREFACE

There is little margin for inadequate preparation in criminal court. Even the most inexperienced legal practitioner is expected to perform competently. Experience is acquired through representation, and, in that process, mistakes may occur. The critical objective for every new legal practitioner is to minimise such mistakes and avoid repeating them. Criminal practice is seldom as straightforward as new practitioners might anticipate; it often requires learning through careful reflection and adjustment.

Competent legal representation plays a vital role in the administration of criminal justice. A failure to consider effective pre-trial strategies may result in a client being denied bail, attending court repeatedly without the matter proceeding to trial, or even being convicted and acquiring a criminal record, notwithstanding that diversion or mediation may have constituted a more appropriate resolution.

This book offers practical guidance on addressing various challenges encountered during criminal pre-trial processes. It explains not only the applicable procedures but also how to implement them in a structured and methodical manner. Full citations, including specific paragraph references, appear on each page, even where the source was cited earlier, in order to assist practitioners in locating authority efficiently and resolving pressing issues without delay. Most of the cases referred to in this book are available on SAFLII and Lawlibrary, making them readily accessible through electronic devices.

The purpose of this work is to bridge the gap between an academic understanding of criminal procedure and its practical application before trial. It seeks to reduce uncertainty regarding the steps that new legal practitioners should take in pursuing appropriate pre-trial remedies for their clients. Legal practitioners bear a professional responsibility to advance well-founded and persuasive arguments that assist the court in reaching carefully considered decisions. This book addresses pre-trial procedures under both the Criminal Procedure Act and the Child Justice Act.

I hope that this publication will prove useful in addressing the day-to-day challenges encountered in criminal practice.

Asante Sana (Thank you very much)

Walter Mahlangu
Pretoria
January 2026

TABLE OF CONTENTS

PART 1:

PROCEDURES AFFECTING AN ADULT CLIENT BEFORE THE TRIAL BEGINS

CHAPTER 1:

VISITING THE ARRESTED CLIENT AT THE POLICE STATION

1.1 Preparing to visit the detained client

In criminal practice, a client or a member of the client's family approaches you because the client is in difficulty with the law. Typically, this occurs because:

1. the client has been arrested;
2. the client has received a summons or a written notice to appear in court; or
3. the client has committed, or is suspected of having committed, an offence.

In most cases, clients seek legal assistance only when faced with an immediate difficulty. While a client remains in police custody, they may observe other detainees being called to consult with their legal representatives and released thereafter. It is therefore common for a detained client to expect a similar outcome when you visit them.

The mechanisms available for securing the prompt release of an adult arrested client prior to first appearance are provided for in the Criminal Procedure Act 51 of 1977 (CPA), namely:

1. a written notice to appear in court;
2. police bail;
3. police warning; and
4. prosecutor's bail.

An understanding of Section 56 of the CPA, which provides for release on written notice; Section 59, read with Part II and Part III of Schedule 2, which governs police bail; Section 72, read with Part II and Part III of Schedule 2, which regulates police warnings; and Section 59A, read with Schedule 7, which governs prosecutor's bail, is essential. Collectively, these provisions establish the four mechanisms by which an arrested client may be released before first appearance.

Attending the police station without first determining whether the client qualifies for any available method of release is professionally ill-advised. You should therefore ensure that you are fully familiar with the applicable procedural steps required to secure release. Where possible, obtain accurate information regarding the charge, together with the client's details and the identity of the police station where the client is detained.

Information conveyed telephonically by a layperson is not always sufficiently precise to determine the exact nature of the charge. However, reference to serious offences such as murder, rape, or armed robbery will generally indicate that release before court appearance is unlikely. In such circumstances, priority should be given to expediting the client's appearance in court while simultaneously gathering all relevant information to ensure readiness for a bail hearing at the first appearance.

The discussion of the circumstances under which a client may qualify for release before first appearance continues in Chapter 2.

1.2 Consultation with the client

Once you arrive at the police station, proceed to the charge office and request to consult with the client. You must be able to establish that you are a qualified legal practitioner. The criminal justice system has encountered instances of bogus legal representatives,[1] and verification of professional status serves to protect detainees from unauthorised access. Your identification should therefore always be readily available.

Although a written brief is not a prerequisite for consulting with a client at a police station, it is prudent to carry one where available. Ensure that the client's full particulars—such as names, charges, and addresses—are accurately recorded. Confidence and preparedness are essential; uncertainty regarding your client's details may unnecessarily complicate access.

Experience shows that, particularly in serious matters, a legal practitioner may be informed upon arrival that access to the client is denied on the instruction of the investigating officer because the client has not yet been formally charged. Under exceptional circumstances, National Instruction 13 of 2019 permits such a limitation.[2] However, like all subordinate legislation and

---

[1] https://www.kaya959.co.za/lineup/point-of-view/how-to-spot-bogus-legal-practitioners/ accessed 4 September 2024. https://www.iol.co.za/news/crime-and-courts/fake-lawyer-who-represented-murder-accused-back-in-court-b18a3796-7569-40ee-b4ce-42e22d5d2697 accessed 04 September 2024.

[2] National Instruction 13 of 2019: Management of Persons in Custody of the South African Police Service para 21(3). Even though this national instruction does not explicitly state so,

internal directives, it is subject to the Constitution and must be applied strictly within its terms.[3]

Legal practitioners often focus primarily on conventional sources of law and may overlook police standing orders or national instructions. Yet these instruments can materially affect access to detained clients. Section 25 of the South African Police Service Act 68 of 1995 empowers the National Commissioner to issue national instructions and standing orders to maintain uniform standards of policing. These instruments are binding on police officials.[4]

National Instruction 13 of 2019 is therefore significant. It permits an investigating officer to apply to the station commander, or acting station commander, for a temporary limitation of access.[5] The authority to decide such an application cannot be delegated.[6] The investigating officer must submit an affidavit setting out reasonable grounds for believing that communication between the accused and a specific legal practitioner would not be in the interests of justice.[7] Such an application may only be made before the accused has been formally charged.[8] An investigating officer may seek to justify that the interests of justice do not permit communication where contact with the specific legal practitioner may:[9]

1. lead to interference with evidence connected with a serious offence or may lead to physical injury to other persons;
2. alert other persons who are suspected to have committed the same offence but are not yet arrested; or
3. obstruct the recovery of property connected to such an offence.

If the station commander is satisfied that it is in the interests of justice not to permit a specific legal practitioner to consult with the detained person, they may, after consulting the legal administrative officer attached to the police

---

it appears to have replaced the Standing Order (G) 361 *Handling of Persons in the Custody of the Service from Arrival at the Police Station*, see written reply to question 1202 of the Minister of Police to Ms Z Majola in the National Assembly dated 07 May 2021, where the minister did not include this standing order as a directive on treatment of detainees by SAPS https://parliament.gov.za/storage/app/media/Docs/exe_rq_na/7c59bfe5-1554-495d-bd6f-dde7d6de26c2.pdf accessed 21 August 2024. Also, see the comment on the October 2019 *African Policing Civilian Oversight Forum Research Paper,* p3, about this national instruction replacing Standing Order (G) 361 https://apcof.org/wp-content/uploads/026-risksofpolicecustody-thepotentialforindependentmonitoringofpolicecustodyinsouthafrica-davidbruce.pdf accessed on 21 July 2024.

[3] Section 35(2) (b) of the Constitution of the Republic of South Africa, 1996 [the Constitution] guarantees the right for every detained person to choose and consult with a legal practitioner of his or her choice and be informed about this right.

[4] Section 25(2) of the South African Police Service Act 68 of 1995.

[5] National Instruction 13 of 2019: Management of Persons in Custody of the South African Police Service para 21(3) (d)

[6] National Instruction 13 of 2019 [*supra*] para 21 (3) (d) (v)

[7] National Instruction 13 of 2019 [*supra*] para 21 (3) (d) (i).

[8] National Instruction 13 of 2019 [*supra*] para 21 (3) (b) (i)

[9] National Instruction 13 of 2019 [*supra*] para 21 (3) (c)

service, issue a written notice in duplicate. The notice must specify the period of prohibition, which may not exceed 12 hours, as well as the reasons for its issuance.[10]

The original must be retained in the 'B' section of the docket,[11] and a copy must be provided to the detained person.[12] Even where such notice has been issued, consultation may still be permitted under specific conditions.[13] The prohibition applies only to the particular legal representative named in the notice.[14] The accused must therefore be allowed to consult with a different legal practitioner.

Where the national instruction does not apply, or once access to the client is secured, begin by greeting the client and explaining the purpose of your visit. It is then important to request the "Notice of Rights" (SAPS 14A). Every detained client should have been issued with SAPS 14A.[15] This document reflects the offence allegedly committed, the date and time of arrest, the Crime Administration System (CAS) number, and the particulars of the arresting officer. Occasionally, the CAS number may not appear on SAPS 14A. This is not necessarily problematic, as it will be recorded in the admission registers, namely the Cell Register (SAPS 14) or the Occurrence Book (SAPS 10).[16] The custody commander—or, at stations without a designated custody commander, the Community Service Centre commander—can assist in obtaining the CAS number.

Once you have established the precise nature of the offence, it is essential to hear the client's version. You should also enquire about previous convictions and pending matters, as these may affect eligibility for release prior to first appearance.

If the client has relevant previous convictions or pending matters involving Schedule 1, 5, or 6 offences, and is currently charged with a Schedule 1 offence, police or prosecutor's bail may not be competent. Release before first appearance is generally intended for less serious matters where the interests of justice clearly favour release.

Where the offence falls within Schedule 5 or Schedule 6, Section 60(11)(a) or Section 60(11)(b) of the CPA applies. In such instances, the applicable onus operates as prescribed by statute, and only the court may determine bail.[17]

---

[10] National Instruction 13 of 2019: Management of Persons in Custody of the South African Police Service para 21 (3) (d) (iii).

[11] To understand sections of the docket, see paragraph 14.1.2.

[12] National Instruction 13 of 2019[*supra*] para 21 (3) (d) (iv).

[13] National Instruction 13 of 2019 [supra] para 21(3)(e).

[14] Ibid.

[15] National Instruction 13 of 2019 [*supra*] para 18 read together with para 19(9).

[16] About police registers, see *Jozela v Minister of Police* (2011/05017) [2013] ZAGPJHC 272 (1 November 2013) para 12.

[17] To understand bail schedules, see paragraph 7.2. Schedules 1, 5, and 6 are discussed in paragraph 8.2-8.5.2.

Police or prosecutor's bail is not designed for contested matters requiring judicial evaluation of evidence and balancing of competing interests. In terms of Section 59A(5) (b), a magistrate retains the authority to review and refuse bail that was incorrectly granted by a prosecutor.

Previous convictions or pending matters can significantly affect the prospects of release prior to first appearance. However, expunged convictions or trivial offences that do not fall within Schedules 1, 5, or 6—such as public drinking or crimen injuria—should not ordinarily preclude release, as they do not alter the applicable bail schedule.[18] Where the accused qualifies for police or prosecutor's bail, it is important to identify the investigating officer responsible for the matter without delay. If no investigating officer has yet been assigned, arrangements should be made with the Client Service Centre commander to facilitate consideration of bail.

[18] Bail Schedules are discussed in paragraph 7.2.

CHAPTER 2

RELEASE OF THE ARRESTED CLIENT BEFORE FIRST APPEARANCE

2.1 Offences falling under the police bail or warning

The accused qualifies for police bail or warning for all offences, except any offence:[19]

1. listed in Part II and Part III of Schedule 2 of the CPA;
2. against a complainant who is in a *domestic relationship* with the accused, as defined in Section 1 of the Domestic Violence Act 116 of 1998;[20]
3. referred to in Section 17(1) (a) of the Domestic Violence Act 116 of 1998;[21]
4. referred to in Section 18(1) (a) of the Protection from Harassment Act 17 of 2011;[22] or

---

[19] For police bail, see Section 59(1) of the CPA, and for police warning, see Section 72(1) of the CPA. The Criminal and Related Matters Amendment Act 12 of 2021 has amended release on bail and warning and strictly prohibits the release of the accused by a police officer where the offence is committed against a complainant who is in a domestic relationship with the accused, or where the offence constitutes a contravention of an order of the court which protects the complainant in terms of the Domestic Violence Act 116 of 1998, the Protection from Harassment Act 17 of 2011, or any other law. See also *Van As v Additional Magistrate Cape Town and Others* (18052/2022) [2023] ZAWCHC 170; [2023] 4 All SA 231 (WCC) (24 July 2023) para 31.

[20] "Domestic relationship', as defined by the Domestic Violence Act 116 of 1998, means a relationship between the accused and the complainant in any of the following ways:
(a) they are married or were married to each other in terms of any law, custom, or religion;
(b) they are cohabiting;
(c) they are the parents of a child, or have or had parental responsibility for a child;
(d) they are related by consanguinity, affinity, or adoption;
(e) they are currently dating, are former intimate partners, or have or had a sexual relationship, irrespective of whether it was a one-night stand or a friends-with-benefits arrangement; or
(f) they are in a close relationship in that they share or have shared the same residence.
In establishing whether there was a close relationship between the accused and the complainant, the court will consider:
(i) the level of trust between them;
(ii) the level of dependence or commitment by one or both towards the other;
(iii) the period for which the relationship has existed;
(iv) how often they have contact with one another; or
(v) the level of intimacy between them.

[21] Contravention of any prohibition, condition, obligation, or order imposed by the court.

[22] Ibid.

5. that criminalises contravention of any prohibition, condition, obligation, or order issued by the court to protect the complainant.

Since offences qualifying for police bail or a warning are not listed in the CPA, the challenge lies in identifying which offences are not listed in Parts II and III of Schedule 2. Identifying what is absent can be more difficult than identifying what is present. Therefore, offences falling under police bail or warning are not only confusing to police officers but also, at times, to legal practitioners. The best way to approach this is to look at what is in Parts II and III of Schedule 2, while still bearing in mind what is in Schedule 7, which is also intended for outside-court bail, albeit by a prosecutor. To sum up, the guiding principles are that the offence should:

1. be less serious;
2. not be included in Part II and Part III of Schedule 2;
3. not be against the complainant who is in a domestic relationship with the accused;
4. not be an infringement of an order of the court which protects the complainant; and
5. not be included in Schedule 7, which deals with offences reserved for the prosecutor's bail.

Part II and Part III of Schedule 2 of the CPA contain the following offences:

Part II offences

1. Treason.
2. Sedition.
3. Murder.
4. Rape or compelled rape as contemplated in Sections 3 or 4 of the Criminal Law (Sexual Offences and Related Matters) Amendment Act 32 of 2007, respectively.
5. Any sexual offence against a child or a person who has a mental disability, as contemplated in Part 2 of Chapter 3 or the whole of Chapter 4 of the Criminal Law (Sexual Offences and Related Matters) Amendment Act 32 of 2007, respectively.
6. Section 4, 5, and 7 offences and involvement in these offences in terms of Section 10 of the Prevention and Combating of Trafficking in Persons Act 7 of 2013.
7. Robbery.
8. Assault GBH.
9. Arson.
10. Breaking or entering any premises, whether under the common law or a statutory provision, with the intent to commit an offence.
11. Theft, whether under the common law or a statutory provision, receiving stolen property knowing it to have been stolen, fraud, forgery or uttering a forged document knowing it to have been forged, in each case if the amount or value involved in the offence exceeds R2 500.00.
12. Any offence under any law relating to the illicit dealing in or possession of precious metals or precious stones.
13. Any offence relating to the coinage.
14. Offences referred to in Section 4(1) and (2) of the Prevention and Combating of Torture of Persons Act 13 of 2013.

15. Any conspiracy, incitement, or attempt to commit any offence referred to in this Part II.

Part III offences

1. Sedition.
2. Public violence.
3. Arson.
4. Murder.
5. Kidnapping.
6. Child-stealing.
7. Robbery.
8. Housebreaking, whether under the common law or a statutory provision, with intent to commit an offence.
9. Contravention of the provisions of Section 1 and 1A of the Intimidation Act 72 of 1982.
10. Offences referred to in Section 4(1) and (2) of the Prevention and Combating of Torture of Persons Act 13 of 2013.
11. Any conspiracy, incitement or attempt to commit any of the above-mentioned offences.
12. Treason.

If you are unable to determine whether the offence falls within police bail or prosecutor's bail, this is not necessarily decisive, as the client may still qualify for release outside of court. Your objective remains to secure the client's release before the first appearance by any legally permissible method. Nevertheless, uncertainty may persist despite careful analysis. For example, the offence of malicious injury to property is not listed in Part II or Part III of Schedule 2. By implication, it would ordinarily fall within the scope of police bail or warning.[23] However, it is expressly listed in Schedule 7, which governs a prosecutor's bail. It therefore qualifies as a prosecutor's bail offence.

The critical concern is to avoid situations where a client who qualifies for an outside-court method of release remains unnecessarily in custody.

Accordingly, it remains essential to identify which offences are specifically covered by police bail. A careful reading of Part II and Part III of Schedule 2, together with Schedule 7, demonstrates that certain offences are excluded from police bail—particularly those committed against a victim in a domestic

[23] *Mvu v Minister of Safety and Security and Another* (07/20296) [2009] ZAGPJHC 5; 2009 (2) SACR 291 (GSJ); 2009 (6) SA 82 (GSJ) (31 March 2009) para 13.

relationship with the accused, as well as offences constituting a contravention of a court order protecting that victim.
Having regard to these exclusions, the following offences generally qualify for police bail or police warning:[24]

1. *Crimen injuria.*
2. Perjury.
3. Bigamy.
4. Obstruction of police in their duties.
5. Assault common.
6. Theft, where the value is less than R2 500.00.
7. Possession of suspected stolen property, where the value is less than R2 500.00.
8. Receiving stolen property knowing that it is stolen, where the value is less than R2 500.00.
9. Forgery or uttering a forged document where the amount or value involved in the offence does not exceed R2 500.00.
10. Fraud, where the value is less than R2 500.00.
11. Driving without a valid driver's licence.
12. Reckless or negligent driving.[25]
13. Failure to stop after an accident.[26]
14. Driving under the influence of liquor.[27]
15. Conspiracy, incitement, or attempt to commit any of the mentioned offences.

2.2 Offences falling under the prosecutor's bail

The prosecutor's bail is governed by Section 59A of the CPA. The bail may be granted by an authorised prosecutor after consultation with the investigating officer, but only for the offences listed in Schedule 7 of the CPA. The prosecutor is strictly prohibited from releasing the accused where the offence is committed against the victim who is in a domestic relationship with the accused, or if the offence is a contravention of an order of the court which protects the victim in terms of the Domestic Violence Act 116 of 1998, or the Protection from Harassment Act 17 of 2011, or any other law.[28] In contrast to police bail offences, the offences that satisfy the criteria for prosecutor's bail are listed. These offences are further qualified by the National Prosecuting Authority (NPA) internal directives, which require prosecutors to release

[24] The list for matters falling under police bail is almost impossible to create because there are many common law and statutory crimes. This list is just a guide of offences that may qualify for police bail.

[25] *Flanagan v Minister of Safety and Security* (497/2017) [2018] ZASCA 96 (1 June 2018) para 1 read together with para 18.

[26] Ibid.

[27] Ibid.

[28] Section 59A(1) of the CPA as amended by the Criminal and Related Matters Amendment Act 12 of 2021. Also see *Van As v Additional Magistrate Cape Town and Others* (18052/2022) [2023] ZAWCHC 170; [2023] 4 All SA 231 (WCC) (24 July 2023) para 31.

detained accused only in less serious offences. Schedule 7 prosecutor's bail offences can be summarised as follows:

1. Public violence [where there is no serious damage to property or injury to persons, not taxi or gang related, and is unlikely to continue].
2. Culpable homicide [either caused by an assault or a motor vehicle, but it must not involve assault by a gang or a hit-and-run accident].
3. Assault GBH.[29]
4. Bestiality.
5. Arson [where there is no death or injury to a person and no gang is involved].
6. Housebreaking with intent to commit an offence [but no other offence must have been committed except for trespassing].
7. Malicious injury to property.
8. Common robbery, where the value of the item(s) does not exceed R20 000.00 [where no mugging or bag snatching at cashpoints, train stations, bus stations, or taxi ranks and where it is not an organised crime].
9. Theft, where the value of item(s) does not exceed R20 000.00.
10. Receiving stolen property, where the value of the item(s) does not exceed R20 000.00.
11. Possession of stolen property, where the value of the item(s) does not exceed R20 000.00.
12. Unauthorised appropriation of another person's property, in contravention of Section 1(1) of the General Law Amendment Act 50 of 1956, where the value of the item(s) does not exceed R20 000.00.
13. Fraud, where the value of the item(s) does not exceed R20 000.00.
14. Extortion, where the value of the item(s) does not exceed R20 000.00.
15. Forgery or uttering where the value of the item(s) involved does not exceed R20 000.00.
16. Unlawful possession of drugs, where no dealing is apparent.[30]

---

[29] Assault involving infliction of grievous bodily harm (GBH) has been broadened by Section 13 of the Criminal and Related Matters Amendment Act 12 of 2021 to include assault where a dangerous wound is inflicted or where the complainant is threatened with GBH or with a firearm or dangerous weapon. Therefore, all assaults with the intent to cause GBH fall under the prosecutor's bail.

[30] Please note that Schedule 5 is applicable. Therefore, a prosecutor's bail is not permissible for possession of drugs under the following circumstances:

(a) If the value is more than R50 000.00, or

(b) If the syndicate is involved and the value is more than R10 000.00, or

(c) If the arrested person is a law enforcement officer.

17. Conspiracy, incitement, or attempt to commit any of the offences mentioned above.

2.3 Negotiating for the police or prosecutor's bail

Bail is inherently urgent.[31] Legal practitioners should not accept unnecessary delays in the consideration of police or prosecutor's bail. At the same time, it is wise to remain polite, even where you disagree with the investigating officer's reluctance to release the client at that stage.

A prosecutor may release an arrested person on bail only after consulting the investigating officer.[32] Although the prosecutor is not bound by the investigating officer's views, those views must be considered when deciding whether to grant or refuse bail.[33] For that reason, engagement with the investigating officer can significantly influence both police bail and prosecutor's bail.

At times, the investigating officer or the prosecutor may be concerned—whether justified or not—that the client's immediate release could lead to further conflict, particularly where the complainant is a neighbour. In such circumstances, it is prudent to consider appropriate bail conditions,[34] such as residence at an alternative address.

Once it becomes apparent that the complainant resides in close proximity to the client, a proactive approach is advisable. This may include arranging an alternative address in advance and, where necessary, providing supporting details to the investigating officer. Such preparation may facilitate earlier release, rather than waiting for the investigation to run its course.

However, an alternative address should be imposed only in deserving cases—namely, where there is a real likelihood of renewed violence and where the accused and the complainant reside in the same vicinity. Criminal procedure, and particularly bail conditions, should not be utilised in a manner that effectively operates as an informal eviction mechanism.

---

[31] *S v Dlamini, S v Dladla and Others; S v Joubert; S v Schietekat* (CCT21/98, CCT22/98, CCT2/99, CCT4/99) [199] ZACC 8; 1999 (4) 623; 1999 (7) BCLR 771 (3 June 1999) para 11. Also see *Majali v S* (41210/2010) [2011] ZAGPJHC 74 (19 July 2011) para 18.

[32] Section 59A(1) of the CPA.

[33] Part 10 of NPA Policy Directives Issued by NDPP 01 June 2014 as quoted in A Kruger *Hiemstra's Criminal Procedure, Criminal Procedure* (2016) 9-5.

[34] Only the prosecutor is permitted to release the accused on bail conditions during the outside court bail. Section 59 of the CPA, which deals with police bail, is silent on bail conditions. Section 59A(3) (a) of the CPA specifically authorises the prosecutor to set conditions of bail in relevant cases.

Prosecutors and police officers are well aware of the implications of *Carmichele v Minister of Safety and Security*.[35] The case established that a failure to oppose bail, where the facts indicate that the accused poses a danger to the public or to witnesses, may, in appropriate circumstances, result in delictual liability if harm arises from that omission.

In the context of bail negotiations, it is therefore prudent to consider solutions tailored to the specific risks posed by the case, rather than merely insisting on the client's immediate release. The potential legal and professional consequences of releasing an accused person who subsequently causes serious harm require careful consideration.

At the same time, investigating officers and prosecutors must exercise their discretion on the basis of objective facts and applicable legal principles, rather than apprehension of future criticism. The decision to grant or refuse bail must be rational, reasonable, and grounded in the available evidence.[36]

2.4 Procedure on police bail

Any police official from the rank of sergeant may release the arrested person after consulting with the investigating officer.[37] The police officer completes the J398 bail form in triplicate and gives the client the original as a bail receipt.[38] The client should keep the receipt safe because they will use it to collect the bail money after the case has been finalised. The police officers deliver the bail money deposited at the police station to the Clerk of the Court. When the matter is finalised, the client will not return to the police station but will collect their bail money from the Clerk of the Court. The client who has been released on bail is compelled to appear at a specified courthouse on a specified date and time.[39] Failure to appear in court while on police bail may lead to the same consequences as if the person failed to appear while released on prosecutor's bail or court bail.[40] A detailed discussion of failure to appear in court when released on police bail appears in paragraph 10.1.2.

---

[35] *Carmichele v Minister of Safety and Security* (CCT 48/00) (2001) ZACC 22 (16 August 2001) para 63 and 74.

[36] *Setlhapelo v Minister of Police and Another* (45031/2012) [2015] ZAGPPHC 363 (20 May 2015) para 41.

[37] Joubert *Applied Law for Police Officials* (2018) 327.

[38] In practice, J399 is sometimes used in the absence of a J398 bail form

[39] Section 59A(4) of the CPA.

[40] Section 67(1) (a) of the CPA.

2.5 Release on police warning

Instead of releasing the arrested client on bail, the police officer may release them on warning.[41] The same requirements regarding the rank of the police officer authorised to grant bail,[42] and the offences for which release on police bail is indicated,[43] are applicable. The difference is that the arrested person does not pay money.[44] The warning must be in writing on the SAPS 496 form.[45] The SAPS 496 must record the offence, date, time, and the court where the client must appear.[46] Failure to appear in court when released on a police warning attracts the same consequences as failure to appear when released by the court on a warning.[47] Failure to appear in court when released on warning is discussed in detail in paragraph 10.1.1.

2.6 Procedure on prosecutor's bail

Every police station with detention custody should have a list of prosecutors on standby. Every police station with detention custody should have a list of prosecutors on standby. Most police stations comply, but not always. If there is no register or it is not updated, you may call any prosecutor to establish who is on standby. Investigating officers usually have prosecutors' phone numbers, as their work requires close collaboration with them. Other legal practitioners who practice in the jurisdiction where the client is detained will certainly have the contact numbers of the prosecutors. If you experience difficulty contacting the on-call prosecutor, or if no on-call list is available, the matter should be escalated immediately to the Senior Public Prosecutor or the Control Public Prosecutor. Such a situation is unacceptable and must be addressed without delay.

The prosecutor can only release the client on bail, not on warning.[48] Therefore, you should ascertain whether the client has a reasonable amount of cash to pay bail before calling the prosecutor. To avoid a conflict of interest, you are not allowed to post bail on behalf of the clients.[49] On arrival, the

---

[41] Section 72 of the CPA.

[42] See para 2.4 above.

[43] See para 2.1 above.

[44] Section 72(1) of the CPA.

[45] Section 72(3) of the CPA.

[46] Ibid.

[47] Section 72(2) (a) read together with Subsection (4) of the CPA.

[48] Section 59A(3) (a) of the CPA. Also see *Matebese v Minister of Police* (2224/2017) [2019] ZAECPEHC 37 (18 June 2019) para 62.

[49] *Code of Conduct for all Legal Practitioners, Candidate Legal Practitioners and Juristic Entities* GN 162 in GG 42337 29 March 2019 para 58.2. Also see *Brown and Another v S* (CC 18/2017) [2018] ZAECPEHC 76; 2019 (1) SACR 691 (ECP) (14 December 2018) para 30.

prosecutor reads the docket and, after consulting the investigating officer, decides whether to grant bail.[50] If the prosecutor decides to grant bail, they will fill in the J398 form in triplicate and give the client the original as a bail receipt.[51] Unlike in police bail, the prosecutor may also attach bail conditions which are reasonable under the circumstances of the case.[52]

Failure to appear when released on this bail may lead to the same consequences as failure to appear on police or court bail.[53] Failure to appear in court while released on the prosecutor's bail is discussed in detail in paragraph 10.1.2. This bail will remain in effect until the first court appearance[54] The court may extend it on the same condition, amend conditions, or add further conditions.[55] The court may even consider the bail issue afresh where it finds that the release was inappropriate, and it retains all the powers provided by Section 60 of the CPA.[56]

2.7 Detained client's right to be promptly informed of their right to apply for police or prosecutor's bail

An arrested client may be released before their first appearance in court only on police bail, police warning, prosecutor's bail, or a written notice to appear.[57] Therefore, the detained client who has not been released on the stated methods of outside court release is not entitled to be brought to court outside ordinary court hours or days for a bail hearing.[58] In simple terms, the arrested person who wishes to be released from police custody is prohibited from approaching the courts to apply for bail outside of ordinary court hours.

To ensure arrested persons who deserve to be released before their first appearance in court are assisted, Section 50(1) (b) of the CPA guarantees the detained person's right to be informed as soon as reasonably possible of their right to apply for bail. As stated in *Setlhapelo v Minister of Police and Another*,[59] this right entitles the detained person to be informed about police bail or prosecutor's bail as soon as reasonably possible after their detention. Failure to promptly inform the detained person of this right may lead to a claim for

---

[50] Section 59A(1) of the CPA.
[51] In certain instances, the J399 form is completed in the absence of the J398 form.
[52] Section 59A(3) (b) of the CPA.
[53] Section 67(1) (a) of the CPA.
[54] Section 59A(4) of the CPA.
[55] Section 59A(5) (a) of the CPA.
[56] Section 59A(5) (b) of the CPA.
[57] The written notice to appear in court is discussed for practical reasons in paragraph 3.3 of the following chapter.
[58] Section 50(6) (b) of the CPA.
[59] *Setlhapelo v Minister of Police and Another* (45031/2012) [2015] ZAGPPHC 363 (20 May 2015) para 42.

delictual damages against the Minister of Police.[60] The investigating officer must plan the investigation so that, immediately after arrest, a prompt decision can be made on whether the accused may be released before the first court appearance.[61] An entry must be made in the Occurrence Book (SAPS 10) and the Investigating Diary (SAPS 5) on whether the detained person should be released.[62] Any refusal of police or a prosecutor's bail must be based on rational grounds to avoid exposure to claims for damages.[63]

2.8 Review where the police or prosecutor's bail is improperly refused

Practitioners frequently encounter difficulty determining the appropriate course of action when outside-court bail is refused or when a police official or prosecutor frustrates its proper consideration. For example, a legal representative may initially consult telephonically with the investigating officer, who appears willing to engage, only to become unreachable thereafter. Attempts to escalate the matter to the station commander may prove equally unproductive, with the response often being that nothing further can be done and that the matter should await the next court sitting.

An appeal against such a refusal is not competent. Section 65 of the Criminal Procedure Act 51 of 1977 provides for appeals against bail decisions of a magistrate, and does not extend to refusals by a police official or prosecutor. Where bail has been considered and refused at the police or prosecutorial level, no internal appeal mechanism exists. The detained accused must instead be brought before a lower court within 48 hours in terms of Section 50(1)(c)(ii) of the Act, where the issue of bail may be reconsidered judicially.[64]

However, where an accused—who has the right to be informed as soon as reasonably possible of their right to apply for police or prosecutor's bail—finds that the consideration of such bail is being frustrated by the conduct of a police official or prosecutor, a constitutional remedy may arise under Section 35(2)(d) of the Constitution.[65] This is because a refusal or failure to consider bail, in

---

[60] *Setlhapelo v Minister of Police and Another* (45031/2012) [2015] ZAGPPHC 363 (20 May 2015) para 42.

[61] Circular 1/1/4/1 Dated 2019/11/19 Instructions Relating to Arrest and Detention of Suspects para 15.

[62] Circular 1/1/4/1 Dated 2019/11/19 [*supra*] para 14.

[63] *Setlhapelo v Minister of Police and Another* [*supra*] para 41.

[64] de Villiers, W.P. "The Interdictum De Homine Libero Exhibendo and the Question Whether it is Incumbent on a Peace Officer to Consider Less Invasive Means to Secure Attendance at Court Before Effecting an Arrest National Commissioner of Police v Coetzee" 2014 *THRHR* p497, http://hdl.handle.net/2263/49125, accessed on 23 September 2023.

[65] Ibid.

circumstances where these officials are legally obliged to do so, may render the continued detention unlawful.[66] Once the detention becomes unlawful, the detained person is entitled to challenge it and, if successful, to be released in terms of Section 35(2)(d) of the Constitution.[67]

Furthermore, there is nothing in principle preventing police bail from being reviewable under the Promotion of Administrative Justice Act 3 of 2000 (PAJA).[68] The decision to grant or refuse a prosecutor's bail does not constitute a decision to institute or continue a prosecution, which is expressly excluded from the definition of "administrative action" under Section 1(b)(ff) of PAJA.[69] It follows that a decision to refuse a prosecutor's bail may also constitute an administrative action and is therefore reviewable under PAJA. Section 1 of PAJA further provides that administrative action includes a failure to take a decision by a natural person exercising a public power or performing a public function under legislation. Accordingly, a failure or refusal to consider a police or prosecutor's bail may amount to a reviewable administrative action.
The principal practical obstacle, however, lies in the requirement to exhaust internal remedies under Section 7(2) of PAJA within the limited period of detention before the first court appearance. Given the short 48-hour timeframe prescribed by the Criminal Procedure Act, the effectiveness of PAJA as an immediate remedy may be limited in urgent bail situations.
The Criminal Procedure Act 51 of 1977 prescribes no internal remedies to be followed where a police official or prosecutor frustrates the consideration of outside-court bail. In such circumstances, the detained person is effectively compelled to endure continued detention until the first court appearance, unless review proceedings are instituted.

Accordingly, where there is a failure or refusal to consider a bail application, an urgent review application should be launched without delay. Given the inherently urgent nature of liberty interests, such proceedings ought to be brought under Rule 6(12) of the Uniform Rules of Court, rather than under Rule 53. Rule 6(12) permits the court to dispense with the ordinary forms and time periods in urgent matters, which is appropriate where continued detention is impugned.

In *Cuniff v Tshite and Others,*[70] the court held that an applicant seeking review has an election to proceed under either Rule 6 or Rule 53 of the Uniform Rules of Court. The primary purpose of Rule 53 is to facilitate access to the record of the proceedings underlying the impugned decision. Accordingly, a

---

[66] de Villiers, W. P. "The Interdictum De Homine Libero Exhibendo and the Question Whether it is Incumbent on a Peace Officer to Consider Less Invasive Means to Secure Attendance at Court Before Effecting an Arrest *National Commissioner of Police v Coetzee*" 2014 THRHR p497, http://hdl.handle.net/2263/49125, accessed on 23 September 2023.
[67] Ibid.
[68] Joubert Applied Law for Police Officials (2018) 327.
[69] Section 1 (b) (ff) of Promotion of Administrative Justice Act 3 of 2000 [PAJA].
[70] *Cuniff v Tshite and Others* (2000) 3 All SA 554 (T) 556.

litigant who elects to proceed under Rule 6 forfeits the procedural advantage of compelling production of the record.[71] In the context of refusal or failure to consider police or prosecutor's bail, no formal record of proceedings is ordinarily created. In such circumstances, an applicant may competently proceed under Rule 6 (general application proceedings), without invoking Rule 53 (review proceedings), as there is no record to be produced.

A notice of motion supported by a founding affidavit is required to start the urgent review proceedings.[72] The notice of motion must set out the relief sought by the applicant and give directions to the respondent as to when and where the application will be heard.[73] The founding affidavit should normally be by the detained person, accompanied by a confirmatory affidavit from their attorney. However, even where the affidavit is made by the attorney and the detained client's spouse, the application may remain competent, as the accused is detained.[74] The founding affidavit must clearly state the reason for urgency and why the remedy cannot be effective if normal rules are observed.[75] The founding affidavit must also set out facts upon which the applicant relies for the relief sought.[76] In the bail application review, it seems enough to state that the application involves interference with personal liberty. Bail applications are, as a rule, urgent.[77] During the hearing, the court will deal with the matter in accordance with the procedure set out in Rule 6, as practically possible and as it deems fit.[78] Where the court finds that the administrator (police officer or prosecutor) failed to exercise their discretion, it must make an order that is just and equitable.[79]

An example of an urgent prosecutor's bail review:[80]

[71] *Mwelase v Minister of Social Development and Others* [CA74/16) [2018] ZAECMHC 16 (22 March 2018) para 33.

[72] Rule 6 (1) of the Uniform Rules of Court.

[73] P van Blerk *Legal Drafting: Civil Proceedings* (2015) para 12.1.

[74] *Coetzee v National Commissioner of Police and Others* (70259/09) (2010) ZAGPPHC 155; 2011 (1) SACR 132 (GNP); 2011 (2) SA 227 (GNP) (11 October 2010).

[75] Rule 6 (12) (b) of the Uniform Rules of the Court.

[76] Rule 6 (1) of the Uniform Rules of Court.

[77] *Setwaba and Others v De Souza NO and Others* (M90/16) [2016] ZANWHC 30 (3 March 2016) para 3.

[78] Rule 6 (12) (a) of the Uniform Rules of Court.

[79] Section 8 of the Promotion of Administrative Justice Act 3 of 2000 [PAJA].

[80] The author confirms that no confidential information or real case material has been used. All names and facts are fictional.

IN THE HIGH COURT OF SOUTH AFRICA

(NORTH WEST DIVISION, MAHIKENG)

BAIL REVIEW CASE NO: A441/2022

In the matter between:

PULE MOLEFE APPLICANT

And

THABO MATJEKE N.O. 1ST RESPONDENT

DIRECTOR OF PUBLIC PROSECUTIONS, MAHIKENG 2ND RESPONDENT

NOTICE OF MOTION

PLEASE TAKE NOTICE that the Applicant intends to make an application to this honourable court on this evening of **24 June 2022** at **09.30 pm** or so soon thereafter as the matter can be heard for orders in the following terms:

1. Declaring the application to be a matter of urgency and dispensing in so far as is necessary in terms of Rule 6 (12) with the usual forms and services provided for in the Uniform Rules of Court;
2. Reviewing and setting aside the decision of the First Respondent on Lomanyaneng Police Station CAS Number 67/06/2022, refusing to consider the release of the Applicant on bail in terms of Section 59A of the Criminal Procedure Act 51 of 1977.
3. Considering the bail application of the Applicant and releasing the Applicant on bail on conditions that the court deems fit.

TAKE NOTICE FURTHER that the affidavit of the Applicant will be used in support of this application.

TAKE NOTICE FURTHER that the Applicant has appointed this email address (**modjadjiattorneys@law.co.za**) of his attorneys as the email address at which it will receive notices and services of all processes in this matter.

TAKE NOTICE FURTHER that if any of the Respondents intend to oppose this application, such Respondent shall:

(i) immediately on receipt of the founding papers, deliver a notice of intention to oppose the application by email to the Applicant's attorneys of record at the following email address: *modjadjiattorneys@law.co.za.*

(ii) further file the opposing papers by no later than this evening at 07.30 pm on 24 June 2022 at *modjadjiattorneys@law.co.za.*

TAKE NOTICE FURTHER that failing to give such notice of intention to oppose and/or failing to file the opposing papers, the application for the relief sought shall be heard on an unopposed basis.

DATED AND SIGNED AT MAHIKENG ON 24 JUNE 2022.

____

MODJADJI ATTORNEYS

APPLICANT'S ATTORNEYS

TO: THE REGISTRAR OF THE ABOVE COURT

TO: MR MATJEKE N.O.

AND TO: THE DIRECTOR OF PUBLIC PROSECUTIONS, MAHIKENG

CHAPTER 3

ALTERNATIVE WAYS TO BRING THE CLIENT BEFORE THE COURT

3.1 Arrest

The arrest is the most drastic way of securing the accused's appearance before the court.[81] Section 40 of the CPA permits an arrest without a warrant. However, the arresting officer must comply with Section 40(1) requirements.[82] If these requirements are satisfied, discretion on whether to effect an arrest or not arises.[83] The discretion to arrest must be exercised *bona fide* and be objective and rational.[84] Whether the discretion has been properly exercised depends on the particular facts of each case. However, the arresting officer must justify the exercise of their discretion on those applicable facts.[85] Where the suspect gives an exculpatory explanation, it should be investigated before arrest.[86] To properly exercise discretion, police officers are guided by the National Instruction 11 of 2019, which applies to all police officers.[87] This national instruction was found to be a sufficient guide in the exercise of the

---

[81] *Tsose v Minister of Justice* 1951 (3) SA 10 (A) p17G-H.

[82] *Groves N.O. v Minister of Police* (CCT 223/22) [2023] ZACC 36; 2024 (1) SACR 286 (CC); 2024 (4) BCLR 503 (CC) (14 November 2023) para 52.

[83] Ibid. See also *Minister of Safety and Security v Sekhoto and Another* [2011] (1) SACR 315 (SCA); [2011] 2 All SA 157 (SCA); 2011 (5) SA 367 (SCA) [2010] ZASCA 141; 131/10 (19 November 2010) para 28.

[84] *Minister of Safety and Security v Sekhoto and Another* [*supra*] para 35 and 36.

[85] *Groves N.O. v Minister of Police* [*supra*] para 52.

[86] Ibid. See also *Minister of Police v Dhali* (CA327/2017) [2019] ZAECGHC 16 (26 February 2019) para 13.

[87] National Instruction 11 of 2019: Arrest, Treatment and Transportation of an Arrested Person, para 3. Even though this national instruction does not explicitly state so, it appears to have replaced Standing Order (G) 341 *Arrest and the Treatment of an Arrested Person Until Such Person is Handed Over to the Community Service Centre Commander*. However, the paragraph on arrest remains unchanged. See written reply to question 1202 of the Minister of Police to Ms Z Majola in the National Assembly dated 07 May 2021, where the minister did not include this standing order as a directive on the treatment of detainees by SAPS. https://parliament.gov.za/storage/app/media/Docs/exe_rq_na/7c59bfe5-1554-495d-bd6f-dde7d6de26c2.pdf accessed 21 July 2024. See also the comment on the October 2019 *African Policing Civilian Oversight Forum Research Paper,* p3, about this national instruction replacing Standing Order (G) 341. https://apcof.org/wp-content/uploads/026-risksofpolicecustody-thepotentialforindependentmonitoringofpolicecustodyinsouthafrica-davidbruce.pdf accessed on 21 July 2024.

discretion to arrest by the Constitutional Court in *Minister of Safety and Security v Van Niekerk.*[88] This national instruction, in short, provides that:[89]

1. Since arrest is a drastic infringement of the rights of an individual, it must be used as a last resort.
2. The police officer, when exercising their discretion, must do so in a proper manner according to the merits of the individual case.
3. Even where the police officer is authorised by law to arrest, they should normally refrain from arresting if:
   a) the attendance of the accused may be secured by using a summons; or
   b) there are reasonable grounds to believe that a court convicting the accused of that offence will not impose a fine exceeding **R5 000.00.**[90] In those circumstances, the 'written notice to appear' (J534) should be used.

Section 43 of the CPA addresses an arrest by warrant. While *Sekhoto*[91] remains the authority for the discretion applicable to an arresting officer when effecting an arrest without a warrant, the position has changed when the arresting officer is executing an arrest based on a warrant (J50). The police officer arresting on the strength of J50 does not have discretion whether to arrest or not because an authorised J50 is subject to processes involving the participation of other role players, such as the prosecutor, the magistrate, or the justice of the peace. Therefore, "it is not only the decision of the arresting officer that determines the fate of the suspect".[92] However, even though the arresting officer does not have discretion on whether to effect an arrest or not, they have discretion on how to effect the arrest and if it must be done there and then.[93] This discretion is about the time, date, and place of the arrest.[94] Since the arresting officer is exercising public power when effecting an arrest, they must act rationally.[95] The arresting officer should make a value

---

[88] *Minister of Safety and Security v Van Niekerk* (CCT74/06) [2007] ZACC 15; 2007 (10) BCLR 1102 (CC); 2008 (1) SACR 56 (CC) (8 June 2007) para 19 and 20. Also see *Mahlanza v Minister of Police* (EL1326/2017) [2019] ZAECELLC (26 November 2019) para 32.

[89] National Instruction 11 of 2019 [*supra*] para 6.

[90] Section 56(1) of the CPA read together with the Determination of Amounts for Purposes of Certain Provisions of the Criminal Procedure Act, 1977, GN R62 in GG 36111 of 30 January 2013.

[91] *Minister of Safety and Security v Sekhoto and Another* [2011] (1) SACR 315 (SCA); [2011] 2 All SA 157 (SCA); 2011 (5) SA 367 (SCA)) [2010] ZASCA 141; 131/10 (19 November 2010) para 28.

[92] *Groves N.O. v Minister of Police* (CCT 223/22) [2023] ZACC 36; 2024 (1) SACR 286 (CC); 2024 (4) BCLR 503 (CC) (14 November 2023) para 53.

[93] *Groves N.O. v Minister of Police* [*supra*] para 60. See also *W.S.L and Another v The Minister of Police and Others* (6467-2020) [2024] ZAGPJHC 181;2024 (1) SACR 546 (GJ) (19 February 2024) para 24.

[94] Ibid.

[95] *Pharmaceutical Manufacturers Association of South Africa and Another: In re Ex Parte President of the Republic of South Africa and Others* (CCT31/99) [2000] ZACC 1; 2000 (2) SA 674; 2000 (3) BCLR 241 (25 February 2000) para 94.

judgment according to the circumstances of the case.[96] For instance, there might be times when the police officer intends to effect an arrest, but the suspect is too ill or is the primary caregiver to minor children.[97]

3.2 Written notice to appear in court

While arrest is the most common method of bringing the accused before the court, other, less severe methods are also available. A written notice to appear in court can be used to secure the accused's attendance in the Magistrates' Court.[98] The J534 is an alternative to arresting suspects of minor offences where the court cannot impose a fine of more than R5 000.00.[99] Even where the arrest was effected, and the client was detained, a J534 may still be used to secure their release. When a police officer issues a J534, it must indicate where the accused must appear, the date and time of appearance, and the amount of the 'admission of guilt fine' (AOG), which may be paid on or before the appearance date.[100]

Payment of the fine stipulated in the J534 is optional. If the accused elects to pay the AOG fine, the matter is finalised. In practice, however, some minor offences are not disposed of by way of a J534 release. Instead, suspects may be presented with the option of paying an AOG fine or remaining in custody pending their first court appearance.[101] This approach has, in certain instances, resulted in detained suspects electing to pay the AOG fine in order to secure prompt release from custody, without fully appreciating that such payment results in a criminal record. [102] Judicial decisions have emphasised the importance of ensuring that accused persons are properly informed of the consequences of paying an AOG fine.[103] In response, a practice has developed of attaching an annexure to the J534 form explaining the implications of an AOG.[104] However, procedural safeguards of this nature are meaningful only if the decision to pay the AOG fine is genuinely voluntary and not influenced by

---

[96] *Groves N.O. v Minister of Police* (CCT 223/22) [2023] ZACC 36; 2024 (1) SACR 286 (CC); 2024 (4) BCLR 503 (CC) (14 November 2023) para 60.

[97] Ibid.

[98] Section 38 of the CPA. See also *Minister of Safety and Security v Sekhoto and Another* [*supra*] para 19.

[99] Section 56 (1) of the CPA read together with the Determination of Amounts for Purposes of Certain Provisions of the Criminal Procedure Act, 1977, GN R62 in GG 36111 of 30 January 2013.

[100] Section 56 (1) (a)-(d) of the CPA.

[101] *S v Elgin* (274/21) [2021] ZAWCHC 147; 2022 (1) SACR 325 (WCC) (5 August 2021) para 9-10.

[102] See *S v Tong* (1287) [2012] ZAWCHC 169; 2013 (1) SACR 346 (WCC) (7 September 2012); *S v Houtzamer* (B7968969/08) [2015] ZAWCHC 25 (10 March 2015); S v Z G (70/W 3389548) [2019] ZAWCHC 45; 2019 (2) SACR 162 (WCC) (27 February 2019); and *S v Matross* (47/2019) [2019] ZAWCHC 68 (13 June 2019).

[103] Ibid.

[104] See the example of the annexure to J534 in *S v Elgin* [*supra*] para 4.

continued detention in circumstances where release would otherwise have been appropriate.

The payment of an admission of guilt (AOG) fine forms an established component of the criminal justice system, as it permits accused persons charged with less serious offences to accept responsibility and contributes to alleviating pressure on congested court rolls.[105] The J534 form has long served as a mechanism for releasing suspects accused of minor offences without immediate payment. Where an accused elects to admit guilt and pays the prescribed fine on or before the date of first appearance, the matter is finalised.[106] This reflects the intended purpose of Section 57 of the CPA. Judicial authority has cautioned against prioritising conviction statistics over substantive justice. In this regard, Thulare J observed that "justice should not be buried in the cemetery of statistics on convictions, for the State to look good on paper, in a battle against crime".[107] The broader principle is that while statistical efficiency is relevant to the functioning of the system, it cannot displace the fundamental requirement that justice be done in each individual case.[108]

It should be noted, however, that while it is common practice to attach an annexure explaining that an AOG fine results in a criminal record, a police officer's failure to provide this explanation or attach the annexure is not, on its own, sufficient reason to set aside the conviction.[109] It should be clear that the accused was misled into paying the AOG fine.[110] While it is a good practice and praiseworthy to attach the annexure, the CPA currently does not impose a duty on police officers to explain the consequences of the AOG payment.[111] Therefore, it is prudent to heed the words of Mpati JP in *National Commissioner of Police and Another v Coetzee*, [112] where it was stated that "[c]ourts must guard against and resist the temptation to impose duties on police officials under the guise of an alleged protection of rights guaranteed in the Bill of Rights, which existing law, in this case the CPA, does not impose".

As a general rule, you should exercise caution before advising a client to pay an AOG, particularly in comparatively minor offences such as assault by

---

105 Dr Llewelyn Curlewis "Sugar-coating guilt: Admission of guilt fines – no easy fix" April 2014 *De Rebus* https://www.derebus.org.za/sugar-coating-guilt-admission-guilt-fines-no-easy-fix/ accessed 29 December 2023.

106 Section 56 (2) read with Section 57 (1) (b) of the CPA.

107 *S v Elgin* (274/21) [2021] ZAWCHC 147; 2022 (1) SACR 325 (WCC) (5 August 2021) para 22.

108 The remark "statistics are good, but justice is much better" was frequently articulated by Ms Lettie Smit, then Acting Regional Magistrate, Brits, in the context of criminal proceedings.

109 *S v Rademeyer* (A186/17) [2017] ZAGPPHC 175 (12 April 2017) para 11-13.

110 Ibid.

111 Ibid.

112 *National Commissioner of Police and Another v Coetzee* (649/11) [2012] ZASCA 161; 2013 (1) SACR 358 (SCA) (16 November 2012) para 16.

pushing, threats, public drinking, crimen injuria, or certain railway offences. Payment of an AOG results in a criminal record and should therefore be considered carefully.

Court rolls are often congested, and prosecutorial resources are typically prioritised for more serious matters. Consequently, less serious and marginal cases may not receive the same degree of prosecutorial attention. In appropriate circumstances, a prosecutor may decline to prosecute, or a court may determine that the conduct is too trivial to warrant conviction, applying the *de minimis non curat lex* principle.[113] If the matter is placed on the roll, it is advisable to make representations to the Control Prosecutor or the Senior Public Prosecutor (SPP) seeking withdrawal of the matter or, at the very least, a recommendation for diversion. Where representations based on the *de minimis* principle or diversion are unsuccessful, the prosecutor may still be approached to consider the imposition of an admission of guilt fine in terms of Section 57A of the CPA.

When a prosecutor considers an admission of guilt fine under Section 57A, that decision constitutes the exercise of public power. As such, it must be exercised lawfully, rationally, and in accordance with constitutional principles.[114]

Failure to appear in court after being properly served with a J534 written notice may result in the issuing of a warrant of arrest. In addition, the court may summarily convict and sentence the accused to a fine not exceeding R10 000.00 or to imprisonment for a period not exceeding three months,[115] where it is satisfied that the accused deliberately failed to appear or to remain in attendance without a satisfactory explanation.[116]

Once the accused has appeared in court pursuant to a written notice and the matter is postponed in terms of Section 168 of the CPA, any subsequent failure to appear on the specified date and time falls within the ambit of Section 170 of the CPA, not Section 55(2). Section 55 regulates failure to appear after service of a written notice by a police official and does not extend to non-appearance at a postponed court date.

---

[113] *De minimis non curat lex* principle in this context means the law does not concern itself with trivial matters. See *S v Visagie* 2009 (2) SACR 70 (W), *S v Kgogong* 1980 (3) SA 600 (A), and *S v Dane* 157 (2) SA 472 (N).

[114] *W.S.L and Another v The Minister of Police and Others* (6467-2020) [2024] ZAGPJHC 181;2024 (1) SACR 546 (GJ) (19 February 2024) para 22.

[115] Considering *Cooper v District Magistrate, Cape* Town (WCC) (1699/2017) [2017] ZAWCHC 140; 2018 (1) SACR 369 (WCC) (24 November 2017) para 21, Section 1(2) of the Adjustments of Fines Act 101 of 1991 is applicable.

[116] Section 55(2) of the CPA is applicable as permitted by Section 56(5) of the CPA.

Confusion between these provisions occasionally arises in practice.[117] It is therefore important to distinguish clearly between failure to appear pursuant to a written notice (Section 55) and failure to appear after a court-ordered postponement (Section 170).[118]

3.3 Summons [J175]

3.3.1 Should it be summons or J50 in recycled cases

Sometimes, instead of arresting the accused, police officers take a warning statement and submit the docket to the prosecutor for a decision on whether to prosecute. If the prosecutor decides to prosecute and no warrant of arrest is issued, the prosecutor may issue a summons (J175) for any case where it is unnecessary to arrest the accused.[119]

Section 54 of the Criminal Procedure Act 51 of 1977 provides for a procedure distinct from arrest and subsequent court appearance. It authorises the issuing of a summons (J175) in respect of any offence, provided that the accused is not in custody and that no warrant of arrest (J50) has been issued or is contemplated. The prosecutor, having been apprised of the facts and procedural history of the matter, retains a discretion—subject to the circumstances of the case—whether to proceed by way of summons (J175) or by warrant (J50). In matters previously withdrawn, struck from the roll, or not enrolled after an earlier appearance—often referred to in practice as "recycled cases"—the issuing of a J175 summons is generally the preferred mechanism for securing the accused's reappearance once investigations have been finalised.

In certain instances, a matter that has previously been withdrawn or struck from the roll is reintroduced through the re-arrest of the accused pursuant to a J50 warrant issued in terms of Section 43 of the CPA. The repeated arrest of an accused for the same offence raises serious concerns regarding procedural fairness and the constitutional right to freedom guaranteed in section 12 of the Constitution, particularly where the re-arrest is not attributable to any fault on the part of the accused. Given that arrest constitutes one of the most invasive methods of securing attendance at court, its repeated use in respect of the same offence warrants careful scrutiny.[120] Where an accused has previously been released through no wrongdoing of their own, a subsequent arrest for the same offence may

---

[117] *Cooper v District Magistrate, Cape* Town(WCC) (1699/2017) [2017] ZAWCHC 140; 2018 (1) SACR 369 (WCC) (24 November 2017) para 13.
[118] Ibid.
[119] Section 54(1) of the CPA.
[120] *Tsose v Minister of Justice 1951* (3) SA 10 (A) p17G-H.

undermine the presumption of innocence and expose the individual to renewed deprivation of liberty and its attendant consequences, including potential reputational and economic harm. Such circumstances call for a principled assessment of whether the re-arrest is objectively justified and consistent with constitutional safeguards.

A challenge to this procedure would require careful consideration of *S v Hewu*[121] and *Conradie v S*,[122] and whether those decisions were correctly decided. In *Hewu*, the matter was struck off the roll by the court.[123] However, the accused were re-arrested almost immediately on a J50 warrant instead of a J175, which is the expected practice.[124] The matter was placed before a different regional magistrate the following day, who struck it off the roll,[125] only for it to reappear on the roll the following week. The magistrate struck it off the roll again.[126] The matter was struck off the roll three times. On review, the court found that there was nothing irregular about re-arresting the accused on a recycled case where the offence is one referred to in Schedule 5 or 6 and is therefore governed by the peremptory terms of Section 60(11) of the CPA, and ordered that the accused may be re-arrested.[127] Section 60(11) of the CPA states that:

> [n]othwithstanding any provision of this Act, where the accused is charged with an offence referred to in Schedule 5 or 6, the court shall order that the accused be detained in custody until he or she is dealt in accordance with the law, unless the accused, having been given a reasonable opportunity to do so, adduces evidence which satisfies the court that he or she complied with requirements of subparagraph (a) or (b), to be released on bail.

A careful reading of *S v Hewu* shows that the interpretation of this section has the effect that in Schedule 5 or 6 offences, the prosecutor does not have a choice between bringing the accused before the court through a J175 or a J50 warrant. The prosecutor should bring the accused before the court through a J50 warrant to ensure the court deals with the accused as provided by Section 60(11).[128] Therefore, it appears that in the peremptory terms of Section 60(11), a suspect in a Schedule 5 or 6 offence must always be arrested, even if

---

[121] *S v Hewu and Others* (170002) [2017] ZAECGHC 44; 2017 (2) SACR 67 (ECG) (06 April 2017) para 6.
[122] *S v Conradie* (A248/2020) [2020] ZAWCHC 177 (11 December 2020).
[123] *S v Hewu and Others* [*supra*] para 3.
[124] Ibid.
[125] *S v Hewu and Others* [*supra*] para 8.
[126] *S v Hewu and Others* [*supra*] para 9.
[127] *S v Hewu and Others* [*supra*] para 11, 14, 21, 23, 24 and 26.
[128] Ibid.

the same case was once withdrawn or removed from the roll.[129] The interpretation of Section 60(11) as governing bail after arrest is phrased in sufficiently broad terms that it may appear to affect the summons procedure under Section 54. Such a broad reading does not always account for the fact that recycled cases arise in different procedural contexts.

For example, where an accused was previously released on bail, and the matter was provisionally withdrawn pending the tracing of witnesses, fingerprint analysis, or DNA results, the completion of investigations may prompt the prosecutor to seek a J50 warrant. If Section 60(11) is applied mechanically, this would require the accused to apply for bail afresh in circumstances where bail had previously been granted.

This approach raises the question whether the compulsory language of Section 60(11) was intended to apply uniformly to all recycled matters, irrespective of the procedural history of the case.[130]

In *S v Conradie*,[131] the matter was struck off the roll after the court found that the accused had appeared unlawfully, as the 48-hour period prescribed by Section 50 of the CPA had expired.[132] The accused was re-arrested a few weeks later on a J50 warrant.[133] The challenge to this supposed irregular procedure did not succeed before the magistrate, and even in the High Court.[134] The High Court ruled that a striking off the roll order can never stop the accused's re-arraignment using legitimate methods in terms of Section 38 of the CPA.[135] If re-arrest remains available regardless of prior non-compliance with section 50, the incentive to ensure timely first appearances may be weakened.

3.3.2 Procedure on summons (J175)

Where the prosecutor has decided to secure the accused's attendance in court through a J175, and it appears that the court may not set a fine above R10 000.00, the prosecutor may also set the AOG amount, which may be paid.[136] The J175 is completed in triplicate: the first document is a return of service, the second document is to be handed to the accused, and the third

---

[129] *S v Hewu and Others* (170002) [2017] ZAECGHC 44; 2017 (2) SACR 67 (ECG) (06 April 2017) para 11, 14, 21, 23, 24 and 26.

[130] See the facts in *W.S.L and Another v The Minister of Police and Others* (6467-2020) [2024] ZAGPJHC 181;2024 (1) SACR 546 (GJ) (19 February 2024) para 13.

[131] *S v Conradie* (A248/2020) [2020] ZAWCHC 177 (11 December 2020) para 6.

[132] Ibid.

[133] *S v Conradie* [*supra*] para 7.

[134] *S v Conradie* [*supra*] para 7-8.

[135] *S v Conradie* [*supra*] para 9.

[136] Section 57(1) (b) of the CPA read with Determination of Amounts for Purposes of Certain Provisions of the Criminal Procedure Act, 1977 GN R2 in GG 3611 of 30 January 2013.

document is the control document, which will be used as a charge sheet. J175 is usually accompanied by an annexure of the charges preferred against the accused. Alternatively, the charge(s) should be written clearly on the face of the J175. The J175 should clearly show where the accused should appear and the date and time of appearance.[137] The J175 has to be issued by the clerk of the court.[138] Therefore, the date stamp and signature should be that of the clerk of the court. To show that it has been properly issued, the summons number will appear in the top-right corner of the J175 document or in the top middle of the electronic version. The J175 must not be short notice.[139] At least 14 days' notice, which excludes Sundays and public holidays, must be given to the accused.[140] The accused is therefore not obliged to attend the court on short notice. Courts usually refuse to issue a warrant of arrest on a defective J175. No outside evidence is needed to prove service, but service must appear on the 'return of service' document itself.[141] Failure to appear in court after being properly served with a J175 may lead to a warrant of arrest being issued and the court may summarily convict and sentence the accused to a fine of not more than R10 000.00, or imprisonment not exceeding 3 months, if it is clear that the accused decided not to appear in court or remain in attendance without a satisfactory explanation.[142]

If the police officer executing the warrant of arrest realises that, although the accused has ignored the J175, they are likely to appear in court if warned, the police may issue a warning to appear in court by completing the SAPS 496 form.[143] If the police officer finds that the accused did not receive the J175 or their failure to appear is not intentional, the police officer may request an affidavit from the accused and must warn them to appear in court.[144] Should the accused fail to appear after being warned, Section 72(4) will be applicable, not Section 55(2) of the CPA.[145] Once the accused appears before the court on a J175 and the matter is postponed by the court, failure to appear in court on a specific date and time falls under Section 170 of the CPA, rather than Section 55(2).[146] Section 55(2) only regulates the failure to appear after receiving a J175 from the police officer, but does not extend after a court appearance.[147] When a J175 is issued, it means the investigations are complete. Therefore, the matter is ready for trial. The application for postponement by

---

[137] Section 54(1) (a) of the CPA.
[138] Ibid.
[139] Section 54(3) of the CPA.
[140] Section 54(3) of the CPA.
[141] Section 54(2) (b) read with Section 55(2) of the CPA.
[142] The amount of R300.00 specified in Section 55(2) of the CPA can be increased in light of *Cooper v District Magistrate, Cape Town* (WCC) (1699/2017) [2017] ZAWCHC 140; 2018 (1) SACR 369 (WCC) (24 November 2017) para 21, which states that Section 1(2) of Adjustments of Fines Act 101 of 1991 is applicable.
[143] Section 55(2) (a) of the CPA.
[144] Section 55(2) (b) of the CPA.
[145] Ibid.
[146] *Cooper v District Magistrate, Cape Town* [*supra*] para 13.
[147] Ibid.

the prosecution to conduct further investigation after it prematurely arraigned the accused on a J175 should be vigorously opposed. In *Sanderson v Attorney-General, Eastern Cape,*[148] the presiding officers were advised to use their experience to determine if a delay is unacceptable. The prosecution is also expected to be mindful of the unreasonable delays and take that into account when arraigning the accused.[149]

---

[148] *Sanderson v Attorney-General, Eastern Cape* (CCT10/97) [1997] ZACC 18; 1997 (12) BCLR 1675; 1998 (2) SA 38 (2 December 1997) para 34. See also *Director of Public Prosecutions, Northern Cape v Brooks and Others* (505/19) [2020] ZASCA 80 (2 July 2020) para 81-83.

[149] Ibid.

CHAPTER 4

OTHER MATTERS WHICH MIGHT AFFECT THE ARRESTED CLIENT BEFORE FIRST APPEARANCE

4.1 The arrested client must be brought to court as early as reasonably possible

Police officers have a duty to bring the detained client to court as soon as they can.[150] To this end, they are expected to make every effort to ensure compliance with this obligation, but where this is not possible, they must take the detained client to court no later than 48 hours after the arrest.[151] Both the CPA and the Constitution make it clear that the detained client must be brought to court as soon as reasonably possible, as a starting point, but not later than 48 hours as a last resort.[152]

If the 48-hour period expires outside of court hours or days, the detained client must be brought to court on the first court day.[153] To determine the date and time of the arrest, you need to check the detained client's notice of rights [SAPS 14A]. That is the only document readily available that gives you the time from which you must start calculating the 48 hours. "It is now settled that the purpose of the arrest is to bring the arrestee before the court for the court to determine whether the arrestee ought to be detained further, for example, pending further investigations or trial."[154] Section 50(1) of the CPA

[150] Section 50(1) (c) of the CPA, Section 35(1) (d) (i) of the Constitution. See also Circular 1/1/4/1 Dated 2019/11/19 Instructions Relating to Arrest and Detention of Suspects, para 14.

[151] Ibid.

[152] *Mashilo v Prinsloo* (576/11) (2012) ZASCA 146 (28 September 2012) para 16-17. See also *Gininda v Minister of Safety & Security* (1322/2016) [2019] ZAECMHC 35 (25 June 2019) para 60 and *Matebese v Minister of Police* (2224/2017) [2019] ZAECPEHC 37 (18 June 2019) para 40.

[153] Section 50(1) (d) (i) of the CPA and Section 35(1) (d) (ii) of the Constitution.

[154] *Naidoo v Minister of Police* (20431/2014) [2015] ZASCA 152; [2015] 4 All SA 609 (SCA); 2016 (1) SACR 468 (SCA) (2 October 2015) para 41.

seeks to ensure that an arrested person is brought before a court without delay, and this "discourages secret and irregular arrests and detentions".[155]

If the arrest occurred on Wednesday at 03.00 pm, then the 48 hours will end at 03.00 pm on Friday.[156] This is clearly 48 hours, which squarely falls within ordinary court hours and court days. Therefore, if the investigating officer only brings the detained client to court at 03.05 pm, technically, the 48 hours have expired. Exceptions to this rule include situations where 48 hours expire outside of court hours or court days,[157] when the accused is ill or injured,[158] or when the accused is being transported from another jurisdiction.[159]
Being brought before the lower court and appearing before the presiding magistrate are distinct procedural events. Once the accused has been brought to court by the police, the timing of their formal appearance falls under the control of the prosecution and the presiding judicial officer. The essential requirement is that the detained person must be removed from police custody. Accordingly, once the accused has been placed in the court's holding cells and the case docket has been handed over to the prosecution, the calculation of the 48-hour detention period ceases, unless the accused is subsequently returned to police custody without having appeared before the court.
If the arrest occurred at 04.05 pm on Wednesday, then the 48 hours would expire at 04.05 pm on Friday.[160] This is outside court hours, as court hours run from 09.00 am to 04.00 pm.[161] Since Saturday and Sunday are not ordinary court days, the client should be brought to court as soon as reasonably possible (Thursday or Friday), but no later than Monday.[162] However, the police officer who arrests on Wednesday or Thursday, but fails to take the accused to court before the weekend starts, is expected to record the reasons in the investigating diary

---

[155] *Minister of Law and Order v Kader* (275/89) [1990] ZASCA 111; 1991 (1) SA 41 (AD); [1991] 1 All SA 256 (A) (27 September 1990) para 20. Also see *Mphohoni v National Police Commissioner and Another* [*supra*] para 11.

[156] Section 50(1) (c) of the CPA and Section 35(1) (d) (i) of the Constitution.

[157] Section 50(1) (d) (i) of the CPA and Section 35(1) (d) (ii) of the Constitution. Also see *Mphohoni v National Police Commissioner and Another* (608/2011) [2014] ZALMPHC 7 (9 September 2014) para 11.

[158] Section 50(1) (d) (ii) of the CPA.

[159] Section 50(1) (d) (iii) of the CPA.

[160] Section 50(1) (d) (i) of the CPA and Section 35(1) (d) (ii) of the Constitution. Also see *Mashilo v Prinsloo* (576/11) (2012) ZASCA 146 (28 September 2012) para 17; *Seleko v Minister of Police* (931/2011) [2014] ZANWHC 47 (30 October 2014) para 83; and *Minister of Police v Ndaba and Others* (A553/2014) [2016] ZAGPPHC 277 (6 May 2016) para 21.

[161] Section 50(2) of the CPA.

[162] Section 50(1) (d) (i) of the CPA and Section 35(1) (d) (ii) of the Constitution. Also see *Mashilo v Prinsloo* [*supra*] para 17 and *Seleko v Minister of Police* [*supra*] para 83.

(SAPS 5), and senior officers are likewise expected to monitor and ensure compliance with this requirement.[163]

For the accused who was arrested on Friday, if they are not brought to court on Friday, they must appear on Monday. Their 48 hours expires on Sunday, which is not an ordinary court day.[164] For those arrested on Saturday, the time at which they were arrested is still a factor, since 48 hours may still fall outside of ordinary court hours on Monday. While there are decisions that, in passing, appear to be contrary and shall be immediately discussed below, it is important to note that weekends and holidays do not stop the hours from continuing to be calculated.[165] If the expiry of 48 hours falls on weekends or holidays, then the client cannot be brought to court since the court would not be sitting. However, the client must be brought to court on the next closest ordinary court day.[166]

In *Khumalo and Another v Minister of Police,*[167] it was stated that the 48-hour calculation stops immediately before the start of the non-court day and only starts at the beginning of the ordinary court day. This appears to be the same position in *Earl Rensburg v Minister of Police and Another,*[168] where the Supreme Court of Appeal (SCA) stated that:

> ...Mr Rensburg was brought to court within a reasonable time, having regard to the fact that he was arrested late on Thursday, 15 September 2016. ...[T]he 48-hour period referred to in terms of s 50 of the CPA had not yet expired, as the previous two days fell on a weekend and <u>were *dies non* for the calculation of this period</u>. Soon thereafter, the police took steps to verify his address, but could not do so, for reasons already alluded to earlier in the judgment. The result reached is that the police cannot be faulted for bringing Mr Rensburg to court on 19 September 2016, which, in my view, was within a reasonable time. Mr Rensburg appeared in court on the first available court day being Monday, 19 September 2016.

While these two decisions correctly found that the weekend or public holiday allowed for the accused person to remain lawfully in detention, it remains

---

[163] Circular 1/1/4/1 Dated 2019/11/19 Instructions Relating to Arrest and Detention of Suspects para 15.

[164] Section 50(1) (d) (i) of the CPA and Section 35(1) (d) (ii) of the Constitution. Also see *Mashilo v Prinsloo* [*supra*] para 17 and *Seleko v Minister of Police* [*supra*] para 83.

[165] Section 50(1) (d) (i) of the CPA. See also *Phaswane v Minister of Police* (735/2014) [2018] ZALMPPHC 48 (6 September 2018) para 22 and 25, and *Minister of Police v Ndaba and Others* [*supra*] para 21.

[166] Section 50(1) (d) (i) of the CPA.

[167] In *Khumalo and Another v Minister of Police* (958/2017&959/2017) [2019] ZANWHC 9 (21 February 2019) para 14.

[168] *Earl Rensburg v Minister of Police and Another* (557/2021) [2022] ZASCA 105 (29 June 2022) para 24, the underlining is my emphasis.

incorrect to say that the hours stopped. If the courts meant to say that once 48 hours have expired on a non-court day, nothing can be done except that the detained person must appear in court before the end of the next ordinary court day, then it would have been understandable. It is respectfully submitted that the reasoning in the above SCA judgment may give rise to some uncertainty. The judgment appears to treat the weekend as *dies non* for the calculation of that period, stating that the detained person was brought before the court on the first available court day and within a reasonable time. In this matter, the accused was arrested late on a Thursday. The following day, Friday (which was not a public holiday), was the first available court day, and Monday was the last permissible day for a lawful first appearance. The wording of the judgment may be understood to suggest that an appearance even on Tuesday would still have been permissible because the weekend is excluded from the calculation of the 48 hours—an interpretation that is irreconcilable with the requirements of Section 50(1) of the CPA and previously decided cases.

In both cases, the issue of stopping hours was mentioned in passing and without consideration of contrary authority; therefore, the decisions are not binding on this issue. The problem with stopping the calculation of hours on non-court days is that police officers might not calculate the hours of persons arrested on weekends and holidays, with the result that those hours would only be calculated from the beginning of the ordinary court day, as occurred in *Seleko v Minister of Police,*[169] where Gutta J correctly stated:

> Officer Tsholetsane testified that if a suspect is arrested on a Saturday or Sunday, the 48 hour period starts to run on Monday at 08h00 and that the plaintiff was taken to court on Wednesday, within the 48 hour period. It is apparent that Officer Tsholetsane misunderstood the provisions of Section 50 of the CPA. The plaintiff was arrested at approximately 03h00 on Sunday, 02 August 2009. Hence, the 48 hour period starts to run from the time of arrest and expires at 03h00 on Tuesday. Hence, the plaintiff should have been taken to Court on Tuesday, 04 August 2009 before 16h00. The plaintiff was taken to court on Wednesday, 05 August 2009.

If the accused cannot be brought before the court within 48 hours due to a medical condition, such as illness or injury, the matter may only be postponed in their absence if an application is made that explains the condition and is supported by a medical practitioner's certificate.[170] This application needs to be made either before the 48-hour deadline or the next normal court day after the 48-hour deadline.[171] In cases where the accused was arrested outside of the jurisdiction of the court, the 48 hours will not expire while the accused is being transported. The period will expire at the end of the following court day

[169] *Seleko v Minister of Police* (931/2011) [2014] ZANWHC 47 (30 October 2014) para 82-83.
[170] Section 50(1) (d) (ii) of the CPA.
[171] Ibid.

after the accused is in the jurisdiction of the court.[172] Assuming the accused arrived within the jurisdiction of the court today (Wednesday), they should be ready to appear before 04.00 pm tomorrow (Thursday).

While the 48-hour rule is a reminder that the arrested person must be brought to court before such hours expire, the police official is not entitled to detain the arrested person for that entire 48-hour period without bringing them to court if it is possible to do so earlier.[173] The police officers are obliged to bring the arrested person before the court as soon as is reasonably possible, whether the 48 hours expire before or during the weekend.[174] The question of when a detained client must be brought to court within 48 hours depends on the circumstances of each case.[175] For example, in matters involving robbery with aggravating circumstances, possession of an unlicensed firearm, or murder with multiple suspects, it may be necessary to conduct an identification parade before the first appearance. This stands in contrast to cases where a single accused is charged with assault GBH, or theft, which may require no further investigation, such as an identification parade. In the second example, it would be justified to approach the High Court urgently if the accused is not brought to court on Friday morning, despite engagement with the investigating officer, and the practitioner is informed that the officer is too busy and intends to charge the accused only on Sunday. Such conduct would be inconsistent with the obligation to bring an arrested person before a court within the prescribed time period and may render the continued detention unlawful. In such circumstances, the High Court may be approached urgently for a mandatory interdict (mandamus).[176] There must be a genuine and lawful reason why an accused is not brought before the court as early as reasonably possible, as obstructive conduct by an investigating officer cannot be countenanced.[177] An example of a mandatory interdict compelling the investigating officer to bring the detained accused before the court for a first appearance may be as follows:

---

[172] Section 50(1) (d) (iii) of the CPA.

[173] *Mashilo v Prinsloo* (576/11) (2012) ZASCA 146 (28 September 2012) para 16. See also *Matebese v Minister of Police* (2224/2017) [2019] ZAECPEHC 37 (18 June 2019) para 40.

[174] Ibid.

[175] Ibid.

[176] Ibid.

[177] Ibid.

IN THE HIGH COURT OF SOUTH AFRICA

(WESTERN CAPE DIVISION, CAPE TOWN)

CASE NO: A77/ 22

In the matter between:

VUYOLWETHU BHAYIBHAYI APPLICANT

And

SIYABULELA BARENDSE N.O. 1ST RESPONDENT

NATIONAL COMMISSIONER OF POLICE 2ND RESPONDENT

NOTICE OF MOTION

PLEASE TAKE NOTICE that the Applicant intends to make an application to this honourable court on this evening of 15 July 2022 at 06.30 pm or so soon thereafter as the matter can be heard for orders in the following terms:

1. Declaring the application to be a matter of urgency and dispensing in so far as is necessary in terms of rule 6 (12) with the usual forms and services provided for in the Uniform Rules of Court;
2. Reviewing and setting aside the decision of the First Respondent in Rondebosch Police Station CAS Number 111/07/2022, refusing to take the Applicant to appear in Cape Town Magistrates' Court for his first appearance and bail application on 15 July 2022;
3. Directing the First Respondent and the Second Respondent to ensure that the Applicant appears at Cape Town Magistrates' Court before 09.00 am on 16 July 2022 for his first appearance and possible bail application;
4. Ordering the First and the Second Respondent, if they oppose this application, to pay the costs;
5. In the event that the First Respondent and the Second Respondent fail to comply with this order, the Applicant shall be entitled to approach this court on the same papers for an appropriate relief on 16 July 2022 at 05.00 pm; and the First Respondent and Second Respondent are hereby directed to appear before this court on 16 July 2022 at 05.00 pm to show cause why they should not pay the costs *de bonis propiis*.

TAKE NOTICE FURTHER that the affidavit of the Applicant will be used in support of this application.

TAKE NOTICE FURTHER that the Applicant has appointed this email address (info@sephumaattorneys.co.za) of his attorneys as the address at which it will receive notices and services of all processes in this matter.

TAKE NOTICE FURTHER that if any of the Respondents intend to oppose this application, such Respondent shall:

(i) Immediately upon receipt of the founding papers, deliver a notice of intention to oppose the application by email to the Applicant's attorneys of record at the following email address: info@sephumaattorneys.co.za

(ii) further file the opposing papers by not later than this afternoon at 04.30 pm on 15 July 2022 at info@sephumaattorneys.co.za.

TAKE NOTICE FURTHER that failing to give such notice of intention to oppose and/or failing to file the opposing papers, the application for the relief sought shall be heard on an unopposed basis.

DATED AND SIGNED AT CAPE TOWN ON 15 JULY 2022.

____

SEPHUMA ATTORNEYS

APPLICANT'S ATTORNEYS

TO: THE REGISTRAR OF THE ABOVE COURT

TO: MR SIYABULELA BARENDSE N.O.

AND TO: NATIONAL COMMISSIONER OF POLICE

Where the 48 hours have expired, but the accused is still held in custody, it amounts to unlawful detention. Therefore, an urgent application to challenge the lawfulness of the accused's detention may be lodged, as explained in paragraph 4.3. Paragraph 6.1 outlines the procedure to follow when the detained client is only brought before the court after 48 hours have passed.

4.2 Torture has no place in police custody

Legal practitioners practising in the field of criminal law are aware that allegations of torture by law enforcement officials arise in certain cases.[178]

[178] Centre for the Study of Violence and Reconciliation "Torture in South Africa: The Act and the Facts" September 2014 p5 https://www.csvr.org.za/pdf/Torture%20in%20South%20Africa.pdf accessed 01 May 2024. See also *S v Gqoki and Others* (CC14/2018) [2020] ZAECMHC 63 (26 February 2020), https://www.saferspaces.org.za/understand/entry/police-brutality-in-south-africa and Bruce D "The Risks of Police Custody: The Potential for Independent Monitoring of Police Custody in South Africa" "October 2019 *African Policing Civilian Oversight Forum*

Despite a comprehensive statutory framework prohibiting such conduct, practitioners may feel uncertain at times. The appropriate legal and procedural steps to advise clients who allege ill-treatment may not always be clear.

Torture is prohibited by the Prevention and Combating of Torture of Persons Act 13 of 2013. Section 4 of this Act stipulates that a police officer can face life imprisonment for torturing the arrested client. The Act establishes a clear legal framework for addressing police brutality and reinforces the constitutional prohibition against torture and cruel, inhuman, or degrading treatment. The prohibition against torture is one of our most fundamental constitutional values since it is one of the most serious violations of human rights.[179] Article 15 of the Convention against Torture and Other Cruel, Inhuman or Degrading Treatment or Punishment [180] prohibits the admissibility of any evidence obtained against the detained client as a result of torture in any proceedings.[181] Accordingly, where allegations of torture arise, it is incumbent upon legal practitioners to ensure that relevant evidence is gathered without delay, since such evidence may have decisive implications for the admissibility of statements or other material alleged to have been procured through torture.

To provide comprehensive advice to the client, it is crucial to understand the definition of 'torture' as defined in Section 3 of Act 13 of 2013. The following describes the requirements for an act to be considered torture in the case of a detained client:

1. The perpetrator of torture must be a public official (police officer, metro police officer, or any person purporting to be a public official).
2. The act of torture can only be committed intentionally.
3. The victim must have suffered severe pain or suffering, whether physical or mental.
4. The purpose of inflicting severe pain or suffering must be to:
   (a) secure information or confession;
   (b) punish the victim for the offence, or
   (c) intimidate or coerce the victim or any other person to do or refrain from doing something.

Torture, as contemplated in the statutory framework, is committed by a public official or person acting in an official capacity who exercises authority over a

Research Paper p5 https://apcof.org/wp-content/uploads/026-risksofpolicecustody-thepotentialforindependentmonitoringofpolicecustodyinsouthafrica-davidbruce.pdf accessed on 01 May 2024.

[179] *S v Mthembu* (379/07) [2008] ZASCA 51; [2008] 3 All SA 159 (SCA); [2008] 4 All SA 517 (SCA); 2008 (2) SACR 407 (SCA) (10 April 2008) para 31.

[180] United Nations Convention against Torture and Other Cruel, Inhuman or Degrading Treatment or Punishment Assembly resolution 39/46 of 10 December 1984, https://www.ohchr.org/sites/default/files/cat.pdf accessed 31 December 2023.

[181] Also see *S v Mthembu* [*supra*] para 32.

detainee, thereby placing that individual in a position of vulnerability.[182] Absent reasonable grounds to believe that torture is imminent or ongoing, an application to court based solely on speculation would not ordinarily satisfy the evidentiary threshold required for judicial intervention.

In certain instances where allegations of ill-treatment arise, access to a detained person may be restricted. Legal practitioners or family members may be informed that the detainee has been taken out for further investigation or that, because formal charges have not yet been instituted, access is limited. Such circumstances require careful scrutiny to ensure that constitutional rights of access to legal representation and family contact are respected.[183] In some instances, a detainee may be held at a police station other than the one initially indicated, ostensibly for purposes of further investigation. Legal practitioners may occasionally encounter additional administrative requirements when seeking access to a detained client, including requests for documentation beyond standard proof of professional status. Where access is delayed or restricted, practitioners should be familiar with the applicable standing orders and national instructions governing detainee rights and legal consultation.

Unlike court proceedings, access disputes at police stations do not occur before a neutral judicial officer. Accordingly, practitioners must rely on their knowledge of the regulatory framework and the constitutional right of access to legal representation to secure compliance.

Where urgent judicial intervention is required, the High Court is ordinarily the appropriate forum. However, such proceedings may not always be practically or financially feasible for every detained person. In practice, familiarity with standing orders and national instructions, coupled with a clear articulation of the legal position, may assist in resolving access difficulties without immediate recourse to litigation.

Where necessary, concerns regarding access or alleged ill-treatment may be escalated to the Community Service Centre (CSC) commander or relevant supervisory personnel. Detainees are entitled to regular monitoring, and responsible officers are required to conduct periodic inspections of holding cells to ensure detainee welfare.[184] Where a detainee raises an allegation of torture while in police custody, the complaint must be reported without delay to the station commander or, where appropriate, to the relevant provincial or

---

[182] Centre for the Study of Violence and Reconciliation "Torture in South Africa: The Act and the Facts" September 2014 p3 https://www.csvr.org.za/pdf/Torture%20in%20South%20Africa.pdf accessed 01 May 2024.

[183] National Instruction 13 of 2019: Management of Persons in Custody of the South African Police Service para 21 (3) deals with a prohibition of communication between a legal practitioner and the detained person, while paragraph 22 (3) deals with the restriction of communication between the detained person and their spouse or next of kin. For more information on the prohibition of consultation between the legal practitioner and their client, see paragraph 1.2 in this book.

[184] National Instruction 13 of 2019 [*supra*] para 25 (6) (a).

divisional commissioner. [185] The commander to whom the complaint is reported is required to notify the appropriate provincial office of the Independent Police Investigative Directorate (IPID). [186] All steps taken following the report must be recorded in the Occurrence Book (SAPS 10) at the station where the complaint was lodged.[187] However, the detained client may also submit a complaint regarding torture directly to the IPID.[188]

The reporting of torture is not always possible or easy because of the vulnerable position the client might find themselves in. Therefore, when you are informed that the client has been tortured, you may lodge a complaint on their behalf. The station commander must ensure that the matter is investigated and steps are taken to protect the client.[189] If the investigation reveals that a police officer has committed, attempted to commit, or acted as an accomplice in the commission of torture, it constitutes serious misconduct.[190] In addition to facing criminal charges, the officer should be subject to immediate disciplinary proceedings.[191] The station commander must report progress monthly to the provincial or divisional commissioner on the disciplinary and/or criminal proceedings against the police officer involved in torture.[192] Every provincial and divisional commissioner must keep a record of all disciplinary and/or criminal proceedings instituted on account of allegations of torture, and of the outcome of each case.[193] The investigation of allegations of torture will inevitably involve an examination by a medical practitioner.[194] Where a state-appointed medical practitioner examines a client alleging torture, the station commander must request a written report that includes:

1. any statements made by the detained person which are relevant to the medical examination;
2. a description of the objective medical findings based on the medical examination; and
3. the conclusions in light of the alleged torture and findings.[195]

Whenever the conclusions reveal signs of torture, the commander must request the medical practitioner to send a copy of the written report to the

---

[185] National Instruction 6 of 2014: The Prevention and Combating of Torture of Persons para 4 (5).

[186] Ibid.

[187] Ibid.

[188] Ibid.

[189] National Instruction 6 of 2014 [*supra*] para 4 (4).

[190] National Instruction 6 of 2014 [*supra*] para 4 (6).

[191] Ibid.

[192] National Instruction 6 of 2014 [*supra*] para 4 (7) and (9).

[193] National Instruction 6 of 2014 [supra] para 4 (8) and (9).

[194] National Instruction 8 of 2016: Medical Treatment and Hospitalization of a Person in Custody para 6 (1).

[195] National Instruction 8 of 2016 [*supra*] para 6 (1) (a)-(c).

nearest IPID office.[196] Where the tortured client is not taken to a district surgeon, or even if they have been attended to by a district surgeon, the client is entitled to be examined by a medical practitioner of their choice, but must pay for medical expenses out of their pocket. Section 35(2) (f) (iv) of the Constitution grants the freedom to exercise this right, and its further regulation is based on Standing Order 349 and National Instruction 8 of 2016.[197]

In light of the prevalence of torture in police custody,[198] and while standing orders and national instructions are against it, if the SAPS is serious about stopping it, every detained person must be informed about the illegality of torture and be advised as to what steps can be taken to report it. This information should be in writing, and every detained person should sign and be provided with a copy of such a document, just as is done regarding SAPS 14A.

4.3 Challenging unlawful arrest and detention before first appearance

Sometimes, the client is arrested and detained without a warrant in cases where the police officers have no authority under Section 40 of the CPA, or the client is kept in custody for more than 48 hours in defiance of Section 50. Where it is clear that the client's arrest and detention are unlawful, the Constitution has created a remedy. In terms of Section 35(2)(d) of the Constitution, every detained person has a right "to challenge the lawfulness of the detention in person before a court and if the detention is unlawful, to be released". This application to challenge the lawfulness of detention should be brought on urgent notice of motion, accompanied by a founding affidavit explaining why the High Court should intervene. Since the challenge concerns the lawfulness of the detention, the affidavit must set out in detail the grounds upon which the detention is alleged to be unlawful.

Urgent applications are dealt with in detail in paragraphs 2.8 and 12.5. It is therefore important to study these paragraphs before drafting an application for the urgent release of a detained client by the High Court.

An example of an application challenging unlawful detention appears below.

---

[196] National Instruction 8 of 2016: Medical Treatment and Hospitalization of a Person in Custody para 6 (2).

[197] National Instruction 8 of 2016 [*supra*] para 7.

[198] See The Centre for the Study of Violence and Reconciliation "Torture in South Africa: The Act on torture" September 2014 p5.

IN THE HIGH COURT OF SOUTH AFRICA

(MPUMALANGA DIVISION, MBOMBELA)

CASE NO:_________

In the matter between:

THAMI MNISI APPLICANT

And

SIPHO NGWANE N.O. 1ST RESPONDENT

NATIONAL COMMISSIONER OF POLICE 2ND RESPONDENT

NOTICE OF MOTION

BE PLEASED TO TAKE NOTICE that the Applicant intends to bring an application on an urgent basis this evening, **16 August 2022,** at **07.30 pm** or so soon thereafter as the honourable court may hear the matter for an order in the following terms:

1. That this honourable court condones the noncompliance by the Applicant with the rules of court regarding the usual forms, time limits and manner of service stipulated therein and hears this application as one of urgency in terms of rule 6 (12);
2. Declaring that the Applicant's detention in Kanyamazane Police Station, Case Number 72/08/2022, is unlawful;
3. Directing the Respondents to release the Applicant from police custody as soon as possible after receiving this order, but not later than 2 hours; and
4. Ordering the Respondents, if they oppose this application, to pay the costs.

TAKE NOTICE FURTHER that the affidavit of the Applicant will be used in support of this application.

TAKE NOTICE FURTHER that the Applicant has appointed this email address (**info@bangiswaniattorneys.co.za**) of his attorneys as the email address at which it will receive notices and services of all processes in this matter.

TAKE NOTICE FURTHER that if any of the Respondents intend to oppose this application, such Respondent[s] shall:

(a) immediately on receipt of the founding papers, deliver a notice of intention to oppose the application by email to the Applicant's attorneys of record at the following email address: **info@bangiswaniattorneys.co.za**;
(b) further, file the opposing papers by not later than **04.30 pm** on **16 August 2022** at **info@bangiswaniattorneys.co.za**.

TAKE NOTICE FURTHER that failing to give such notice of intention to oppose and/or failing to file the opposing papers, the application for the relief sought shall be heard on an unopposed basis.

DATED AND SIGNED AT **MBOMBELA** ON **16 AUGUST 2022**.

____

Bangiswani Attorneys

APPLICANT'S ATTORNEYS

TO: THE REGISTRAR OF THE ABOVE COURT

TO: MR SIPHO NGWANE N.O.

AND TO: NATIONAL COMMISSION OF POLICE

CHAPTER 5

GENERAL PREPARATION FOR FIRST APPEARANCE

5.1 There are unnecessarily difficult presiding officers

Many presiding officers are exemplary in their conduct, treating both legal practitioners and members of the public with respect, patience, and professionalism. However, it must be acknowledged that some court experiences are made unnecessarily difficult by presiding officers whose conduct may be perceived as impatient, dismissive, or sarcastic. It can be especially challenging for practitioners to appear before a judicial officer who appears unwilling to engage meaningfully with counsel, reaches premature conclusions, or does not provide a fair opportunity to present the client's case.

Surely, many legal practitioners have, at some point, encountered a presiding officer who asserts that "this is my court," followed by a directive to adhere to a particular established practice. If you have not yet had such an experience, you are either very new to the profession or fortunate—at least for now. These instances often occur in open court, in the presence of clients and members of the public. Given the authority of the presiding officer, such remarks can carry significant weight and, at times, may unintentionally result in embarrassment—even for seasoned practitioners. The imbalance of courtroom power makes it imperative that judicial authority is exercised with both firmness and fairness.

In 2002, in *Terry v Botes and Another*,[199] the legal practitioner was unnecessarily criticised for their dress code,[200] and later was not allowed to address the court about the accused's failure to appear in court while released on bail.[201] When the sickly accused was forced to come to court and testify, his phone unfortunately rang and his testimony was abruptly stopped by the court, which commented that he was now in trouble, and he was remanded in custody for

[199] *Terry v Botes and Another* (1868/2002) ZAWCHC 22; [2002] 3 All SA 798 (C); 2003 (1) SACR 206 (C) (30 April 2002).
[200] *Terry v Botes and Another* [*supra*] p6-7.
[201] *Terry v Botes and Another* [*supra*] p8.

seven days before the inquiry could proceed again.[202] In this case, Foxcroft J had the following to say after reviewing the conduct of the magistrate:

> This whole unhappy saga reminds one of days when members of the public and legal representatives were treated in some cases with great indifference, and occasional rudeness, in superior and inferior courts. The Constitution insists that people be treated fairly and properly, and the attitude displayed by [the] First Respondent in this matter was reprehensible and cannot be left without criticism.

Ratshibvumo J, in *S v Mashego,*[203] also dealt with this problem almost two decades after Foxcroft J's comments under what was termed "Court's decorum flowing from the bench". While the accused in that case was unrepresented, the judgment goes a long way in reminding the presiding officers of how to conduct themselves properly when administering justice in court. In a guiding voice, the learned judge stated the following:[204]

> The authority we are endowed with as judicial officers is from the public and it is not meant to intimidate it, but to execute justice to its members with respect and humility. We are not in these positions because we are indomitable. If we did not volunteer our service, there would be others doing exactly what we are doing and maybe even better. When the time is due, we will be replaced and justice will continue being meted out to the public in our absence.

At times, attempts to refer to case law are cut short by presiding officers who insist they are already familiar with it, discouraging further argument. Remaining calm is necessary when faced with these circumstances. It is submitted that, while courts must manage time efficiently—particularly in light of increasingly congested case rolls—this responsibility must be balanced against the principle of *audi alteram partem*, which guarantees each party the right to be heard. Therefore, legal practitioners should not be dissuaded by perceived judicial impatience, but should continue to advocate—firmly yet respectfully—for the time and opportunity necessary to ensure the fair and lawful conduct of proceedings. Ultimately, this calls for a careful balancing of competing interests: judicial efficiency on the one hand, and procedural fairness on the other.

The conduct of presiding officers—whether marked by impatience, sarcasm, or an appearance of egotism—may, at times, be shaped by how we present

---

[202] *Terry v Botes and Another* (1868/2002) ZAWCHC 22; [2002] 3 All SA 798 (C); 2003 (1) SACR 206 (C) (30 April 2002) p10.

[203] *S v Mashego* (R24/2021; A360/2020) [2021] ZAMPMBHC 36; 2021 (2) SACR 520 (MM) (10 August 2021) para 28-31.

[204] *S v Mashego* [*supra*]) para 30.

ourselves in court: our level of preparation, our clarity of purpose, and our ability to argue persuasively. It is therefore vital that we approach every court appearance with thorough preparation, clear objectives, and a readiness to engage constructively, even in the face of difficulty.

5.2 There are applications in criminal proceedings, not mere requests

From the beginning, you should know that there are no requests in criminal proceedings, only applications. Informal applications are ordinarily made orally from the bar without the filing of written documents. They are used where facts are not in dispute. Formal applications require supporting evidence, either through affidavits or witness testimony. Even if the prosecution makes an informal application, you may still lead evidence. In cases of opposed applications, evidence is usually necessary, whether in the form of affidavits or witness testimony.

5.3 Good manners and respect in court are not negotiable

As a legal practitioner and officer of the court, you are expected to conduct yourself with the highest degree of integrity, to ensure that the dignity and decorum of the court are maintained, and to have the highest respect for the legal order.[205] For the courts to effectively function and to properly administer justice, they depend heavily on how legal practitioners discharge their duties to the court.[206] You must always be sensitive to your choice of words in court because "[i]nsulting, vulgar and disparaging language by a legal practitioner cannot be tolerated".[207] Legal practitioners are always expected and are bound to "deal with the judicial officer, court staff and all other persons in court with civility and respect".[208] "It will be difficult to expect members of the public to respect and uphold the decorum of the court if this is not adhered to by members of the court."[209]

No eating or drinking is permitted in court, except for still water contained in a transparent bottle or glass. The requirement that the container be transparent is intended to avoid any misconception regarding its contents. The

---

[205] *Goane Jack Montshiwa (Ex Parte Application)* (672/2021) [2023] ZASCA 19 (3 March 2023) para 36.
[206] Ibid.
[207] *Goane Jack Montshiwa* [supra] para 36.
[208] *Code of Conduct for all Legal Practitioners, Candidate Legal Practitioners and Juristic Entities* GN 162 in GG 42337 29 March 2019 para 61.6.
[209] *Yuma v S* (A09 / 2022) [2022] ZAMPMBHC 7 (3 February 2022) para 21.

prescribed uniform for legal practitioners must be strictly adhered to. Compliance with court dress is not optional. Legal practitioners should also refrain from engaging in conversations while the court is in session, as such conduct undermines the dignity of the proceedings.

Cell phones must be switched off or placed in flight mode. Merely placing a cell phone on silent is inadequate. Any legal practitioner who has applied for court transcripts will be familiar with portions of the record marked "inaudible". In many instances, this is not because the witness was unclear, but because mobile network signals interfered with the court's recording equipment. When stenographers listen through earphones, they often detect that a cell phone is on and that its signal is interfering with the recording. However, this interference may not always be immediately detected, as stenographers also perform other administrative duties. Legal practitioners must therefore ensure that their cell phones are completely switched off, particularly as they are officers of the court and are seated closest to the recording devices.

Legal practitioners have designated seating in court, which they are expected to occupy throughout the proceedings. Where a practitioner appears in a particular court for the first time and is the only legal practitioner present, it is advisable to enquire where one should sit. Although courtroom layouts are generally similar, variations do exist. In most courts, the legal practitioner's podium faces the presiding officer directly, while the prosecutor's podium is positioned to the side, facing the witness stand.

When the presiding officer enters the courtroom, all persons present are required to stand. Before taking their seat, the presiding officer will make a slight bow, which is reciprocated by the officers of the court. Whenever the court addresses a legal practitioner, or whenever a legal practitioner addresses the court, the practitioner must stand fully and respectfully. It is insufficient merely to gesture or partially rise.

At every court appearance, the legal practitioner must first place their appearance on record by confirming that they appear on behalf of the accused before making any submissions. If it becomes necessary, while addressing the court, to take brief instructions from the client, the practitioner must first seek the court's leave and wait for it to be granted. If leave is granted, the communication must be limited to whispering. Upon completion, it is appropriate to thank the court for the indulgence and request permission to proceed. Upon concluding submissions, the practitioner should indicate this by stating, "as the court pleases". Similarly, once the court delivers a ruling on any application, both the legal practitioner and the prosecutor must show respect for the ruling—whether they agree with it or not—by responding, "as the court pleases".

In the High Court, it is not customary to request to be excused once a matter is finished. In the Magistrates' Court, a legal practitioner must request to be excused before another matter is called. Typically, you would state: "Your

Worship, that concludes my roll; may I be excused." When entering or leaving the courtroom during a session, stop at the doorway, face the presiding officer, and bow slightly before entering or leaving.

5.4 It is important to arrive early for the first appearance

Although the court commences at 09:00 and you are duty-bound to be present before proceedings begin, [210] it is essential to arrive early for the first appearance of your matter, particularly where the accused is in custody.

Arriving early enables the legal practitioner to engage with the prosecutor regarding the preferred charge and the State's attitude toward bail or the matter generally. It must always be borne in mind that the offence initially preferred by the police is not binding on the prosecutor.

A practitioner may attend court under the impression that the matter concerns a Schedule I offence, such as common robbery, only to discover that the prosecutor has elected to prefer a charge of robbery with aggravating circumstances. In such circumstances, the matter falls immediately under Schedule 6, requiring a formal bail application. Early engagement with the prosecutor allows the practitioner to inform the client timeously and to prepare an affidavit in anticipation of that application. One of the most difficult situations for a client is to learn, for the first time while already standing in court, that the offence falls under Schedule 6 and that bail will be opposed.

In some instances, the prosecutor may indicate that the matter will not be placed on the roll. This may occur because there are no reasonable prospects of a successful prosecution (nolle prosequi), or because the matter is provisionally withdrawn pending the completion of outstanding investigations, in which event it is marked as not enrolled. Informing the client and their family of such a decision before it is formally announced in court reflects professionalism and reinforces confidence in the representation.

5.5 Duty to introduce yourself to the presiding magistrate

Where a matter is placed on the roll, and a legal practitioner appears for the first time before a particular presiding officer, it is necessary to introduce oneself before appearing in that court.[211] In the Magistrates' Courts, such an introduction does not require the presence of the prosecutor. Waiting for the

---

[210] *Code of Conduct for all Legal Practitioners, Candidate Legal Practitioners and Juristic Entities* GN 162 in GG 42337 29 March 2019 para 60.3.

[211] *Code of Conduct* [*supra*] para 61.4.

prosecutor to become available for this purpose is impractical. Prosecutors often carry heavy rolls, sometimes exceeding fifty matters in a single court. Requiring them to accompany practitioners for introductions would unnecessarily disrupt trial preparation. In practice, prosecutors simply do not have the capacity to do so.

The appropriate approach is to liaise with the court clerk assigned to the particular magistrate and request assistance in facilitating the introduction.[212]

When introducing yourself, you must have all the necessary documentation confirming that you are duly qualified to practise. This should not present a difficulty, particularly since the Legal Practice Council now issues digital identity cards that allow verification by scanning a QR code.[213] The digital identity card serves as an important safeguard against the appearance of unqualified or fraudulent representatives.

If you are a briefed advocate, you should also have a written brief available.

Presiding officers are obliged to ensure that all court officials, including legal practitioners, are properly qualified.[214] If you were unable to introduce yourself beforehand—as sometimes occurs—you should apologise before placing yourself on record and have your documentation available should the court require proof of your status.

---

[212] *Code of Conduct for all Legal Practitioners, Candidate Legal Practitioners and Juristic Entities* GN 162 in GG 42337 29 March 2019 para 61.4.

[213] https://lpc.org.za/legal-practitioners/identity-card-application/ accessed 02 July 2024.

[214] Criminal Practice Directives for the Regional Court of South Africa, 2023, para 3.3.

CHAPTER 6

ISSUES WHICH ARE STRICTLY APPLICABLE TO OR MIGHT NEED TO BE ADDRESSED ON FIRST APPEARANCE

6.1 Fighting unlawful arrest and detention on first appearance

6.1.1 Unlawful detention in general

Legal practitioners may encounter matters in which an accused remains in custody, only to realise that the arrest ought not to have occurred. This arises where the nature of the offence and the circumstances under which it was allegedly committed do not justify an arrest, or where the detention has exceeded 48 hours. In such cases, it becomes apparent that the police officer acted without lawful authority, either by effecting an arrest without a warrant contrary to Section 40(1) of the Criminal Procedure Act, or by detaining the accused beyond the period permitted by Section 50(1) of the Act.

These provisions are of central importance in limiting unjustified infringements of the right to freedom. They ensure that arrests without a warrant are effected only where the offence and surrounding circumstances warrant such intervention, and that an arrested person is brought before a court for a first appearance at the earliest available opportunity. This ensures that any further detention takes place under the supervision of the court. An arrest or detention effected in breach of Sections 40(1) and 50(1) constitutes a clear case of unlawful arrest and detention.[215] It amounts to a deprivation of freedom that is arbitrary or without just cause, in contravention of Section 12(1)(a) of the Constitution. In *Mahlangu and Another v Minister of Police*,[216] the Constitutional Court recently reminded us that the "unlawful deprivation of

---

[215] See *De Klerk v Minister of Police* (CCT 95/18) [2019] 32; 2019 (12) BCLR 1425 (CC); 2020 (1) SACR 1 (CC); 2021 (4) SA 585 (CC) (22 August 2019), *Mashilo and Another v Prinsloo* (576/ 2011) [2012] ZASCA 146 and *Seleko v Minister of Police* (938/2011) [2014] ZANWHC 47 (30 October 2014).

[216] *Mahlangu and Another v Minister of Police* (CCT 88/20) [2021] ZACC 10; 2021 (7) BCLR 698 (CC); 2021 (2) SACR 595 (CC) (14 May 2021) para 27.

liberty, as inescapably accompanied by a breach of the right to human dignity, is always taken as a grave wrong and a serious inroad into the freedom and rights of a person". The court quoted *Thandani v Minister of Law and Order,*[217] where it was stated that:

> ... sight must not be lost of the fact that the liberty of the individual is one of the fundamental rights of a [person] in a free society which should be jealously guarded at all times and there is a duty on our Courts to preserve this right against infringement. Unlawful arrest and detention constitutes a serious inroad into the freedom and the rights of an individual.[218]

Looking at Section 40, it is clear that arrest without a warrant is not permitted under certain circumstances, while Section 50(1) explains that detention should never exceed 48 hours. However, neither of these Sections provides a remedy in the event of a breach. While it is clear "that the State may not deprive its citizens of liberty for reasons that are not acceptable",[219] the lack of a clear remedy or procedure as to what should be done is a problem on its own, since the Magistrates' Court are 'creatures of statute'. Therefore, all the powers they exercise are derived from statute.[220] The jurisdiction of the lower courts is dependent on any statute granting such jurisdiction.[221] The question

---

[217] *Thandani v Minister of Law and Order* 1991 (1) SA 702 (E) 707A-B.

[218] Ibid.

[219] *Mahlangu and Another v Minister of Police*: (CCT 88/20) [2021] ZACC 10; 2021 (7) BCLR 698 (CC); 2021 (2) SACR 595 (CC) (14 May 2021) para 28.

[220] *S v Naidoo* (A 293/2011) [2011] ZAWCHC 448; 2012 (2) SACR 126 (WWC) (6 December 2011) para 12, the court emphasised that powers and jurisdiction of Magistrates' Courts "are limited to those which have been expressly provided by statute". It quoted *Minister of Safety and Security and Another v Bosman* 2010 (2) SA 148 (C) para 10: "Our law is replete with case law and legal authority that the jurisdiction of magistrates' courts is established in the statute under which the courts are constituted. This applies not only to the empowering sections of the Magistrates' Courts Act, but also to the Rules. A magistrate cannot exercise powers which are not expressly stated in the Act or the Rules. There may be instances where authority may be implied, since it has been held that the purpose of an Act is not to be defeated because the ancillary powers which are necessary to enforce a judgment have not been especially mentioned".

[221] *Naidoo v Regional Magistrate for Durban Magistrates' Court, Mr M Maharaj and Another* (AR769/14) [2017] ZAKZPHC 19; 2017 (2) SACR 244 (KZP) (23 May 2017) para 13 and the footnote appearing thereto: *Ndamase v Functions 4 All* 2004 (5) SA 602 (SCA) para 5, reads:"It is well-established that the Magistrates' Court has no jurisdiction and powers beyond those granted by the Act (compare *Riversdale Divisional Council v Pienaar* (1885) 3 SC 252 at 256; *Stork v Stork* (1903) 20 SC 138 at 139; *Gqalana and Others v Knoesen and Another* 1980 (4) SA 119 (E) at 120; *Mason Motors (Edms) Bpk v Van Niekerk* 1983 (4) SA 406 (T) at 409E-F; *Venter v Standard Bank of South Africa* [1999] 3 All SA 278 (W) at *280i-j*) and that in this context, jurisdiction means 'the power vested in a court by law to adjudicate upon, determine and dispose of a matter' (see *Ewing McDonald & Co. Ltd v M & M Products Co* 1991 (1) SA 252 (A) at 256G-H; *Graaff-Reinet Municipality v Van Ryneveld's Pass Irrigation*

is what should be done when you encounter either of these two problems (where either Section 40 or 50 has been breached)?

6.1.2 Unlawful detention due to the expiration of 48 hours and struck off the roll order

What should be done on the first appearance when the accused person is brought before the court after 48 hours have expired? The courts usually strike the matter from the roll once it becomes clear that 48 hours have expired.[222] While the authority for the court to strike the matter from the roll is sometimes questionable, Section 50(1) of the CPA's use of "shall be brought before lower court as soon as reasonably possible, but not later than 48 hours after the arrest" seems decisive that the lower court cannot deal with the detained client if brought later than 48 hours. If the prosecutor enrols the matter, the court may strike it from the roll. While the authority of a magistrate to strike the matter off the roll is not expressed in Section 50(1) (c) of the CPA, it appears to be implied. The authority is deemed to be implied where it is clear that the purpose of the legislation would be defeated because the ancillary or incidental powers necessary to enforce a judgment have not been expressly conferred.[223] The implied power to strike the matter from the roll is necessary for the court to exercise the expressed power in

---

Board 1950 (2) SA 420 (A) at 424; *Spendiff NO v Kolektor (Pty) Ltd* 1992 (2) SA 537 (A) at 551C). It is also well-established that powers may be conferred expressly or by implication. Where the Act is silent on a matter, the general rule is that by expressly conferring on the Magistrates' Courts' jurisdiction in respect of a particular matter, the Act confers by implication the ancillary powers necessary to give effect to that jurisdiction. Concerning matters specifically provided for in the Act, the Act will govern that situation (compare *Reuters v Clarke* 1922 EDL 303 at 305; *Van der Merwe v De Villiers and Another* 1953 (4) SA 670 (T) at 672F-673C; *Hatfield Town Management Board v Mynfred Poultry Farm (Pvt) Ltd* 1963 (1) SA 737 (SR) at 739E-F). The primary question to be answered, therefore, is whether the Act expressly or by implication confers on a magistrates' court jurisdiction to grant a provisional sentence. Also see LAWSA Vol 11 (2 ed) para 534, which reads as follows: "The magistrates' courts are creatures of statute and have no jurisdiction beyond that granted by the Constitution or the statute creating them. They have no inherent jurisdiction to develop the common law since they have not been empowered by the Constitution to develop the common law, taking into account the interests of justice, but must, in their decisions, apply the provisions of the Bill of Rights, by which they are bound, as organs of state" (Footnotes omitted).

[222] See *Mphohoni v National Police Commissioner and Another* (608/2011) [2014] ZALMPHC 7 (9 September 2014) para 12. Also see *S v Conradie* (A248/2020) [2020] ZAWCHC 177 (11 December 2020) para 6.

[223] *Minister of Safety and Security and Another v Bosman* (A725/2007, 4261/2007) [2008]; 2010 (2) SA 148 (C) (4 June 2008) para 10, is also quoted in *S v Naidoo* (A293/2011) [2011] ZAWCHC 448; 2012 (2) SACR 126 (WWC) (6 December 2011) para 12.

Section 50(1) (c) of the CPA.[224]

It is therefore submitted that the court in enforcing Section 50(1) of the CPA has the implied authority to strike the matter off the roll. Apart from bringing the application, which is squarely dependent on the CPA as discussed, non-compliance with the 48-hour rule may also be addressed in conjunction with the detained client's right to challenge the lawfulness of their detention before the court in terms of Section 35(2) (d) of the Constitution, as discussed in paragraphs 6.1.4 and 6.1.5. In *National Commissioner of Police v Coetzee,*[225] the Supreme Court of Appeal (SCA) was also of the view that Section 50 of the CPA, which deals with the procedure after arrest, should also be interpreted in the context of Section 35 (2) (d) of the Constitution.

6.1.3 Unlawful detention due to arrest without a warrant in defiance of Section 40(1) of the CPA

What should happen when the accused appears on their first appearance in court after being detained for an offence for which they were not supposed to be arrested? While Section 40 of the CPA sets out the offences and situations that permit arrest without a warrant, it does not expressly give magistrates the power to inquire into or issue orders where it appears that the detention is unlawful, and no implied power appears competent. Consequently, it appears that in terms of the CPA, the magistrate is not obliged to conduct an inquiry about the lawfulness of the arrest of the detained person appearing before them.[226]

An early interpretation of the court's competence to entertain enrolled matters involving all arrested persons at their first appearance—including those unlawfully arrested—was considered in *Mthimkhulu v Minister of Law and Order.*[227] The court held that a lawful arrest (including compliance with Section 40 of the CPA) is a prerequisite for an accused to be lawfully dealt with by the court at their first appearance in terms of Section 50(1) of the CPA; thus, if the arrest is unlawful, it cannot be regarded as valid, and anything flowing from such an arrest is equally invalid and unlawful.[228] However, the Appellate Division in *Isaacs v Minister van Wet en Orde,*[229]

---

[224] *AmaBhungane Centre for Investigative Journalism NPC and Another v Minister of Justice and Correctional Services and Others; Minister of Police v AmaBhungane Centre for Investigative Journalism NPC and Others* (CCT 278/19;CCT 279/19) [2021] ZACC 3;2021 (4) BCLR 349 (CC); 2021 (3) SA 246 (CC) (4 February 2021) para63-68.

[225] *National Commissioner of Police v Coetzee* (649/11) [2012] ZASCA 161 (16 November 2012) para 6.

[226] E DuToit et al *Commentary on the Criminal ProcedureAct* (2023 RS 70) (5–44).

[227] *Mthimkhulu v Minister of Law and Order* 1993 (3) SA 432 (E) at438C-F.

[228] Ibid.

[229] *Isaacs v Minister vanWet en Order* [1995] ZASCA 152;1996 (1) SACR 314 (A) 323H-I.

found that the *lawful arrest prerequisite* established in *Mthimkhulu* was incorrect. It stated that when Section 50(1) refers to someone who is 'arrested', it is not limited to a lawfully arrested person, but "it includes someone who, under an attempt to exercise the power of arrest, was brought under the arrestor's control".[230] The SCA in *Minister of Safety and Security v Tyokwana,*[231] reiterated the position in *Isaacs* and stated that:

> ...what was decided in Isaacs, is that the prior lawful arrest of a person is not a prerequisite to the provisions of s 50(1) of the CPA coming into effect. Put differently, it was held that the fact that the person may have been arrested unlawfully, does not preclude him or her from being remanded lawfully in terms of s 50(1) of the CPA. However, what was not held in Isaacs, is that an arrested person's continued detention by virtue of an order of the court remanding him or her in custody in terms of s 50(1) of the CPA, will automatically render such continued detention lawful.

This pronouncement appears to suggest that the court may, for procedural purposes, treat a person who has allegedly been unlawfully arrested and detained as if they were lawfully arrested, and, if necessary, may remand such a person in custody—although such an order does not, in itself, rectify the underlying unlawfulness of the detention. Nevertheless, it is submitted that while this position is our law, these cases were not interpreted against the backdrop of Section 35(2) (d) of the Constitution, where the detained person challenges their unlawful arrest before the court on first appearance. Therefore, the question is still open to interpretation.

6.1.4 Detained client's constitutional right to challenge unlawful detention before the court

Section 35(2) (d) of the Constitution guarantees every detained person's right "to challenge the lawfulness of the detention in person before a court and if the detention is unlawful, to be released". It appears that the Constitution provides a remedy where the detention is found to be unlawful. Nonetheless, the question arises whether the proper interpretation of the term *"court"* in section 35(2)(d) of the Constitution confines the power contemplated therein to the Superior Courts, thereby excluding the

---

[230] The translated version as appearing in *De Klerk v Minister of Police* (CCT 95/18) [2019] 32; 2019 (12) BCLR 1425 (CC);2020 (1) SACR 1 (CC);2021 (4) SA 585 (CC) (22August 2019) para 38.

[231] *Minister of Safety and Security v Tyokwana* (827/13) [2014] ZASCA 130 (23 September 2014) para 38.

Magistrates' Courts, where the first appearance of almost all the accused takes place. It is submitted that the definition of the 'court' in Section 35(2)(d) of the Constitution includes the court in which the accused appears for their first appearance. The jurisdiction of the Magistrates' Court here is clearly being extended by the Constitution.[232] The Magistrates' Court's power to directly apply the Bill of Rights is constrained under Section 170; therefore, it cannot directly craft constitutional remedies or challenge legislation. However, Sections 39(1) and (2) of the Constitution require the courts to apply the Bill of Rights indirectly when interpreting legislation.[233] This limited application of the constitutional provision by inferior courts is called indirect or incidental jurisdiction.[234] Froneman J, in *Qozeleni v Minister of Law and Order & another*,[235] emphasised jurisdiction as a means of giving access to justice in the following way:

> In my view, it seems inconceivable that those provisions of chapter 3 of the Constitution which are meant to safeguard the fundamental rights of citizens should not be applied in courts where the majority of people would have their initial and perhaps only contact with the provisions of the Constitution, viz the lower courts. Such an interpretation of the Constitution would frustrate its very purpose of constituting a bridge to a better future. It would negate the principle of accountability or justification in those courts where most of the day to day administration of justice takes place.

In *National Director of Public Prosecutions v King*,[236] it was stated that the Constitution requires a generous approach when it is interpreted to give effect to the fundamental rights and freedoms that it creates. When interpreting legislation, every court must promote the spirit, purport, and objects of the Bill of Rights.[237] In this context, the interpretation and implementation of Section 50 of the CPA "must affirm the democratic values of human dignity, equality and freedom".[238] Mohamed AJ (as he was known

---

[232] Also see LAWSA Vol 11 (2nd ed) para 534, which reads: "The magistrates' courts are creatures of statute and have no jurisdiction beyond that granted by the Constitution or the statute creating them".

[233] *Naidoo v Director of Public Prosecutions and Others* (12180/2017) [2020] ZAKZDHC 39 (13 August 2020) para 122.

[234] *Naidoo v Director of Public Prosecutions and Others* [*supra*] para 123.

[235] *Qozeleni v Minister of Law and Order & another* 1994 (2) SACR 340(E).

[236] *National Director of Public Prosecutions v King* (86/09) [2010] ZASCA 8; 2010 (2) SACR 146 (SCA); 2010 (7) BCLR 656 (SCA); [2010] 3 All SA 304 (SCA) (8 March 2010) para 4.

[237] *Mafe v Acting Director of Public Prosecutions Western Cape and Another* (871/2022) [2022] ZAWCHC 63; 2022 (2) SACR 54 (WCC) (29 April 2022) para 13.

[238] Ibid.

then), in *S v Acheson,*[239] stressed the importance of the Constitution and the rights protected therein. Albeit referring to the Namibian Constitution of 1990, he said the following:

> The constitution of a nation is not simply a statute which mechanically defines the structures of government and the relations between the government and the governed. It is a 'mirror reflecting the national soul', the identification of the ideals and aspirations of a nation, the articulation of the values bonding its people and disciplining its government. The spirit and the tenor of the constitution must therefore preside over and permeate the processes of judicial interpretation and judicial discretion.
>
> Crucial to that tenor and that spirit is its insistence upon the protection of personal liberty..., the respect for human dignity ..., the right of an accused to be brought to trial within a reasonable time...and the presumption of innocence...
>
> ...No judicial officer should ignore that culture, where it is relevant, in the interpretation or application of the law or in the exercise of a discretion.

It is submitted that Section (35)(2) (d) allows the magistrate, on first appearance, to look at the issue of unlawful detention if they perceive such or if an application is brought. In *Mafe v S,*[240] the court was of the view that the detained client's right to challenge the lawfulness of the detention before the court may be exercised at his first appearance in the magistrates' court. In *National Commissioner of Police v Coetzee,*[241] the Supreme Court of Appeal remarked, in passing, that Section 50 of the Criminal Procedure Act, which regulates procedure after arrest, must be interpreted within the framework of Section 35(2)(d) of the Constitution.

6.1.5 Proposed approach to unlawful arrest during first appearance

Where an accused is unlawfully detained, the appropriate course is to challenge the lawfulness of the detention immediately after placing an appearance on record, rather than following the ordinary procedures applicable to a first appearance. If the application is unsuccessful, the practitioner should then proceed with the normal processes, including a bail

[239] *S v Acheson* 1991 (2) SA 805 (Nm) at 813A-D.
[240] *Mafe* v S (A49/22) [2022] ZAWCHC 108 (31 May 2022) para 55.
[241] *National Commissioner of Police v Coetzee* (649/11) [2012] ZASCA 161 (16 November 2012) para 6.

application. This approach is generally sound and, at the very least, warrants careful consideration. A legal practitioner is required to advance the client's cause without undue apprehension of failure; the greater disservice lies in failing to raise a meritorious challenge at all.

The prosecutor who screened the docket, or the prosecutor appearing in court, should be informed of the alleged unlawfulness of the detention, whether arising from a breach of Section 50(1) or Section 40(1) of the CPA.[242] The prosecutor should be informed before the matter is entered in the court book, because once it is recorded, the matter must be formally withdrawn before the court. This has implications for the prosecutor's withdrawal statistics.

Prosecutors manage heavy caseloads, and the enrolment of such matters is not always deliberate. Where the prosecutor is not persuaded that the challenge advanced is legally sound, a legal practitioner should place a properly motivated challenge before the court. Immediately after placing an appearance on record, the court should be informed that a challenge is being made on the basis that the accused is unlawfully before the court. Such a challenge may be made informally from the bar, particularly where the issue relates to the expiry of the 48 hours, as the 'notice of rights' (SAPS 14A) will ordinarily reflect the date and time of arrest, and the date of appearance will be apparent. However, where a dispute is likely to arise—most commonly in cases involving detention flowing from an allegedly unlawful arrest—a more formal approach may be required, such as the use of an affidavit or oral evidence. The legal practitioner must carefully assess which approach is appropriate in the circumstances. Should you elect to proceed informally, the challenge may be presented as follows:

1. **Introduction of the application**

   Your Worship, this is an application to declare that the accused is unlawfully before this court.

2. **Constitutional basis**

   This application is founded on Section 35(2) (d) of the Constitution, which provides that:
   "Every detained person has the right to challenge the lawfulness of the detention in person before a court and, if the detention is unlawful, to be released."

3. **Grounds of unlawfulness**
   (Select the applicable contravention)

   3.1 The 48-hour rule

   The accused was arrested at approximately 12:00 p.m. on Friday and was

---

[242] In practice, the prosecutor who appears in court is often not the same prosecutor who initially considered the new docket and took the decision to prosecute. "Docket screening" refers to the process of deciding whether a case should be enrolled.

only brought before this honourable court today, Tuesday. In terms of Section 50(1) (a) of the CPA, an arrested person must be brought before a court as soon as reasonably possible, but not later than 48 hours after the arrest. The 48-hour period expired at 12:00 p.m. yesterday. The failure to bring the accused before the court within this period constitutes a procedural irregularity and a violation of the accused's constitutional rights under Section 35(1) (d) of the Constitution.

3.2 Unlawful arrest in terms of Section 40 of the CPA

The accused was arrested without a warrant for the offence of common assault. This offence does not fall under Schedule 1 of the CPA. Section 40(1) (b) of the CPA permits a peace officer to arrest without a warrant only where there is a reasonable suspicion that a person has committed a Schedule 1 offence. Furthermore, the offence was not committed in the presence of the arresting officer, did not arise within a domestic relationship, and did not involve a contravention of a court order protecting a complainant under any law.

The arresting officer, therefore, acted ultra vires and without lawful authority. In the circumstances, the appropriate and legally permissible mechanism for securing the accused's attendance in court was the issuing of a written notice to appear in terms of Section 56 of the CPA (J534). The use of arrest was unnecessary and unlawful, particularly given the availability of a less invasive, statutorily sanctioned alternative.

4. **Constitutional infringement**

The arrest and detention amounted to a deprivation of freedom arbitrarily or without just cause, in violation of Section 12 of the Constitution.

5. **Principle of legality**

The State is required to respect the law and act within its confines. This did not occur in the present matter. The conduct complained of, therefore, constitutes a breach of the principle of legality and the rule of law, which are foundational values of the Constitution.[243]

6. **Relief sought**

In terms of Section 35(2) (d) of the Constitution, the appropriate remedy is the immediate release of the accused. Accordingly, it is submitted that the matter should be struck from the roll. Such an order would serve not only to vindicate the accused's rights, but also to discourage both the police and the prosecution from placing matters of this nature on the court roll.

---

[243] Section 1 of the Constitution.

6.2 Approach where the issue of torture is raised on first appearance

The issue of torture was addressed in paragraph 4.2. It is now approached in passing as the procedure outlined there, with necessary adjustments, also applies on first appearance.

It is important to inform the court when the accused complains during the first appearance that they were tortured, so that such an allegation may be recorded. In some cases, injuries are visible in areas where the court can observe them without compromising the dignity of the accused. Therefore, they may be brought to the court's attention. Where the accused remains in custody, you should specifically apply that the "warrant of detention" (J7) be endorsed and that the accused be referred to a medical practitioner on their arrival in prison. The accused may still be visited by their medical practitioner in prison, if they wish.[244] Where the accused is released from custody, they should visit the medical practitioner immediately to strengthen their criminal or civil claim against the police.

A case of torture can lead to imprisonment for life,[245] and since it constitutes serious misconduct, it calls for the immediate institution of disciplinary proceedings.[246] However, very few cases are reported. You must advise the client and assist them in lodging a complaint with the station commander and/ or IPID in a manner already explained in paragraph 4.2.

6.3 The importance of ascertaining the age of youthful clients on their first appearance

When you are instructed to represent a client who appears young, do not simply accept the age you see in the charge sheet or that you get from the client after merely asking how old they are. This is more important to the Legal Aid legal representatives who meet with the client briefly in court at the first appearance. Many 17-year-old clients are quick to say they are 18 years old, but when you ask their date of birth, you realise they will be 18 years old in months to come. It might be because they erroneously calculate their age from 1 January instead of their birthdays, or simply because they waited their entire lives to become adults. Sometimes children are brought to

---

[244] Section 35(2) (f) (iv) of the Constitution.

[245] Section 4 of the Prevention and Combating of Torture of Persons Act 13 of 2013.

[246] National Instruction 6 of 2014:The Prevention and Combating ofTorture of Persons of 2014 para 4(6).

court through the normal procedure as if they were adults.[247] You have to make a proper inquiry into the age of a youthful client.[248] If their family is present, try to confirm their age from them or get the birth certificate. The worst thing that can happen under your watch is to let a child be dealt with as if they are an adult and miss out on the opportunities available for the child accused.

It is also important to check the date on which the offence was committed in relation to the age of the youthful client. You might find that they allegedly committed the crime while they were a child, and they qualify to be dealt with as if they were a child in terms of Section 4(2) of the Child Justice Act 75 of 2008 (CJA). While a child is a person under the age of 18 years,[249] the CJA also provides that someone who committed an offence while under 18 years old, but is between 18 and 21 years at the time of arrest, receiving a written notice to appear in court (J534) or a summons (J175), may still be treated as a child in certain circumstances.[250] Thus, they may be assessed by the probation officer, attend the preliminary inquiry, and be eligible for diversion by the prosecutor before the preliminary inquiry or be diverted by the court at the preliminary inquiry.[251] Managing an adult as if they were a child can only be directed at a Director of Public Prosecutions (DPP) level.[252] The DPP may direct that such an accused be dealt with as if they were a child:[253]

1. in Schedule 1 offences of CJA;
2. if the co-accused is a child;
3. if he or she was used by an adult to commit the offence;
4. if there is a doubt about his or her age; or
5. where exceptional circumstances exist, such as:[254]
   5.1 low-level development of such an accused;
   5.2 he or she faces a particular hardship, vulnerability, or handicap;
   5.3 the victim prefers diversion or does not want to testify;
   5.4 witnesses for the State are fragile and or unwilling to testify; or
   5.5 continuing with the trial would be potentially damaging to the child witness or victim.

---

[247] See *S v LJ* (346/22) [2023] ZAWCHC 6; 2023 (1) SACR 396 (WCC) (24 January 2023) and *S v LC* (R12/2022; R13/2022) [2022] ZAMPMBHC 86; 2023 (1) SACR 578 (MM) (30 November 2022).

[248] *S v LJ* [supra] para 24.

[249] Section 28(3) of the Constitution and Section 1 of the CJA.

[250] Section 1 read with Section 4(2) of the Child Justice Act 75 of 2008 [hereinafter referred to as "the CJA"], also read together with Child Justice Act (75/2008): Directives by NDPP in terms of Section 97(4), No. R. 252 (31 March 2010) para M.

[251] The Child Justice Act (75/2008): Directives by NDPP [*supra*] para M2.

[252] Section 4(2) of the CJA.

[253] The Child Justice Act (75/2008): Directives by NDPP [*supra*] para M4.

[254] The Child Justice Act (75/2008): Directives by NDPP [supra] para M4(f) read with J2.

Where the co-accused was already an adult at the time of the commission of the offence, the DPP will rarely direct that the client be dealt with as a child, unless the client was used by the adult co-accused in the commission of the offence.[255] While it is the prosecutor who should request the DPP's directive as early as possible, even telephonically,[256] you can also approach the prosecutor to consider this option. Because the client was a child when the offence was committed, you may request adult diversion by the prosecutor if the client is charged with the offence falling under CJA Schedule 1.[257] If the prosecutor refuses to refer the matter to the DPP to issue this directive, you may request a postponement to make the written representations to the DPP. If your problem is regarding the prosecutor's refusal to divert the accused as an adult, then you can make your representations starting from the Senior Public Prosecutor (SPP) upwards. See paragraph 15.1 for a detailed discussion on representations.

6.4 Address in terms of Section 60(11B) (a)

You must be ready on the first appearance to address the court in terms of Section 60(11B) (a) of the CPA. This will happen immediately after placing yourself on record. Such an address entails dealing with the following:

1. **Previous convictions and pending matters**

   You must address whether the accused has any previous convictions or pending matters.

   (a) Previous convictions
   Where the accused has a previous conviction, you must state:

   (i) the offence of which the accused was convicted;

   (ii) the date of the conviction; and

   (iii) the court where the conviction took place.

   (b) Pending matters
   Where the accused has a pending matter, you must state:

   (i) whether the accused is in custody, on bail, or released on warning in respect of that matter;

   (ii) the offence with which the accused is charged;

   (iii) the court where the matter is pending; and

   (iv) the next court date.

---

[255] The Child Justice Act (75/2008): Directives by NDPP [*supra*] para M5.

[256] The Child Justice Act (75/2008): Directives by NDPP [*supra*] M6.

[257] The Child Justice Act (75/2008): Directives by NDPP [*supra*] para M7.

Note:

- References to previous convictions do not include expunged records.[258]
- References to pending matters do not include withdrawn cases.

2. **Protection orders**

You must address whether the accused is subject to any protection order issued under the Domestic Violence Act 116 of 1998, the Protection from Harassment Act 17 of 2011, or any other law protecting the complainant in the matter under consideration.[259]

(a) Where such an order exists, you must state:

(i) the date on which the order was issued;

(ii) the name of the court that issued the order; and

(iii) the material terms of the order.

3. **Status as a sentenced offender**

You must address whether, at the time of the commission of the offence, the accused was a sentenced offender placed under correctional supervision, day parole, parole, or medical parole.[260]

(a) Where the accused is a sentenced offender, you must provide:

(i) details of the offence in respect of which the sentence was imposed;

(ii) the name of the correctional centre;

(iii) the name of the correctional officer responsible for supervision;

(iv) the date on which correctional supervision or parole commenced; and

(v) the anticipated date of completion of the sentence.

Failure to disclose previous convictions, pending matters, protection orders, correctional supervision, or any parole is a criminal offence punishable by up to R40 000.00 in fines or 2 years of imprisonment.[261] The practical way of dealing with Section 60(11B) is explained in conjunction with an application

---

[258] *Molefe v S* (A129/18) [2018] ZAGPPHC 271 (18 April 2018) para 12.

[259] Section 60(11B) (a) (iii) of the CPA as amended by the Criminal and Related Matters Amendment Act 12 of 2021.

[260] Section 60(11B) (a) (iv) of the CPA as amended by the Criminal and Related Matters Amendment Act 12 of 2021.

[261] Section 60(11B) (d) of the CPA as amended by the Criminal and Related MattersAmendment Act 12 of 2021.

for Schedule I bail in paragraph 8.2.2.

CHAPTER 7

PREPARATION FOR BAIL APPLICATION

7.1 Preparation for bail in general

The basic objective of bail is to maximise personal liberty", thereby minimising "interference with the lawful activities of an accused".[262] To successfully secure the personal liberty of the client before trial, it is very important to thoroughly apply your mind to the facts of every specific bail application, because every application must be approached differently. Where the client is an illegal immigrant, you should know that such status is a relevant consideration on bail but is not a deciding factor.[263] Accordingly, it is imperative to compile all available evidence demonstrating that, notwithstanding your client's immigration status, they possess substantial emotional, familial, community, or occupational ties within the country.[264]
When preparing for a bail application, you should also consider whether the matter is opposed or not. It is customary that in Schedule 1 unopposed bail, no affidavit needs to be prepared. However, the issue of bail is handled promptly with the address in terms of Section 60(11B) (a) of the CPA.[265] In unopposed Schedule 5 and 6 matters, the accused can only adduce evidence either *viva voce* or by way of affidavit.[266]

It is best to always have a draft bail affidavit on your laptop. Since bail is urgent, you should be able to draft bail affidavits urgently. Although handwritten affidavits are acceptable, they take time to prepare due to the requirements of Section 60(4) of the CPA, and the situation is even worse if there is no commissioning stamp. The draft affidavit should be used only for unopposed bail applications, and one should still be mindful that every bail application must set out its facts. The affidavit must be signed by the accused, not their

---

262 *Zwakala v S* (CA&R10/23) [2023] ZANCHC 20 (14 April 2023) para 86.

263 *Alehi v S* (A173/2021) [2021] ZAGPPHC 492; 2022 (1) SACR 271 (GP) (10 August 2021) para 16.

264 *Namlela and Another v S (Bail Appeal)* (CA&R 16/2024) [2024] ZAECGHC 25 (7 March 2024) para 22.

265 Section 60(11B) together with a Schedule 1 bail is dealt with in para 8.2.

266 *Mofokeng v S* (A212/2021) [2021] ZAGPPHC 522; 2022 (2) SACR 184 (GP) (12 August 2021) para 7.

legal representative.[267] In *Mofokeng v S,*[268] the court found that the statement signed by the legal representative on behalf of the accused, even if it was read into the record, cannot constitute a sworn statement by the accused. Therefore, there was no evidence led on behalf of the accused, which the court had to consider in terms of Section 60(11) of the CPA.[269] The affidavit must be properly commissioned.[270] In *S v Deyi,*[271] the court found that the requirements of Regulation 4(2) of the Regulations issued in terms of Section 10 of the Justices of the Peace and Commissioners of Oaths Act 16 of 1963 were not complied with because the magistrate's stamp was used as a date stamp and there was no area of appointment. Therefore, the accused led no evidence as required by Section 60(11) of the CPA because they had made an unsworn statement.[272]

Opposed cases generally demand more preparation than unopposed applications. Therefore, if a postponement is necessary to do such preparation, you should apply for it. Firstly, it is important to establish with the prosecutor or the investigating officer the reasons for opposing the bail application. Once the reasons are known, you should gather evidence that might undermine the State's expected evidence or try to show the court that, despite the opposition, the bail conditions may be effective.[273]

Before dealing with bail, you should also be aware of the topics to be discussed in this chapter, and if applicable, you should be able to use them to the client's advantage.

7.2 Understanding bail schedules

When a client appears in court while in custody, an inquiry into the client's release on bail will be held if the prosecution does not apply for a postponement under Section 50(6) of the CPA. A bail application in court is dealt with under Section 60 of the CPA. During bail hearings, the court will deal with Schedule 1, 5, or 6 bail matters. Whether a matter falls under Schedule 5 or Schedule 6 is generally not confusing, as the CPA is clear and straightforward. However, Schedule 1 sometimes requires clarification.

The current Schedule 1 of the CPA plays a dual role: it guides police officers on the offences in respect of which they may arrest a suspect without a warrant under Section 40 of the CPA, and it serves as a bail schedule for less serious offences. When the CPA was published on 6 May 1977, it did not

---

[267] *Mofokeng v S* (A212/2021) [2021] ZAGPPHC 522; 2022 (2) SACR 184 (GP) (12 August 2021) para 7.
[268] Ibid.
[269] Ibid.
[270] Ibid.
[271] *Deyi v S* (A16/13) [2013] ZAGPPHC 75 (6 March 2013) para 5, 17 and 20.
[272] Ibid.
[273] *Sibeko v S* (BA17/2020) ZAMPMHC 13 (30 May 2020) para 23.

contain Schedules 5 and 6. Schedule 1's primary role was to guide officers on the offences in respect of which they could arrest a suspect without a warrant in terms of Section 40 of the CPA. All the offences for which the accused were arrested in terms of Section 40 of the CPA were subject to the same standard.[274] Following the amendment of the CPA by the Criminal Procedure Second Amendment Act 85 of 1997, Schedules 5 and 6 provided for the classification of offences according to their seriousness and established different requirements that must be met before an accused is released on bail.[275] This development underscored the importance of bail schedules during bail applications. Consequently, because of this dual purpose, Schedule 1 contains both less serious and more serious offences.

A reading of Schedule 1 reveals that it includes a wide range of offences, including those mentioned in Schedule 5, because the Section 40 guidance remains important. Therefore, the appropriate method for determining whether a matter constitutes a Schedule 1 offence for purposes of a bail application is to begin by reading Schedules 5 and 6. Any offence listed in Schedule 1 but not repeated in Schedule 5 or 6 remains a Schedule 1 offence for bail purposes. Put differently, the offence must appear in Schedule 1 but not be repeated in Schedule 5 or 6.

For example, murder is listed in Schedule 1 but is repeated in Schedule 5; it is therefore not a Schedule 1 offence for bail purposes. Assault GBH,[276] is referred to in Schedule 1 and is not repeated in Schedule 5; it therefore remains a Schedule 1 offence for purposes of bail.

When applying the technique explained above—namely, identifying offences listed in Schedule 1 that are not repeated in Schedules 5 or 6—the Schedule 1 offences for bail purposes are as follows:

1. Sedition.
2. Public violence.
3. Attempted murder with no infliction of GBH.
4. Culpable homicide.
5. Sexual assault compelled sexual assault, or compelled self-sexual

---

[274] *S v Hlongwa* 1979 (4) SA 112 (D) as discussed in *Mbaleki andAnother v S* (2853/2011) [2011] ZAKZDHC 68; 2013 (1) SACR 165 (KZD) (1 April 2011) para 9; and *S v Sithole and Others* (7032/11) [2011] ZAKZDHC 36;2012 (1) SACR 586 (KZD) (19August 2011) para 18.Also see *Prokureur-generaal van die Witwatersrandse Plaaslike Afdeling v CJ van Heerden en Andere* 1994 (2) SACR 469 (W) 471 a-b and *Magano v Magistrate Johannesburg and Others* 1994(2) 304 (W) 306 g-j.

[275] The Purpose of the Criminal Procedure Second Amendment Act 85 of 1997. Also see Combrinck H "'He's out again': The role of the prosecutor in bail for persons accused of sexual offences" 2001 *Law, Democracy & Development* p32 https://journals.co.za/doi/pdf/10.10520/EJC162740 accessed 18 July 2024.

[276] Assault, when a dangerous wound is inflicted, has been amended by Section 11 of the Criminal and Related Amendment Act 12 of 2021 to cover assault GBH in general.

assault, where the victim is older than 16 years.

6. Using children or mentally disabled persons for the benefit of child pornography.
7. Bestiality.
8. Robbery.
9. kidnapping.
10. Child stealing.
11. Assault GBH.[277]
12. Arson.
13. Malicious injury to property.
14. Breaking or entering any premises, whether under the common law or a statutory provision.
15. Theft, whether under the common law or a statutory provision.
16. Receiving stolen property knowing it is stolen.
17. Fraud.
18. Forgery or uttering a forged document, knowing it is forged.
19. Offences relating to the coinage.
20. Escaping from lawful custody, where the accused is in such custody in respect of Schedule 1 or in respect of the offence of escaping from lawful custody.
21. Any statutory offence, the punishment of which may be a period of imprisonment exceeding six months without the option of a fine.[278]
22. Torture.
23. Any conspiracy, incitement, or attempt to commit any offence referred to in this Schedule.

Once you have mastered the offences listed in Schedule 1 of the CPA, understanding the classification of Schedule 5 bail offences becomes more straightforward. However, it is important to note that Section 60 (11) (c) of the CPA effectively elevates certain offences—specifically those committed in the context of a domestic relationship or involving a contravention of a court order protecting a complainant—to be treated as Schedule 5 offences for bail purposes. To fully grasp the bail framework and its application, it is

[277] The offence of assault where a dangerous wound is inflicted has been amended by Section 11 of the Criminal and Related Matters Amendment Act 12 of 2021 to include assault involving GBH, as well as instances where the complainant is threatened with GBH or with a firearm or other dangerous weapon. Accordingly, all assaults with intent to cause GBH fall within Schedule 1 for purposes of bail.

[278] It was made clear that this provision was never intended to apply to common-law crimes, but rather to cover statutory offences not specified in Schedule 1. This was stated in the minority judgment in *De Klerk v Minister of Police* (329/17) [2018] ZASCA 45 (28 March 2018) at para 21, where the court cited *Areff v Minister van Polisie* 1977 (2) SA 900 (A) at 913b as authority for this position.

essential to consider the implications of Section 60(11)(c) when determining whether an offence qualifies as a Schedule 5 offence. This provision ensures that certain serious offences, although not expressly listed in Schedule 5, are subject to the same bail threshold and procedural requirements as those expressly listed in Schedule 5. The following are Schedule 5 offences:

1. Treason.
2. Murder.
3. Attempted murder involving the infliction of GBH.
4. Rape or compelled rape as contemplated in Section 3 or 4 of the Criminal Law (Sexual Offences and Related Matters) Amendment Act 32 of 2007, respectively, in circumstances other than those referred to in Schedule 6.
5. Section 5, 6, 7, 8 (1), and 23 offences and involvement in these offences in terms of Section 10 of the Prevention and Combating of Trafficking in Persons Act 7 of 2013.
6. Any offence referred to in Section 13 (f) of the Drugs and Drug Trafficking Act 140 of 1992, if it is alleged that:
   a) the value of the dependence-producing substance in question is more than R50 000.00; or
   b) the value of the dependence-producing substance in question is more than R10 000.00, and that the offence was committed by a person, group of persons, syndicate, or any enterprise acting in the execution or furtherance of a common purpose or conspiracy; or
   c) the offence was committed by any law enforcement officer.
7. Any offence relating to the dealing in or smuggling of ammunition, firearms, explosives, or armament or the possession of an automatic or semi-automatic firearm, explosives, or armament.
8. Any offence in contravention of Section 36 of the Arms and Ammunition Act 75 of 1969 on account of having more than 1,000 rounds of ammunition intended for firing in an arm contemplated in Section 39(2) (a)
   (i) of that Act.
9. Any offence relating to exchange control, extortion, fraud, forgery, uttering, theft, or any offence referred to in Parts 1 to 4, or Section 17, 20, or 21 (in so far as it relates to the aforementioned offences) of Chapter 2 of the Prevention and Combating of Corrupt Activities Act 12 of 2004:
   a) involving amounts of more than R500 000.00; or
   b) involving amounts of more than R100 000.00, if it is alleged that the offence was committed by a person, group of persons, syndicate, or any enterprise acting in the execution or furtherance of a common purpose or conspiracy; or

c) if it is alleged that the offence was committed by any law enforcement officer:

   i) involving amounts of more than R10 000.00; or
   ii) as a member of a group of persons, syndicate, or any enterprise acting in the execution or furtherance of a common purpose or conspiracy.

10. Sexual assault compelled sexual assault, or compelled self-sexual assault as contemplated in Section 5, 6, or 7 of the Criminal Law (Sexual Offences and Related Matters) Amendment Act 32 of 2007, in respect of a child under the age of 16 years.
11. An offence referred to in Schedule 1:

    a) and the accused has previously been convicted of an offence referred to in Schedule 1;

    b) which was allegedly committed whilst they were released on bail in respect of an offence referred to in Schedule 1.

12. The offences referred to in Section 4(2) or (3), 13, or 14 (as far as it relates to the aforementioned Sections) of the Protection of Constitutional Democracy against Terrorist and Related Activities Act, 2004.
13. The offences referred to in Sections 2, 4, 6, or 9 of the Prevention of Organised Crimes Act 121 of 1998.
14. The offence referred to in:

    a) Section 54(1) of the International Trade Administrative Act 71 of 2002;

    b) Section 32(1) (a), (b), (c), or (d) as far as the paragraph relates to Section 21(1), (l), (m), or (o) of the Second-Hand Goods Act 6 of 2009; or

    c) Section 36 or 37 of the General Law Amendment Act 6 of 1955, if it is alleged that ferrous or non-ferrous metal, which formed part of essential infrastructure, is involved as defined in Section 1 of the Criminal Matters Amendment Act 18 of 2015.

15. Theft of ferrous or non-ferrous metal, which formed part of essential infrastructure, as defined in Section 1 of the Criminal Matters Amendment Act 18 of 2015:

    a) if it is alleged that it caused or has the potential to:

       i) interference or disruption of any basic service to the public as defined by Section 1; or
       ii) damage to such essential infrastructure; or

    b) if it is alleged that it was committed by or with the collusion or assistance of:

       i) a law enforcement officer; or
       ii) a security officer who was required to protect or safeguard such essential infrastructure; or
       iii) an employee or a contractor appointed by the owner or the person in charge of such essential infrastructure; or
       iv) a group of persons, syndicate, or any enterprise acting in execution or furtherance of a common purpose or conspiracy.

16. Any offence referred to in Section 3 of the Criminal Matters Amendment Act 18 of 2015.
17. Contravention of Sections 8, 9, and 10 of the Cybercrimes Act 19 of 2020:
    a) involving amounts of more than R50 000.00; or
    b) involving amounts of more than R100 000.00, if it is proven that it was committed by:
       i) a person, group of persons, syndicate, or any enterprise acting in execution or furtherance of a common purpose or conspiracy; or
       ii) a person or with the collusion or assistance of another person, who, as a part of their duties, functions, or lawful authority, was in charge of, in control of, or had access to data or a computer programme, a computer data storage medium, or a computer system of another person in respect of which the offence in question was committed; or
    c) if it is proven that it was committed by a law enforcement officer:
       i) involving amounts of more than R10 000.00; or
       ii) as a member group of persons, syndicate, or any enterprise acting in execution or furtherance of a common purpose or conspiracy; or
       iii) with the collusion or assistance of another person, who, as a part of their duties, functions, or lawful authority, was in charge of, in control of, or had access to data or a computer programme, a computer data storage medium, or a computer system of another person in respect of which the offence in question was committed; or
18. Contravention of Section 11(2) of the Cybercrimes Act 19 of 2020.

<u>CPA Schedule 6 bail offences are:</u>

1. Murder, when:
    a) it was planned or premeditated; or
    b) the victim was:
       i) a law enforcement officer performing their functions as such, whether on duty or not, or a law enforcement officer who was killed because they hold such a position; or
    c) a person who has given or was likely to give material evidence about any offence referred to in Schedule 1; the death of the victim was caused by the accused in committing or attempting to commit or after having committed or attempted to commit one of the following offences:
       i) rape or compelled rape as contemplated in Section 3 or 4 of the Criminal Law (Sexual Offences and Related Matters) Amendment Act 32 of 2007, respectively; or
       ii) robbery with aggravating circumstances; or
    d) the offence was committed by a person, group of persons, or syndicate acting in the execution or furtherance of a common purpose or conspiracy.
2. Rape or compelled rape as contemplated in Section 3 or 4 of

the Criminal Law (Sexual Offences and Related Matters) Amendment Act 32 of 2007, respectively:

a) when committed:

i) in circumstances where the victim was raped more than once, whether by the accused or by any co-perpetrator or accomplice; or

ii) by more than one person, where such persons acted in the execution or furtherance of a common purpose or conspiracy; or

iii) by a person who is charged with having committed two or more offences of rape; or

iv) by a person, knowing that they have the Acquired Immune Deficiency Syndrome (AIDS) or the Human Immunodeficiency Virus (HIV); or

b) where the victim:

i) is a person under the age of 16 years; or

ii) is a physically disabled person who, due to their physical disability, is rendered particularly vulnerable; or

iii) is a person who is mentally disabled as contemplated in Section 1 of the Criminal Law (Sexual Offences and Related Matters) Amendment Act 32 of 2007; or

c) involving the infliction of GBH.

3. Section 4 offences and involvement in these offences in terms of Section 10 of the Prevention and Combating of Trafficking in Persons Act 7 of 2013.

4. Robbery, involving:

a) the use by the accused or any co-perpetrators or participants of a firearm; or

b) the infliction of GBH by the accused or any of the co-perpetrators or participants; or

c) the taking of a motor vehicle.

5. An offence referred to in Schedule 5:

(a) and the accused has previously been convicted of an offence referred to in Schedule 5 or this Schedule; or

(b) the offence was allegedly committed whilst the accused was released on bail in respect of an offence referred to in Schedule 5 or this Schedule.

6. The offences referred to in Section 2, 3(2) (a), 4(1), 5, 6, 7, 8, 9, 10, or 14 (in so far as it relates to the aforementioned Sections) of the Protection of Constitutional Democracy against Terrorist and Related Activities Act 33 of 2004, Section 2(1) and (2) of the Civil Aviation Offences Act 10 of 1972, Section 26(1) (j) of the Non-proliferation of Weapons of Mass Destruction Act 87 of 1993, and Section 56(1) (h) of the Nuclear Energy Act 46 of 1999.

It is submitted that bail schedules should be understood and applied as follows:

1. **Multiple charges under the same schedule**
   The number of simultaneous charges against the accused does not, by itself, affect the relevant bail schedule.[279] For instance, if the accused faces two charges of fraud and three of theft, the case remains under Schedule 1 bail. Likewise, if charged with three counts of murder, the application remains a Schedule 5 bail.[280]

2. **Previous convictions outside Schedules 1, 5, or 6**
   A prior conviction for an offence outside Schedules 1, 5, or 6 does not escalate a Schedule 1 offence to Schedule 5. For example, earlier convictions for common assault, crimen injuria, public drinking, or mandrax possession do not elevate a theft charge to Schedule 5.[281]

3. **Release on bail versus release on warning**
   Only a release on bail affects the bail schedule; a release on warning does not. If an accused is released on warning and then commits a Schedule 1, 5, or 6 offence, the bail schedule remains unchanged. The legislature consistently separates bail from warning and assigns distinct consequences to their breach. Thus, legislative references to bail exclude release on warning.

4. **Schedule 5 offence with prior Schedule 1 conviction or bail**
   If the accused is charged with a Schedule 5 offence and has a prior Schedule 1 conviction, or was on Schedule 1 bail when the Schedule 5 offence occurred, the bail schedule does not rise from Schedule 5 to Schedule 6. For example, a prior assault GBH (Schedule 1) conviction does not upgrade a Schedule 5 bail to Schedule 6. Simply put, 1 + 5 = 5.

5. **When a Schedule 6 bail arises**
   An accused will face a Schedule 6 bail only where they have:
   a) committed a Schedule 6 offence; or
   b) committed a Schedule 5 offence while having a previous conviction for a Schedule 5 or Schedule 6 offence; or
   c) committed a Schedule 5 offence while released on bail for a Schedule 5 or

---

[279] *S v Vermaas* 1996 (1) SACR 528 at 530 g-h.

[280] In *Mfeketho and Others v S* (CA&R193/2014) [2014] ZAECGHC 67 (21 July 2014) para 1, 2, 21, and 23, the accused were charged with four counts of murder, but the bail proceedings were conducted as a Schedule 5.

[281] In *Matebese v Minister of Police* (2224/2017) [2019] ZAECPEHC 37 (18 June 2019) para 2 read with para 3, 7, 38, and 39, the court in passing rejected the argument, and even the agreement between the parties, that an offence of possession of drugs, in general, was a Schedule 1 offence and therefore the accused's previous conviction remained irrelevant for purposes of increasing a purported Schedule 1 to Schedule 5. In statutory offences, the prosecution should first prove that the punishment for the offence is a period of imprisonment exceeding six months, without an option of a fine, as stated in *Areff v Minister van Polisie* 1977 (2) SA 900 (A) 913b.

Schedule 6 offence.

6. **Schedule 1 offence with prior Schedule 6 conviction or bail**
   If the accused faces a Schedule 1 offence but has a prior conviction for a Schedule 6 offence or was on bail for a Schedule 6 offence while committing the Schedule 1 offence, the bail application will proceed under Schedule 5.

7. **Robbery with aggravating circumstances**
   The definition of robbery with aggravating circumstances in Section 1 of the CPA should be approached with caution for bail purposes, as not all such robberies fall under Schedule 6. For a robbery to qualify as a Schedule 6 offence, there must be the use of a firearm, the infliction of GBH, or the taking of a motor vehicle. Where a knife was merely wielded, the offence remains a Schedule 1 robbery, unless the victim was stabbed or the robbery involved the taking of a motor vehicle.

Occasionally, the issue arises of when a prior conviction can be disregarded in determining bail. Section 271A(b) explicitly provides:

> any offence in respect of which a sentence of imprisonment for a period not exceeding six months without the option of a fine may be imposed, that conviction shall fall away as a previous conviction if a period of 10 years has elapsed after the date of conviction of the said offence, unless during that period the person has been convicted of an offence in respect of which a sentence of imprisonment for a period exceeding six months without the option of a fine, may be imposed.

In *S v Rabele,*[282] the court held that a previous conviction must be disclosed during bail proceedings, even if it is old or has "fallen away". The court reasoned that Section 271A of the CPA applies strictly to sentencing proceedings and does not govern disclosure under Section 60(11B) of the CPA.

This reasoning appears to draw support from Section 60(5), particularly Section 60(5)(e) of the CPA, which requires a court to consider the accused's previous convictions and past conduct when determining bail. From that perspective, the State may contend that full disclosure is necessary for the court to properly assess the risks contemplated in Section 60.

However, conceptual difficulty arises where a conviction has been expunged or has legally fallen away. Once expunged in terms of Section 271A of the CPA, the conviction is, in law, treated as though it does not exist. It is therefore problematic to require an accused to disclose something which the law has effectively extinguished. To insist on disclosure in such circumstances places

---

[282] *S v Rabele* (76/2014) [2016] ZAFSHC 178 (29 September 2016) para 23.

the accused in an untenable position: they are compelled to revive a conviction that has been reduced to nothing by operation of law.

Furthermore, it is difficult to conceive how a court, acting judiciously, could refuse or cancel bail solely because the accused failed to disclose a conviction that has legally fallen away. Bail proceedings under Section 60 of the CPA are concerned with risk assessment—not with penalising an accused for failing to resurrect legally extinguished history. The ancient past, particularly where expungement has occurred, cannot logically serve as a basis for denying bail.

In contrast, *Molefe v S*,[283] adopts a different approach. The court held that a prior conviction expunged under the law should be disregarded for bail purposes. This approach is arguably more consistent with the legal fiction created by expungement: once removed, the conviction should not reappear indirectly during bail proceedings.

The divergence between *Rabele* and *Molefe* demonstrates that the High Courts are not in agreement on the correct interpretation of the CPA in this context. Until authoritative clarification is provided, practitioners must be mindful of the jurisdictional position and prepared to advance arguments on statutory interpretation and the constitutional implications of resurrecting expunged convictions during bail proceedings.

7.3 When the bail schedule is in dispute

To determine the applicable bail schedule, you must begin with the charge sheet. In most instances, you will already be aware of any previous convictions or pending matters involving your client. That information, read together with the charge, will usually indicate which schedule applies.
Where the bail schedule is determined purely by the nature of the charge, the jurisdictional facts relied upon by the prosecution should appear ex facie the charge sheet, unless a written certificate has been issued by the Director of Public Prosecutions (DPP). [284] For example, where the State relies on premeditation in a murder charge in order to invoke Schedule 6, that allegation should be expressly reflected on the charge sheet unless supported by a DPP certificate.[285] The same principle applies where the value of property involved

---

[283] *Molefe v S* (A129/18) [2018] ZAGPPHC 271 (18 April 2018) para 9 and 12. Also see *Zwakala v S* (CA&R10/23) [2023] ZANCHC 20 (14 April 2023) para 14, where a previous conviction of assault that was older than 10 years was disregarded for purposes of bail.

[284] *Nwabunwanne v S* (CA&R114/2016) [2017] ZANCHC 9; 2017 (2) SACR 124 (NCK) (31 January 2017) para 12. Also see *S v Kock* (670/02) [2003] ZASCA 1; [2003] 1 All SA 551 (SCA); 2003 (2) SACR 5 (SCA) (14 February 2003) para 25.

[285] *Kula v S* (CAB 02/2023) [2023] ZANWHC 35; 2023 (2) SACR 52 (NWM) (4 April 2023) para 31.

in an offence has the effect of elevating the matter to a higher bail schedule.[286]

In practice, it frequently occurs that the prosecution and the defence do not agree on the applicable bail schedule prior to the commencement of the bail proceedings. This dispute arises most commonly in murder matters. The prosecution may allege that the offence was premeditated and therefore falls under Schedule 6, while the defence contends that there is insufficient proof of premeditation and that the matter properly falls under Schedule 5.

The court should resolve the issue of the applicable bail schedule timeously—preferably before the bail application commences.[287] It must be clear from the outset what the accused must prove to secure release. The evidential burden under Section 60(11) of the CPA differs materially between Schedule 5 and Schedule 6 matters, and uncertainty at the commencement of proceedings undermines procedural fairness.

The most appropriate method for resolving a dispute regarding the bail schedule is for the prosecutor to present to the court a written confirmation issued by the DPP.[288] In practice, however, such confirmation is seldom readily available. Without a DPP certificate, courts often ask both the legal practitioner and the prosecutor to address the issue from the bar and then make a quick ruling. This approach needs careful scrutiny. Section 60(2)(b) of the CPA allows courts to get information informally, but only for undisputed matters.[289] Section 60(2)(c) of the CPA makes it clear that where issues are in dispute during a bail application, evidence must be adduced. Determining the nature of the charge affects the bail schedule and the accused's burden of proof. It is a major disputed issue and should be handled formally.[290] This is particularly important given the far-reaching consequences of Section 60(11) of the CPA.[291] If the bail schedule is disputed, the prosecutor must provide either the DPP's written confirmation or supporting evidence. Such evidence is often presented by way of an affidavit from the investigating officer setting out the jurisdictional facts relied upon.[292]

Even where a DPP certificate has been issued, and the bail schedule is contested, the court should still consider the evidence placed before it before

---

[286] *Nwabunwanne v S* (CA&R114/2016) [2017] ZANCHC 9; 2017 (2) SACR 124 (NCK) (31 January 2017) para 13.

[287] *Nel and Others v S* (A508/2017) [2017] ZAGPJHC 296; 1018 (1) SACR 576 (GJ) (17 October 2017) para 10; *Molefe v S* [*supra*]) para 12; and *Kula v S* [*supra*] para 21.

[288] Section 60(11A) (c) of the CPA.

[289] *Phadi and Another v S* (A1/2024) [2024] ZAFSHC 169 (3 June 2024) para 21.

[290] *Josephs v S* 2001 (1) SACR 659 (C) at 661f-h and *Kula v S* [*supra*] para 21-23.

[291] Ibid.

[292] *S v Kock* (670/02) [2003] ZASCA 1; [2003] 1 All SA 551 (SCA); 2003 (2) SACR 5 (SCA) (14 February 2003) para 6, *Nel and Others v S* (A508/2017) [2017] ZAGPJHC 296; 1018 (1) SACR 576 (GJ) (17 October 2017) para 4 and *Kula v S* [*supra*] para 22-23.

making a ruling. The certificate constitutes prima facie proof only; it is not conclusive. However, where no evidence is led on behalf of the bail applicant to challenge the applicability of the schedule, the certificate—although merely prima facie proof—will become conclusive proof of the applicable bail schedule.[293]

7.4 Importance of *S v M* during bail application of a primary caregiver

It is important to note the significance of *S v M*,[294] in bail applications for primary caregivers of minor children. Although *S v M* was decided in the context of sentencing, its principles are not confined to that stage of the criminal process. The Constitutional Court emphasised that where a primary caregiver of minor children is before the court, the child's best interests must be treated as of paramount importance.

The applicability of these principles to bail proceedings was confirmed in *S v Petersen*.[295] The court recognised that although bail inquiries focus on the interests of justice, they cannot be divorced from constitutional considerations, particularly where the detention of an accused directly affects minor children.

When dealing with a bail application by a primary caregiver, the court must consider the interests of justice under Section 60 of the CPA. However, it must simultaneously take into account, as a relevant and weighty factor, the child's right "to family care or parental care, or to appropriate alternative care when removed from the family environment," as guaranteed by Section 28(1)(b) of the Constitution.[296] The detention of a primary caregiver may have immediate and profound consequences for minor children, and those consequences form part of the broader enquiry into whether detention is justified.

It is essential not to conflate a primary caregiver with a mere breadwinner. A primary caregiver is "the person with whom the child lives and who performs everyday tasks like ensuring that the child is fed and looked after and that the

[293] *Gumede v S* (A51/2017) [2021] ZAMPMHC 22 (24 May 2021) para 34.

[294] *S v M* (CCT 53/06) [2007] ZACC 18; 2008 (3) SA 232 (CC); 2007 (12) BCLR 1312 (CC) (26 September 2007).

[295] *S v Petersen* (A717/07) [2008] ZAWCHC 11; [2008] 3 All SA 301 (C); 2008 (2) SACR 355 (C) (27 February 2008) para 63. Also see *Gombe v S* (CA&R 06/2024) [2024] ZAECMHC 22 (2 May 2024) para 28.

[296] Ibid.

child attends school regularly".[297] The enquiry is functional and fact-specific; it concerns who actually performs the day-to-day caregiving responsibilities.

It is submitted that even a postponement of bail in terms of Section 50(6)(d) of the CPA, where it results in the continued detention of a primary caregiver, must be approached in light of the best interests of the child principle. Although such a postponement may be procedurally authorised, the constitutional imperative requires the court to consider the immediate impact on the child and to ensure that the child's rights are not overlooked in what may otherwise appear to be a routine remand.

7.5 Fighting the strength of the State's case during bail

In bail applications under Schedule 5 or 6 of the CPA, how strong the State's case always matters.[298] In Schedule 6 matters, a key distinction arises: the strength or weakness of the State's case is relevant to the existence of exceptional circumstances, as contemplated in Section 60(11)(a) of the CPA.[299] Notably, a demonstrably weak case may, depending on the facts, establish exceptional circumstances that justify release.

By contrast, in Schedule 5 matters, the strength of the State's case is still relevant but serves a different function. In Schedule 5 matters, it is a relevant factor in determining where the interests of justice lie.[300] It is important to note that questioning the strength of the State's case is not always needed to get bail under either schedule.[301] Bail hearings are not full trials. The accused can succeed for other reasons, such as strong personal circumstances, a low risk of running away, or none of the risk factors listed in Section 60(4) being present.[302]

There are, nevertheless, circumstances in which a practitioner has little choice but to engage directly with the merits. This commonly arises in Schedule 5 or Schedule 6 bail applications where the Section 60(4) factors operate against the accused—for example, where the accused has relevant previous

---

[297] *S v M* (CCT 53/06) [2007] ZACC 18; 2008 (3) SA 232 (CC); 2007 (12) BCLR 1312 (CC) (26 September 2007) para 28.

[298] *S v Viljoen* (286/2002) [2002] ZASCA 81; [2002] 4 All SA 10 (SCA); 2002 (2) SACR 550 (SCA) (27 August 2002) para 11. See also *S v Kock* (670/02) [2003] ZASCA 1; [2003] 1 All SA 551 (SCA); 2003 (2) SACR 5 (SCA) (14 February 2003) para 15.

[299] *S v Kock* [*supra*] para 15.

[300] *Mfeketho and Others v S* (CA&R193/2014) [2014] ZAECGHC 67 (21 July 2014) para 11.

[301] *Mathebula v S* (431/2009) [2009] ZASCA 91; 2010 (1) SACR 55 (SCA); [2010] 1 All SA 121 (SCA) (11 September 2009) para 12.

[302] *Mfeketho and Others v S* [*supra*] para 23.

convictions or is alleged to have committed the offence while on bail, yet denies committing it. In such instances, the perceived strength of the State's case may significantly influence the court's assessment of risk.

This issue also arises in Schedule 6 cases when the accused argues that the State's case is so weak as to constitute a special reason for bail. To do this, the accused must show, more likely than not, that they will be found not guilty.[303] Just saying they did not do it is not enough. The court requires cogent evidence that the likelihood of conviction is minimal, thereby rendering further detention unjustified. Where the strength of the State's case is challenged, the presentation of an affidavit alone is insufficient; the accused must ordinarily be subjected to cross-examination.[304]

Legal practitioners should therefore approach this strategy with caution. An attack on the merits requires sufficient factual material—usually by way of oral evidence—to demonstrate that the State's case is unreliable, contradictory, or inherently weak. Unsupported assertions will carry little, if any, weight.

7.6 The role of the presumption of innocence on bail

There are conflicting judicial decisions on whether the presumption of innocence applies to bail applications under the CPA. Some courts have held that the presumption of innocence is a trial right and does not apply at the bail stage.[305] According to this view, bail proceedings concern risk assessment and the interests of justice, not guilt determination.

Other decisions, however, have accepted that the presumption of innocence "does not take a break during a bail inquiry".[306] On this approach, although

---

[303] *Mathebula v S* (431/2009) [2009] ZASCA 91; 2010 (1) SACR 55 (SCA); [2010] 1 All SA 121 (SCA) (11 September 2009) para 12. Also see *Mazibuko and Another v S* (8774/09) [2009] ZAKZPHC 61; 2010 (1) SACR 433 (KZP) (19 November 2009) para 23; and *S v Botha en 'n Ander* [2001] ZASCA 146 (30 November 2001]); [2002] 2All SA 577 (A); 2002 (1) SACR 222 (SCA) para 21.

[304] *Mahendren v S* (SSCC3/2022; A34/2022;10/2/5/2-2022) [2022] ZAGPJHC 251 (25 April 2022) para 19.

[305] *Shabangu v S* (A727/2014) [2014] ZAGPPHC 832 (17 October 2014) para 20, *Mbaleki and Another v S* (2853/2011) [2011] ZAKZDHC 68; 2013 (1) SACR 165 (KZD) (1 April 2011) para 14. *S v Conradie* (A248/2020) [2020] ZAWCHC 177 (11 December 2020) para 19-20.

[306] See *Mgijima v S* (CA&R 13/23) [2023] ZANCHC 18 (28 April 2023) para 11; *Majali v S* (41210/2010) [2011] ZAGPJHC 74 (19 July 2011) para 20; *Mafe v S* (A49/22) [2022] ZAWCHC 108 (31 May 2022) para 72 [majority judgment] and 142-143 [dissenting judgment]; *Gombe v S* (CA&R 06/2024) [2024] ZAECMHC 22 (2 May 2024) para 19; *Namlela and Another v S (Bail Appeal)* (CA&R 16/2024) [2024] ZAECGHC 25 (7 March

bail is not a determination of guilt, the accused remains constitutionally presumed innocent, and that status must inform the court's evaluation of detention.

In *S v Barends and Others,*[307] the court considered these divergent authorities and concluded that, even if the presumption of innocence applies during bail proceedings, it plays a limited role. It does not entitle an accused to release on bail, nor does it displace the statutory onus imposed in Schedule 5 and Schedule 6 matters. Rather, it is one factor to be considered together with others, including the strength of the State's case and the risks contemplated in Section 60(4) of the CPA.[308]

While it remains debatable whether the presumption of innocence plays a limited role or no role at all in bail proceedings, it is important to bear in mind that Section 58 of the CPA makes it clear that bail is non-penal in character. The proper refusal of bail should therefore never be viewed as a form of anticipatory punishment for the offences with which the accused is charged.[309] Detention pending trial is justified only where the interests of justice so require—not because the accused is presumed to be guilty, but because identifiable risks outweigh the accused's right to liberty pending trial.

7.7 Application for disclosure for purposes of bail application

Despite Section 60(14) of the CPA,[310] it is clear that disclosure may be permissible during bail proceedings, particularly where an accused bears the heavy burden of proving exceptional circumstances in a Schedule 6 application.[311] Although Section 60(14) limits the right to disclosure at the bail

2024) para 18; and *Alehi v S* (A173/2021) [2021] ZAGPPHC 492; 2022 (1) SACR 271 (GP) (10 August 2021) para 15. *S v M* (CCT 53/06) [2007] ZACC 18; 2008 (3) SA 232 (CC); 2007 (12) BCLR 1312 (CC) (26 September 2007) para 28.

[307] *S v Barendse and Another* (A01/2023) [2023] ZAWCHC 63 (22 May 2023) para 27.

[308] Ibid.

[309] *Johannes v S* (A218/2023) [2023] ZAWCHC 312; 2024 (2) SACR 318 (WCC) (1 December 2023) para 35.

[310] Section 60 (14) of the CPA appears to be against disclosure during bail, but this subsection cannot be interpreted as allowing a total refusal to disclose the information even where that would constitute a 'reasonable opportunity' in terms of Section 60(11) (a) and (b) of the CPA. See *S v Dlamini, S v Dladla,* and *Others; S v Joubert; S v Schietekat* (CCT21/98, CCT22/98, CCT2/99, CCT4/99) [199] ZACC 8; 1999 (4) 623; 1999 (7) BCLR 771 (3 June 1999) para 84.

[311] *S v Dlamini, S v Dladla and Others; S v Joubert; S v Schietekat* [*supra*] para 83 and 84.

stage, it does not impose an absolute bar. An accused facing a Schedule 6 bail application must prove exceptional circumstances in terms of Section 60(11)(a) of the CPA. In order to discharge that onus meaningfully, access to certain information in the State's possession may be necessary. Similarly, an accused in a Schedule 5 bail application may require limited disclosure in order to satisfy the requirement of being afforded a "reasonable opportunity" to adduce evidence in terms of Section 60(11)(b). Even the accused facing a Schedule 5 bail application may be granted disclosure to satisfy the requirement of being given a 'reasonable opportunity' as stated in Section 60(11) (b) of the CPA.[312]

In *S v Green*,[313] the court ordered the prosecution to allow the defence to view video footage linking the accused to the offence. The court recognised that, in appropriate circumstances, fairness may require limited disclosure to enable the accused to address the strength of the State's case. The applicable test is whether the State would suffer prejudice if disclosure were granted while the investigation is ongoing.[314] Where there is no real risk of interference with the investigation, witness intimidation, or evidence tampering, and where the material is necessary to enable the accused to rebut the statutory onus under Schedule 5 or Schedule 6, courts may permit disclosure during bail proceedings.

It must be emphasised, however, that disclosure at the bail stage remains the exception rather than the rule. Bail proceedings are not intended to become a vehicle for full pre-trial discovery. Disclosure for purposes of bail is generally granted only in exceptional circumstances, where fairness and the proper ventilation of the bail issues require it.

As confirmed in *S v Green*, a refusal to grant disclosure for purposes of bail is interlocutory in nature. The court retains the discretion to revisit the issue and may grant access at a later stage should circumstances change or should the interests of justice so require.[315]

---

[312] *While the court in S v Dlamini, S v Dladla and Others; S v Joubert; S v Schietekat* [*supra*] dealt with disclosure in the context of a Schedule 6 bail application, the term 'reasonable opportunity' is also used in Schedule 5.

[313] *S v Green and Another (008/06) [2006] ZASCA 3; 2006 (1) SACR 603 (SCA) (3 March 2006) para 25.*

[314] *S v Green and Another* [*supra*] para 23.

[315] *S v Green and Another* [*supra*] para 24.

CHAPTER 8

APPLICATION TO BE RELEASED ON BAIL OR WARNING IN COURT

8.1 Procedural right to a speedy bail hearing versus Section 50(6) (d) application

In terms of Section 50(6) (a) (i) of the CPA, an accused is entitled to apply for release on bail at their first appearance, subject to the limited exceptions contemplated in Section 50(6) (d) and Section 60 of the CPA. Notwithstanding this, a growing tendency has emerged in the courts to postpone the issue of bail merely because it is the accused's first appearance, the applicable bail schedule is 5 or 6, or on the basis of minimal information placed on record by the prosecutor, purportedly in reliance on Section 50(6) (d) of the CPA.[316] Section 50(6) (a) (i) confers the right on all accused persons, irrespective of the bail schedule, to be heard on bail at the first appearance. While postponements in opposed bail applications may be justified in appropriate circumstances, unopposed bail applications should be heard irrespective of the bail schedule. The higher courts have commented on postponements before bail or during bail proceedings in the magistrates' courts as follows:

1. The Constitutional Court in *De Klerk v Minister of Police*[317] stated that magistrates have to "apply their mind to the question of bail at the first appearance". In this case, the magistrate, as a 'reception court', had postponed the matter without determining the issue of bail.
2. The SCA in *Matshikwe NO v M* [also known as *Magistrate Stutterheim v Mashiya*][318] stated that the right to a quick bail decision is a "procedural right independent of whether the right to liberty entitles the accused to bail". In this case, the magistrate who presided over the bail application postponed the judgment thereof until nine days later.

---

[316] De Ruter N and Hardy K "Study on the use of bail in South Africa" May 2018 *African Policing Civilian Oversight Forum Research Paper* para 2.2, http://apcof.org/wp-content/uploads/023-apcof-research-study-on-the-use-of-bail-in-south-africa-nicola-de-ruiter-and-kathleen-hardy-.pdf, accessed on 03 July 2023.

[317] *De Klerk v Minister of Police* (CCT 95/18) [2019] ZACC 32 (22 August 2019) para 49.

[318] *Matshikwe NO v M* [also known as *Magistrate Stutterheim v Mashiya*] (102/2002) [2003] ZASCA 54; [2003] 3 All SA 11 (SCA) (30 May 2003) para 16.

3. In *Setwaba and Others v De Souza NO and Others,*[319] the magistrate had postponed the unopposed and opposed bail applications in the public violence case for 17 days to hear the evidence of the employer of the bail applicants. he High Court, as an urgent review court, highlighted that a bail application by a detained person and its finalisation are always matters of urgency because they affect personal liberty.[320]
4. In *Hans v District Court Magistrate, Cape Town and Others,* [321] The magistrate had postponed the bail hearing to 28 days, on agreement between the parties. The court stated that, while it is understandable that the issue of court bail is not entertained during weekends for logistical reasons, "it cannot be that the goalposts for a bail hearing continue to be shifted by the lower courts as a result of the logistical and co-ordination challenges even on weekdays ... [O]vercrowding of court rolls ... should not be allowed to trump the constitutional rights of those detained who seek an audience with a court, to challenge the lawfulness of their continued detention within the prescribed limits".
5. In *Mafe v S,*[322] the court stressed that "[t]he first appearance of an accused person, in our constitutional judicial system, is not a traditional gathering where the rituals of postponement and further detention are announced by magistrates. It is intended to examine the reasons for the detention and if needs be to place the further detention of an accused under judicial oversight. The courtroom in the first appearance of an accused is the theatre where especially the charge and the detention of the accused undergo analytical, precise, dispassionate and excellent judicial operative procedure by the Specialist Constitutional Surgeon, the Magistrate".

In *Majali v S,*[323] the accused applied for bail, but the prosecution wanted the matter to be postponed in terms of Section 50(6) (d) of the CPA. The review court stressed the following summarised points, which you should never forget when dealing with this application:

1. Postponement in bail proceedings is not for the asking, but there must be persuasive, sustainable reasons justifying the granting of such postponement.[324]
2. Given that the prosecution seeks an indulgence to investigate certain aspects before bail, it must prove that what it wants to investigate is

[319] *Setwaba and Others v De Souza NO and Others* (M90/16) [2016] ZANWHC 30 (3 March 2016) para 8.
[320] *Setwaba and Others v De Souza NO and Others [supra]* para 3.
[321] *Hans v District Court Magistrate, Cape Town and Others* (19047/19) [2020] ZAWCHC 17 (4 March 2020) para 15.
[322] *Mafe v S* (A49/22) [2022] ZAWCHC 108 (31 May 2022) para 52.
[323] *Majali v S* [*supra*] para 28.
[324] *Majali v S* [*supra*] para 24.

based on a reasonable belief and is relevant to the issue of bail.[325]

3. The presiding officer should consider the strength of the reasons on which the prosecutor's application for postponement is based and use its inquisitorial powers in terms of Section 60(3) of the CPA to conduct an inquiry to determine whether the prosecutor has placed all relevant information or evidence before the court to assist it to properly exercise its discretion to postpone the bail application.
4. The presiding officer should evaluate and weigh the strength of the reasons given as a foundation for the application for a postponement and balance these against the liberty of the accused, "and basic objectives traditionally ascribed to the institution of bail".[326]
5. Finally, the presiding officer has to make a value judgment on whether it would be in the interests of justice to grant the postponement.[327]

If bail is genuinely urgent, the investigations preceding it should be equally urgent. Where a client resides within the court's jurisdiction and is arrested on a Friday or Saturday, it is not unreasonable to expect that their address will have been verified by the time they appear in court on the following Monday. If the address has not been confirmed and the prosecution seeks a postponement for that purpose, it is reasonable to expect the investigating officer to either depose to an affidavit or testify, explaining the reasons for the requested postponement.

Where the accused's address has been confirmed, and identity documents have been submitted, the verification of previous or pending cases should not require a postponement of seven days. The investigating officer can utilise CAS Function 5.13.6 to confirm any previous or pending cases.[328] While it is accepted that profiles may contain inaccuracies where an accused has previously used false names,[329] any information later shown to be false may constitute a basis for cancellation of bail under Section 68(1) (e) and (f) of the CPA. In addition, Section 60(11B) (d) of the CPA obliges an accused to disclose previous or pending cases, and a failure to do so constitutes a criminal offence.

Where the prosecution fails to confirm the client's address, the defence may call a relevant witness who resides at, or has knowledge of, the accused's address, or attach a confirmatory affidavit to the bail application. Even where a postponement appears necessary, or where such postponement is granted, the practitioner should still address the court on the reasonable period

---

[325] *Majali v S* (41210/2010) [2011] ZAGPJHC 74 (19 July 2011) para 28.

[326] *Majali v S* para [*supra*] 26.

[327] Ibid. See also *De Klerk v Minister of Police* (329/17) [2018] ZASCA 45 (28 March 2018) para 14.

[328] Information was gathered after interviewing investigating officers and profilers who wished to remain unnamed sources.

[329] Ibid.

justified in the circumstances, as the application for bail remains urgent. The period of seven days represents the maximum period for which a matter may be postponed before bail is entertained,[330] and this period includes weekends and public holidays.[331] A postponement in terms of Section 50(6) should not be interpreted to mean that every matter must be postponed for seven days. Postponing bail for the full seven-day period where the accused's address falls within the court's jurisdiction is difficult to justify, as the urgency of bail does not thereby fall away.

There should be no presumption that investigating officers are generally too busy with other cases, as is sometimes readily assumed by presiding officers. A court may take judicial notice only of facts that are "so notoriously or clearly established that evidence of their existence is unnecessary".[332] A court may not take judicial notice of facts that do not constitute common knowledge. The alleged busyness of a particular investigating officer cannot be inferred without supporting facts. While an investigating officer may have been occupied with a serious matter, such as a murder case, over a weekend, reliance on workload as a basis for postponement must be supported by evidence. An investigating officer can readily generate a printout of cases allocated to them using CAS Function 4.15.1.1 to substantiate any claim of busyness.[333]

Given that Section 50(6) of the CPA is among the most frequently misapplied provisions, it is imperative for legal practitioners, prosecutors, and magistrates to reflect critically on its practical operation. To gain a clearer appreciation of the realities faced by remand detainees—particularly overcrowding and prolonged detention—it would be beneficial for role players to visit remand detention facilities within their respective jurisdictions. Such exposure is likely to promote a more informed, balanced, and empathetic approach to bail proceedings. A *Practical Guide to Court and Case Flow Management* similarly encourages such visits as a means of advancing a fair, efficient, and humane criminal justice system.[334]

---

330 *Setwaba and Others v De Souza NO and Others* (M90/16) [2016] ZANWHC 30 (3 March 2016) para 12.

331 *S v Mashego* (R24/2021; A360/2020) [2021] ZAMPMBHC 36; 2021 (2) SACR 520 (MM) (10 August 2021) n1.

332 *MEC Department Police Roads & Transport, FS Province v Roberts and Another* (A116-2019) [2020] ZAFSHC 23; 2020 (3) SA 478 (FB) (13 February 2020) para 17.

333 Information was obtained through interviews with investigating officers and profilers who wished to remain anonymous.

334 *A Practical Guide: Court and Case Flow Management for Regional and District Criminal Courts in South African Lower Court Division*, 2010, p36.

8.2 Analysis and approach to Schedule 1 bail application

8.2.1 Schedule 1 bail application in general

Offences falling under Schedule 1 are listed and discussed in paragraph 7.2. In a Schedule 1 bail application, the accused is entitled to be released on bail unless the court finds that such release is not in the interests of justice.[335] In Schedule 1 matters, courts generally lean in favour of the accused's liberty, provided that the interests of justice are not prejudiced.[336] It is trite that where the State opposes the accused's release on bail in a Schedule 1 matter, it bears the onus of adducing evidence to establish that the interests of justice do not permit such release.[337] Opposition to bail in Schedule 1 matters is therefore relatively uncommon.

8.2.2 Unopposed Schedule 1 bail application

The interests of justice in relation to the granting or refusal of bail are concerned primarily with "securing the attendance of the accused at trial and preventing the accused from interfering with the proper investigation and prosecution of the case".[338] Where the State does not oppose release on bail, it indicates that, based on the information available to the investigating officer, the accused does not present a risk of absconding.[339] In such circumstances, release on bail should not present difficulty.

An unopposed Schedule 1 bail application is informal, and no affidavit in support of release on bail is required. Submissions from the bar are ordinarily sufficient. Following a Section 60(11B) (a) inquiry, the practitioner will submit that the accused's release on bail is in the interests of justice and indicate the amount of bail the accused can afford. The prosecutor will then either confirm that amount or suggest a different amount for the court's consideration. The court will usually determine the amount of bail or enquire further into the accused's financial circumstances before fixing bail. The application generally

---

[335] *Gcwabe v S* (CA&R 03/2012) [2012] ZAECPEHC 23 (17 April 2012) para 17.

[336] *S v Smith and Another* 1969 (4) SA 175 (N) at 177 e-f.

[337] *S v Dlamini, S v Dladla and Others; S v Joubert; S v Schietekat* (CCT21/98, CCT22/98, CCT2/99, CCT4/99) [1999] ZACC 8; 1999 (4) 623; 1999 (7) BCLR 771 (3 June 1999) para 13 and 38. See *S v Vermaas* 1996 (1) SACR 528 at 530 d-e. Also see *Gcwabe v S* [*supra*] para 17 and *Nwabunwanne v S* (CA&R114/2016) [2017] ZANCHC 9; 2017 (2) SACR 124 (NCK) (31 January 2017) para 11.

[338] *S v Dlamini, S v Dladla and Others; S v Joubert; S v Schietekat* [*supra*] para 52.

[339] *Mvambi v S* (A113/2021) [2022] ZAGPJHC 157 (4 February 2022) para 28.

proceeds as follows:

1. **Prosecutor:** Calling case number B123/2020, *S v Chris Maswanganyi*, first appearance. The accused is represented by Advocate Khumalo. [The prosecutor hands the charge sheet (J15) to the magistrate.]

2. **Defence:** *[Stands]* Your Worship, I confirm my appearance on behalf of the accused. *[If a briefed advocate:]* I hold a brief from Bangiswani Attorneys. *[The brief is handed up to the court through the interpreter, court orderly, court clerk, or prosecutor.]* In terms of Section 60(11B) (a) of the CPA, the accused has no previous convictions and no pending cases. There is no protection order issued against the accused under the Domestic Violence Act 116 of 1998, the Protection from Harassment Act 17 of 2011, or any other law protecting the complainant in this matter. The accused is not a sentenced offender placed under correctional supervision, day parole, parole, or medical parole. The consequences of failing to disclose, or of furnishing incorrect information, have been explained to the accused. Accordingly, based on the charge of theft, the defence submits that this is a Schedule 1 bail. It is further submitted that the interests of justice permit the accused's release on bail. The accused can afford bail in the amount of R500.00, as the court pleases.

3. **Magistrate**: Accused, do you confirm that you have no previous convictions or pending cases? Do you further confirm that there is no protection order issued against you under the Domestic Violence Act 116 of 1998, the Protection from Harassment Act 17 of 2011, or any other law protecting the complainant in this matter? Do you also confirm that you are not presently a sentenced offender placed under correctional supervision, day parole, parole, or medical parole?

   You are warned that, should you fail to disclose, or should you furnish false information regarding your previous convictions, pending cases, protection orders relating to the same complainant, or your status as a sentenced offender under correctional supervision, day parole, parole, or medical parole, you may be convicted and be liable to a fine not exceeding R40 000.00 or to imprisonment for a period not exceeding two years.

4. [*After the accused confirms*]

5. **Magistrate:** Prosecution, on bail and the amount suggested by the defence?

6. **Prosecutor:** The State does not oppose the accused's release on bail, and submits that an amount of R500.00 is fair and equitable.

7. **Magistrate:** Bail is set at R500.00, on condition that you attend this court (Court B) at 8:30 a.m. on every date to which this matter is adjourned. Failure to comply with this condition will result in your bail

being cancelled and the bail money being forfeited to the State. Do you understand?

While Schedule I bail should be dealt with swiftly, it is important to place sufficient information before the court regarding the accused's financial resources and why the suggested amount is fair and equitable. This ensures that, if the court sets a higher amount and the accused is unable to pay it, the explanation can later be relied upon when applying for a reduction of the bail amount.

8.2.3 Opposed Schedule 1 bail application

Where bail is opposed, submissions from the bar carry less weight than evidence placed before the court by way of affidavit.[340] Therefore, in opposed bail applications, it is generally necessary to prepare a bail affidavit or to lead viva voce evidence. However, calling the accused to testify is not always desirable, as any admissions made may be admissible at the subsequent trial.[341] It must also be borne in mind that affidavit evidence, because it is not subjected to cross-examination, is ordinarily less persuasive than viva voce evidence.[342] Affidavits in bail applications are commonly used as a time-saving measure, particularly in unopposed matters.[343] They should therefore not be relied upon without making the accused available for cross-examination, unless the prosecution—being the party upon whom the onus rests—also relies solely on affidavit evidence. Properly utilised, an affidavit assists in presenting focused evidence while avoiding unnecessary disclosure of information that may be admissible at the pending trial. The practical approach to applying this method in opposed bail applications, irrespective of the schedule, is as follows:

1. **Defence introduces the affidavit**

Your Worship, an affidavit in support of bail has been prepared. May I beg leave of the court to read the same into the record?

[Court grants leave]

---

[340] *Pretorius v S* (CC91/2003) [2011] ZAGPPHC 65 (29 April 2011) para 21.

[341] Section 60(11B) (c) of the CPA.Also see *Madlala v S* (A387/2013) [2014] ZAGPJHC 258 and *Pataka v S* (A337/2017) [2018] ZAGPJHC 73, 2018 (2) SACR 135 (GJ) (23 April 2018) para 25.

[342] *S v Mathebula* (431/2009) [2009] ZASCA 91; 2010 (1) SACR 575 (SCA); [2010] 1 All SA 121 (SCA) (11 September 2009) at para 11.

[343] *Pretorius v S* [*supra*] para 23.

2. **Reading the affidavit**

The defence reads the affidavit into the record, commencing from the citation of the court ("In the Magistrates' Court for the District of ...") and concluding with the final prayer ("Wherefore, I pray that ...").

Unless directed otherwise by the court, the affidavit should never be read beginning with "I, the undersigned ...". The proper commencement is the court citation, as the affidavit constitutes formal evidence before court.

3. **Handing in the affidavit**

Your Worship, the affidavit is duly signed and commissioned. Before begging leave of this honourable court to hand it in as an exhibit, may I beg leave to call the accused to the witness stand to adopt the affidavit and subject himself to cross-examination?

[Court grants leave]

4. **Accused sworn in**

The accused enters the witness stand and takes the oath (or affirms).

5. **Identification of the affidavit**

Mr Ndlovu, I have a document before the court. Kindly look at it and confirm whether this is your affidavit, which has just been read into the record. With the leave of the court, may the document be handed to the accused?

[Court grants leave. The orderly, interpreter, or clerk hands the affidavit to the accused.]

6. **Confirmation of ownership**

Do you confirm that this is your affidavit, which has been read into the record?

[Accused confirms]

As ownership is not ordinarily in dispute, confirmation is sufficient.

7. **Confirmation of signature**

Does your signature appear on the last page of the affidavit?

[Accused confirms]

8. **Confirmation of contents**

Do you agree with the contents of the affidavit as they were read into the record?

[Accused confirms]

9. **Conclusion of evidence-in-chief**

Is there anything further you wish to add?

[Accused confirms that there is nothing further]

Your Worship, that is all for this witness.

[Defence resumes seat, indicating conclusion of evidence-in-chief.]

10. **Cross-examination**

Should the prosecutor attempt to cross-examine the accused on the detailed merits of the pending trial—particularly where such questioning goes beyond what is necessary for purposes of assessing bail—the defence must object.[344]

Bail proceedings are not a trial. The purpose of cross-examination in bail is to test:

1. The credibility of the accused.
2. The reliability of the affidavit.
3. The existence of risks contemplated in Section 60(4) of the CPA.

It is not to secure admissions on disputed trial issues or to convert the bail hearing into a premature merits enquiry. An objection may be framed as follows:

Your Worship, I object. The question relates to the detailed merits of the pending trial and exceeds what is necessary for the purposes of this bail application. The accused's trial rights may be prejudiced if he is compelled to answer at this stage.

8.3 Analysis of Schedule 5 bail

In a schedule 5 bail application, the onus rests on the accused to prove, on a balance of probabilities, that the interests of justice permit their release on bail.[345] The interests of justice have been described as a "value judgment of

---

[344] *Pretorius v S* (CC91/2003) [2011] ZAGPPHC 65 (29 April 2011) para 21. Also see *Johannes v S* (A218/2023) [2023] ZAWCHC 312; 2024 (2) SACR 318 (WCC) (1 December 2023) para 32.

[345] Section 6011(b) and (c) of the CPA as amended by the Criminal and Related Matters Amendment Act 12 of 2021. See also *Nwabunwanne v S* (CA&R114/2016) [2017] ZANCHC 9; 2017 (2) SACR 124 (NCK) (31 January 2017) para 10 and *Killian v S* [2021] ZAWCHC 100 (24 May 2021) para 3.

what would be fair and just to all concerned".[346] In this bail application, the defence must first lead evidence to satisfy the court, on a balance of probabilities, that it is fair and just to both society and the complainant that the accused be released on bail.[347] To determine whether the interests of justice favour society or the accused, the court must balance the factors set out in Section 60(4) of the CPA against those contained in Section 60(9) of the CPA and decide whether the accused should be released on bail. In essence, the accused's interests in liberty, as contemplated in Section 60(9) of the CPA, are weighed against the factors that militate against release on bail in the interests of society and the complainant, as set out in Section 60(4) of the CPA.[348] Note that Section 60(4) (e) comes into operation only in exceptional circumstances.[349] It should be "taken into account only in those rare cases where it is really justified".[350] The presiding officer will rely on this factor "with great circumspection in the knowledge that the Constitution protects the liberty interests of all".[351]

It is not enough to merely reiterate Section 60(4) factors in the bail affidavit.[352] You have to place evidence before the court which negates the existence of the Section 60(4) factors.[353] Therefore, if you put forward evidence which shows that there is no likelihood that the client might infringe any factor contained in Section 60(4) of the CPA, you should have succeeded in proving on the balance of probabilities that the interests of justice permit the client's release.[354] The term 'likelihood' used in Section 60(4) of the CPA should be understood to mean that, based on available evidence, it is probable that the risk of infringing Section 60(4) factors will occur, but not to mean a mere possibility or suspicion that such risk will occur.[355] In *S v Diale and Another*,[356] the court stressed this point in the following way:

> A court cannot find that refusal of bail is in the interest of justice merely because there is a risk or possibility that one or more of the consequences mentioned in s60(4) will

---

[346] *S v Dlamini, S v Dladla and Others; S v Joubert; S v Schietekat* (CCT21/98, CCT22/98, CCT2/99, CCT4/99) [199] ZACC 8; 1999 (4) 623; 1999 (7) BCLR 771 (3 June 1999) para 46.

[347] *S v Porthern and Others* (A736/2003) [2003] ZAWCHC 36 (21 August 2003) para 60 read together with Section 60(10) of the CPA as amended by the Criminal and Related Matters Amendment Act 12 of 2021.

[348] *S v Dlamini, S v Dladla and Others; S v Joubert; S v Schietekat* [*supra*] para 65.

[349] *S v Dlamini, S v Dladla and Others; S v Joubert; S v Schietekat* [*supra*] para 57. *Zwakala v S* (CA & R 10/23) [2023] ZANCHC 20 (14 April 2023) para 66.

[350] Ibid.

[351] Ibid.

[352] *Barendse and Another v S* (A01/2023) [2023] ZAWCHC 125 (22 May 2023) para 91. See also *Motsi v S* (A37/22) [2022] ZAWCHC 151; 2023 (1) SACR 218 (WCC) (15 August 2022) para 27 and 28.

[353] *S v Dlamini, S v Dladla and Others; S v Joubert; S v Schietekat* [*supra*] para 65.

[354] Ibid.

[355] S v Dlamini, S v Dladla and Others; S v Joubert; S v Schietekat (CCT21/98, CCT22/98, CCT2/99, CCT4/99) [199] ZACC 8; 1999 (4) 623; 1999 (7) BCLR 771 (3 June 1999) para 65.

[356] *S v Diale and Another* 2013 (2) SACR 85 (GNP) para 14.

> result. The court must not grope in the dark and speculate; a finding on the probabilities must be made. Unless it can be found that one or more of the consequences will probably occur, detention of the accused is not in the interest of justice, and the accused should be released.

Even where there is a likelihood that one or more of the factors contained in Section 60(4) might be at risk if bail is granted, that is not the end. The court must still weigh such factors against the right of the accused to their personal freedom, in particular, the prejudice they are likely to suffer if not released on bail.[357] Before reaching its decision on bail, the court will take into account the pre-trial report, if any, that has been placed before it and the views of the complainant about their safety. [358] Any offence committed against a complainant who is in a domestic relationship with the accused by virtue of such relationship becomes elevated to Schedule 5 status. When the court decides that it is in the interests of justice to release the accused who is in a domestic relationship with the complainant, but there is no existing protection order issued in terms of the Domestic Violence Act 116 of 1998, it must hold an inquiry regarding the issuing of a protection order.[359] If such a protection order is issued, the provisions of the Domestic Violence Act become applicable.[360] It is therefore important to channel the court to this point from the beginning of the bail affidavit after consulting the client by stating that the client is willing and will abide by any condition of the protection order issued by this court in terms of Section 60(12) (b) of the CPA. What constitutes a domestic relationship is explained in footnote 21.

8.4 Analysis of Schedule 6 bail

In a Schedule 6 bail application, the onus is on the bail applicant to prove that there are exceptional circumstances which, in the interests of justice, permit their release on bail.[361] The purpose of Section 60(11) (a) is to ensure that it is difficult to obtain bail for Schedule 6 offences.[362] Therefore, you should not be surprised when courts are reluctant to grant bail in Schedule 6 offences.

---

[357] *S v Dlamini, S v Dladla and Others; S v Joubert; S v Schietekat* ([*supra*] para 53.

[358] Section 60(2A) of the CPA as amended by the Criminal and Related Matters Amendment Act 12 of 2021.

[359] Section 60(12) (b) of the CPA as amended by the Criminal and Related Matters Amendment Act 12 of 2021.

[360] Ibid.

[361] *S v Dlamini, S v Dladla and Others; S v Joubert; S v Schietekat* (CCT21/98, CCT22/98, CCT2/99, CCT4/99) [1999] ZACC 8; 1999 (4) 623; 1999 (7) BCLR 771 (3 June 1999) para 61.

[362] *S v Dlamini, S v Dladla and Others; S v Joubert; S v Schietekat* [*supra*] para 64. See also *S v Mabena and Another* (373/06) [2006] ZASCA 178; [2007] 2 All SA 137 (SCA); 2007 (1) SACR 482 (SCA) (17 October 2006) para 6.

Schedule 6 covers the most serious offences. In *S v Dlamini,*[363] the court emphasised that:

> Section 60(11)(a) contemplates an exercise in which the balance between the liberty interests of the accused and the interests of society in denying the accused bail will be resolved in favour of the denial of bail, unless "exceptional circumstances" are shown by the accused to exist.

The legislative policy involved in Section 60(11) (a) of the CPA is that, unless in exceptional circumstances, public interest recommends that accused persons charged with more serious offences listed in Schedule 6 of the CPA should forfeit their freedom until the courts have determined whether they are guilty or innocent.[364] Put differently, the accused charged with a Schedule 6 offence should be denied bail even if it is in the interests of justice to release them, simply because of the seriousness of the charge they are facing, until they prove that there are exceptional circumstances which, in the interests of justice, permit their release.[365] Therefore, the court presiding on a bail application under Schedule 6 evaluates the evidence before it and decides whether such evidence is persuasive enough to show that an exception should be made to the normality of keeping the accused arrested for Schedule 6 offences in custody until the outcome of their criminal proceedings.[366] Before reaching its decision on bail, the court will take into account the pre-trial report, if any, that has been placed before it and the views of the complainant about their safety.[367]

8.4.1 Meaning of exceptional circumstances

What constitutes exceptional circumstances is often problematic, and courts may require an accused to identify what exceptional circumstances arise from the facts of their particular case.[368] While it is frequently argued that exceptional circumstances are vague and incapable of precise definition, this absence of definition serves an important purpose. It allows the court to consider each matter on its own facts and affords the accused a broader scope

---

[363] *S v Dlamini, S v Dladla and Others; S v Joubert; S v Schietekat* [*supra*] para 64. See also *S v Mabena and Another* [*supra*] para 6.
[364] *S v Porthern and Others* (A736/2003) [2003] ZAWCHC 36 (21 August 2003) para 17.
[365] *S v Conradie* (A248/2020) [2020] ZAWCHC 177 (11 December 2020) para 11.
[366] *Killian v S* [2021] ZAWCHC 100 (24 May 2021) para 5.
[367] Section 60(2A) of the CPA as amended by the Criminal and Related Matters Amendment Act 12 of 2021.
[368] *S v Dikhusooka* (18/2002) [2002] ZANWHC 25 (20 June 2002) para 10.

to establish exceptional circumstances which, in the interests of justice, permit their release on bail.[369]

In proving exceptional circumstances, it is not decisive whether the circumstances relied upon relate to the nature of the offence, the personal circumstances of the bail applicant, or any other factor that appears persuasive.[370] The onus on the accused is limited to showing, on a balance of probabilities, that circumstances exist which entitle them "in the interests of justice to be admitted to bail and to be treated as an exception to the general position advanced by Section 60(11) (a) of the Act that accused persons charged with Schedule 6 offences shall remain in custody".[371] This onus does not require the accused "to absolutely convince the court of the existence of exceptional circumstances".[372] Nor is the accused required to rely on a predetermined list of circumstances that are inherently distinctive.[373] The existence of exceptional circumstances must be assessed on a case-by-case basis, as each bail application is inherently unique and depends on the specific facts and context presented.[374] The courts have provided guidance on the meaning and application of *exceptional circumstances* in bail applications as follows:

1. In *S v Vanqa*,[375] it was held that an accused is not required to prove the existence of factors different from the normal considerations listed in Sections 60(4) to (9). What is required is to show that such usual or common factors are, in the context of the particular case, blended with an element of exceptionality.
2. In *S v Bruintjies*,[376] the court held that, in determining whether exceptional circumstances exist, all relevant factors must be considered and assessed, whether individually or cumulatively, to decide whether they justify such a finding. What is exceptional cannot be determined in isolation from the facts, but it should be apparent that the facts are out of the ordinary.
3. In *S v Zwakala*,[377] the court stated that the existence of exceptional circumstances must be determined within the context of each particular case, bearing in mind that facts which may be sufficient in one case may not be sufficient in another.

---

[369] *S v Dlamini, S v Dladla and Others; S v Joubert; S v Schietekat* (CCT21/98, CCT22/98, CCT2/99, CCT4/99) [1999] ZACC 8; 1999 (4) 623; 1999 (7) BCLR 771 (3 June 1999) para 75.

[370] *S v Dlamini, S v Dladla and Others; S v Joubert; S v Schietekat* [*supra*] para 76.

[371] *Mququ v S* (CA&R78/2019) [2019] ZAECGHC 55; 2019 (2) SACR 207 (ECG) (14 May 2019) para 20.

[372] Ibid.

[373] *Killian v S* [2021] ZAWCHC 100 (24 May 2021) para 4.

[374] Ibid.

[375] *S v Vanqa* 2000 (2) SACR 371 (TkHC) at 376 c-d.

[376] *S v Bruintjies* (676/2002) [2003] ZASCA 4 (25 February 2003) *para* 6.

[377] *Zwakala v S* (CA&R10/23) [2023] ZANCHC 20 (14 April 2023) para 80. See also *S v Porta* 2004 (2) SACR 242 (WCD) para 12.

4. In *S v Porthern and Others*,[378] it was held that the determination of exceptional circumstances involves a value judgment as to whether the proven circumstances are of such a nature that they may properly be described as exceptional.

5. In *S v Petersen*,[379] the court stated that the exceptionality of the circumstances must be such that it would be in the interests of justice to order the accused's release on bail. This approach allows for some flexibility, recognising that what may be exceptional can differ from case to case.

6. In *Rudolph v S*,[380] it was stated that exceptional circumstances do not mean circumstances that are "above and beyond, and generally different from those enumerated" in Sections 60(4) to (9). Ordinary circumstances, when present to an exceptional degree, may justify a finding that release on bail is warranted.

7. In *S v Mazibuko and Another*,[381] the court held that, for circumstances to qualify as exceptional and justify release on bail, they must weigh exceptionally heavily in favour of the accused, thereby rendering the case for release on bail exceptionally strong or compelling.

8. In *S v Dlamini*,[382] the court emphasised that, in conducting the final analysis on whether exceptional circumstances exist in the interests of justice, the court must act wisely and focus on substance rather than form.

8.5 Approach to Schedule 5 and 6 bail applications

8.5.1 Unopposed Schedule 5 or 6 bail application

When the prosecutor does not oppose the accused's release on these two schedules, the court shall require the prosecutor to provide reasons on the record.[383] Therefore, in arguments, you should also use these reasons to persuade the court to grant bail. As a result of the onus, which is on the accused, you must lead evidence first in Schedule 5 or 6 bail applications.[384] Even when bail is unopposed, the evidence must be submitted either by affidavit or oral testimony. When bail is unopposed, the affidavit is usually sufficient because there is no dispute over whether the accused should be

---

[378] *S v Porthern and Others* (A736/2003) [2003] ZAWCHC 36 (21 August 2003) para 12.

[379] *S v Petersen* (A717/07) [2008] ZAWCHC 11; [2008] 3 All SA 301 (C); 2008 (2) SACR 355 (C) (27 February 2008) para 56.

[380] *Rudolph v S* (484/2009) [2009] ZASCA 133; 2010 (1) SACR (SCA); [2010] 2 All SA 178 (SCA) (30 September 2009) para 9.

[381] *Mazibuko and Another v S* (8774/09) [2009] ZAKZPHC 61; 2010 (1) SACR 433 (KZP) (19 November 2009) para 19.

[382] *S v Dlamini, S v Dladla and Others; S v Joubert; S v Schietekat* CCT21/98, CCT22/98, CCT2/99, CCT4/99) [1999] ZACC 8; 1999 (4) 623; 1999 (7) BCLR 771 (3 June 1999) para 75.

[383] Section 60(2) (d) of the CPA.

[384] *S v Porthen and Others* [*supra*] para 60. See also *Gcwabe v S* (CA&R 03/2012) [2012] ZAECPEHC 23 (17 April 2012) para 20.

released on bail. However, you should be mindful that even when the bail is unopposed, the court is not bound by the State's attitude.[385] The court must still weigh the accused's personal interests against the interests of justice, including the complainant's safety.[386] Nevertheless, if the substantial evidence presented by the bail applicant is uncontroverted, the court will rarely deny bail, because, although a bail application is less formal than a trial, it remains a legal court process that is adversarial in nature.[387] Consequently, the court cannot, without a factual basis, conclude that it is not in the interests of justice to release the accused on bail.[388] Where the court is of the view that certain crucial evidence has not been placed before it, it may use its inquisitorial powers in terms of Section 60(3) of the CPA to call for such evidence to be presented. However, nothing in the CPA prohibits you from applying to reopen the bail applicant's case to shed more light on the evidence solicited by the court. The term 'reasonable opportunity' used in Section 60(11) (a), (b), and (c) of the CPA requires the court to give the bail applicant a fair chance.[389]

<u>An example of an affidavit in support of an unopposed Schedule 5 bail:</u>

IN THE MAGISTRATES' COURT FOR THE MAGISTERIAL DISTRICT OF SARAH BAARTMAN

[HELD AT MAKHANDA]

CASE NO: CA405/2024

In the matter between:

VUYOLWETHU MGQAMQHO APPLICANT

And

THE STATE RESPONDENT

---

[385] Section 60(10) of the CPA as amended by the Criminal and Related Matters Amendment Act 12 of 2021. See also *Mbaleki and Another v S* (2853/2011) [2011] ZAKZDHC 68; 2013 (1) SACR 165 (KZD) (1 April 2011) para 12; *Mfeketho and Others v S* (CA&R193/2014) [2014] ZAECGHC 67 (21 July 2014) para 9; and *S v Sithole and Others* (7032/11) [2011] ZAKZDHC 36; 2012 (1) SACR 586 (KZD) (19 August 2011) para 11,13, and 21.

[386] Ibid.

[387] *Majali v S* (41210/2010) [2011] ZAGPJHC 74 (19 July 2011) para 25. See also *S v Mabena and Another* (373/06) [2006] ZASCA 178; [2007] 2 All SA 137 (SCA); 2007 (1) SACR 482 (SCA) (17 October 2006) para 7 and *Mgijima v S* (CA&R 13/23) [2023] ZANCHC 18 (28 April 2023) para 12-13.

[388] *Crossberg v S* (439/2007) [ZASCA] 93 (22 August 2007) para 19. See also *Johannes v S* (A218/2023) [2023] ZAWCHC 312; 2024 (2) SACR 318 (WCC) (1 December 2023) para 30.

[389] *S v Dlamini, S v Dladla and Others; S v Joubert; S v Schietekat* [*supra*] para 80, as read together with Section 60 (11) of the CPA as amended by the Criminal and Related Matters Amendment Act 12 of 2021.

AFFIDAVIT IN SUPPORT OF SCHEDULE 5 BAIL APPLICATION

I, the undersigned VUYOLWETHU MQGAMQHO, do hereby make an oath and say:

1. I am the Accused in this matter and the Applicant in this bail application. I am making this declaration freely and voluntarily without undue influence. The facts herein contained are within my personal knowledge, save where the context indicates otherwise, and to the best of my knowledge and belief, are true and correct.

2. I make this affidavit to persuade the court to release me on bail. I will therefore inform this honourable court about my circumstances, deal with the allegations levelled against me, and further deal with the factors to be considered by the court in terms of Sections 60(4) to 60(9) of the CPA.

3. I have been advised that the record of this bail application, excluding the information provided in terms of Section 60(11B) (a) of Act 51 of 1977, can and may be used against me in my subsequent trial. Therefore, I am aware that if I provide information that goes to the merits of the charge, I may be cross-examined on that information during trial.

4. I further confirm that I have been warned about the consequences of non-disclosure and of furnishing wrong information about my previous convictions, pending cases, protection orders protecting the complainant issued against me, and being a sentenced offender placed under correctional supervision, day parole, parole, or medical parole. I have been informed that I may be liable to a fine not exceeding R40 000.00 or imprisonment not exceeding two years should I ignore the above warning. With that in mind, I state that I have no previous convictions or pending cases. I further confirm that there is no protection order issued against me in terms of the Domestic Violence Act 116 of 1998, the Protection from Harassment Act 17 of 2011, or any other law that protects the complainant of this case, and I am not a sentenced offender placed under correctional supervision, day parole, parole, or medical parole.

5. I am charged with rape in terms of Section 3 of the Criminal Law (Sexual Offences and Related Matters) Act 32 of 2007. I have been advised that my case falls under Schedule 5 of the Criminal Procedure Act 51 of 1977. Therefore, I bear the burden of proving, on the balance of probabilities, that the interests of justice permit my release on bail, and I have a duty to start leading the evidence. Therefore, I place the following on record to show the court on the balance of probabilities that the interests of justice permit my release on bail:

   5.1 I am a 40-year-old South African male with identity number 8406246236080. I am staying at 324 Ncame Street, Extension 4, Joza

Location, Makhanda. I have been staying at this address for the past 15 years. I am not married, but I have a live-in partner, Nongqesho Radebe, and we have two minor children: Vuyokazi Radebe, 05 years old and Athenkosi Radebe, 2 years old. I have no passport and no relatives, friends, or businesses outside the borders of the Republic of South Africa.

5.2 I own the following assets: Erf 324 Ncame Street, Extension 4, Joza Location, which is valued at R550 000.00, furniture to the value of R80 000.00, and a 1991 BMW 325is motor vehicle valued at R250 000.00. I am employed as a chef at Piet my Vrou Cocktail Lounge. I earn R10 500.00 per month. I have been employed by the same lounge for the past five years. I am the breadwinner since my partner is unemployed.

5.3 On 23 June 2024, I left my workplace at around 10.00 pm and went home. When I arrived home, my partner informed me that an investigating officer had come by looking for me and left his cell phone number. I decided to call the investigating officer the following day, since it was already night. The following morning, 24 June 2024, I was informed by the investigating officer to come to the police station, as a case had been opened against me. I went to the police station, and I was arrested. I was informed that Nonhle Jaca (the complainant) had opened a case of rape against me. I know the complainant as my neighbour. We have known each other for the past 12 years. On 22 June 2024, at around 08.00 pm, I met the complainant at CoolSpot Tavern, and she asked me to buy her beers. I bought her eight 440ml cans of Heineken, and we drank until the tavern closed at 2.00 am. I accompanied her home, where she invited me into her backroom. We then engaged in consensual sexual intercourse once, and I went home since I was supposed to go to work at 10.00 am. At around 9.00 am on 23 June 2024, I was on my way to work when I met the complainant. She asked me to buy her beers as she was experiencing a hangover. I told her that I did not have money, and she became angry, stating that I owed her and warning that if I thought I was clever, I would see.

5.4 I have a strong defence in this case, and should I be released on bail, I will comply with the requirements of Section 60(4) of Act 51 of 1977. I have a strong defence in this case, and should I be released on bail, I will comply with the requirements of Section 60(4) of Act 51 of 1977. I have never attempted, and I will not, after release on bail, endanger the safety of the public, the complainant, or myself, or commit an offence. I maintain good relationships with people, I hold no grudges against anyone, and I am not a violent person. Even though I know the complainant in this case, I will never intimidate or influence her or any other witness. I do not know what kind of evidence the State has against me, but I will not conceal or destroy it. I have been staying in Makhanda for the rest of my life, and I also work here. I cannot afford to leave my family and job just to evade this trial, as I believe the State has a weak case against me. I will not undermine or jeopardise the objectives or the proper functioning of the criminal justice system, including the bail system. My release on bail will not, in exceptional circumstances, disturb public order, undermine public peace, or compromise public security.

5.5 I am willing to abide by all bail conditions which the honourable court may impose. My nearest police station is Makhanda Police Station.

5.6 When the court assesses the affordability of bail amount as a separate inquiry in terms of Section 60(2B) of Act 51 of 1977, I request that it take into account that I earn only R10 500.00 and that I am the only income earner in my family. In addition, I pay a monthly bond amount of R5 500.00.

5.7 I will afford bail in the amount of R1 000.00. The said amount is fair and reasonable for someone in my situation, and I cannot afford to lose it.

Wherefore, I pray that the honourable court finds that the interests of justice, considerations of prejudice and the balancing of relevant interests favour my release on bail.

____

SIGNATURE OF THE DEPONENT

The deponent having acknowledged that he knows and understands the contents of this affidavit, that it is both true and correct to the best of his knowledge and belief, that he has no objection to taking the prescribed oath and that the prescribed oath will be binding on his conscience.

____

COMMISSIONER OF OATHS

FULL NAME: **AVIWE NZAMA**

DESIGNATION: **CONSTABLE**

ADDRESS: MAKHANDA POLICE STATION

<u>An example of an affidavit in support of unopposed Schedule 6 bail:</u>

IN THE MAGISTRATES' COURT FOR THE MAGISTERIAL DISTRICT OF MADIBENG

[HELD AT BRITS]

CASE NO: B212/2024

In the matter between:

MOTLALEPULA MODISANE APPLICANT

And

THE STATE RESPONDENT

AFFIDAVIT IN SUPPORT OF SCHEDULE 6 BAIL APPLICATION

I, the undersigned Motlalepula Modisane, do hereby make oath and say:

1. I am the Accused in this matter and the Applicant in this bail application. The facts hereinafter deposed to fall within my personal knowledge, save where the contrary appears from the context and are, to the best of my knowledge and belief, both true and correct.

2. I have been advised that the record of this bail application, excluding the information provided in terms of Section 60(11B) (a) of Act 51 of 1977, can and may be used against me in my subsequent trial. Therefore, I am aware that if I provide information that goes to the merits of the charge, I may be cross-examined on that information during trial. I have been warned that I must disclose my previous convictions and pending cases, and not provide incorrect information about them. I must also provide correct information about any protection orders issued against me for the protection of the complainant, if any, and I must inform the court if I am a sentenced offender placed under correctional supervision, on day parole, parole, or medical parole. I have been informed that if I fail to comply with the above warning, I may be liable to a fine not exceeding R40 000.00 or imprisonment not exceeding two years. With that in mind, I state that I have no previous convictions or pending cases. I further confirm that there is no protection order issued against me in terms of the Domestic Violence Act 116 of 1998, the Protection from Harassment Act 17 of 2011, or any other law that protects the complainant of this case, and I am not a sentenced offender placed under correctional supervision, day parole, parole, or medical parole.

3. I am charged with contravention of Section 3 of the Criminal Law (Sexual Offences and Related Matters) Act 32 of 2007.

4. I have been informed that my case falls under Schedule 6 of the Criminal Procedure Act 51 of 1977, as the victim is 15 years old. Therefore, the onus rests on me to prove on the balance of probabilities that there are exceptional circumstances which, in the interests of justice, permit my release. I shall therefore proceed to place the following on record to demonstrate to the court, on a balance of probabilities, that there are exceptional circumstances which, in the interests of justice, warrant my release on bail:

   4.1. I am a 21-year-old male and a South African citizen staying at 44 Vuka Section, Oukasie, Brits. I have lived at this address since I was born. I am not married, and I have no children. I am the only child of Boipelo Modisane and Tshepo Modise. My father (Tshepo Modise) is employed at Nissan Plant I Rosslyn as a Toolmaker. He is earning R20 000.00 per month. My mother (Boipelo Modisane) is unemployed. I am also unemployed, and I rely on my parents for financial support. I am a final-year full-time BSc (Chemistry) student at the University of Pretoria, under student number 2043032 (A1-A2). When I attend my classes, I stay at House Nala Residence in Hatfield, Pretoria. I have no passport and no relatives, friends, or business outside the borders of the Republic of South Africa.

   4.2. On 23 June 2024, I finished writing my first-semester exams, and on the same day, I decided to go home to Oukasie. I took a taxi from Pretoria Bloed Mall to Brits. In the taxi, I met with the victim, who did not appear to be 15 years old. I started a conversation with her as we were sitting in the same seat. I found out that she is also staying at Oukasie. We travelled together until we arrived in Oukasie, and when the taxi was near her street, I asked for her phone number, and she gave it to me. On the morning of 24 June 2024, I called her and invited her to visit me at my home. She came to visit me at around 01.00 pm. I was alone at home when she arrived. We were sitting in my back room and listening to music. I professed my love to her, and she accepted me, and we had sexual intercourse once without a condom. At around 06.00 pm the same day, I accompanied her back to her home. On 25 June 2024, I returned to my university residence and did not call her again. On 14 August 2024, I received a text message from her, informing me that she was pregnant, her parents were very angry, and she did not know what to do. I ignored the message since I thought she was joking, or it was a way to come back to me because I had not called her since we had sexual intercourse. On 15 August 2024, at around 06.00 pm, my father contacted me and told me to return home quickly because the police were looking for me. On the morning of 16 August 2024, I went back home. When I arrived home, my father took me to the police station, where we met the investigating officer. The officer informed me that the parents of the complainant had opened a case of rape against me on the basis that the complainant was underage and pregnant, after which I was arrested. I never raped the complainant, and I was not aware that she was 15 years old, and she does not look that young.

4.3. I apply to be released on bail and will comply with the provisions of Section 60(4) of Act 51 of 1977. I have never attempted, and I will not, after release on bail, endanger the safety of the public, the complainant, or myself, or commit an offence. Even though I know the complainant in this case, I will never intimidate or influence her or any other witness. I do not know what kind of evidential material the State has against me, but I will not conceal or destroy it. I have been living in Oukasie for most of my life, even though I am also studying at Hatfield. I cannot afford to leave my family and my university studies to evade this trial. I will not undermine or jeopardise the objectives or the proper functioning of the criminal justice system, including the bail system. The court must note that I did not supply any incorrect information during my arrest. I am not in custody in another matter, nor am I on parole. I have never failed to comply with any bail conditions. The public order factor, which arises only in exceptional circumstances, is not applicable, as my release on bail will not disturb public order or undermine public peace or security

4.4. My continued incarceration will severely prejudice me as a full-time university student because I would not be able to attend classes or write tests and examinations. My father has already paid this year's tuition fee, and there will be no refund. I have only three months left to complete my degree. I am also scheduled to attend practicals on organic chemistry, time-series analysis, numerical analysis, and cell structure and function from 05 September 2024 to 04 October 2024 [see practical schedule, Annexure B]. I have to pass these practicals to write examinations.

4.5. I am willing to abide by all bail conditions that the honourable court may impose. My nearest police station is the Brits Police Station.

4.6. When the court assesses the affordability of the bail amount as a separate inquiry in terms of Section 60(2B) of Act 51 of 1977, I request that it take into account that I am a student, and I am dependent on my parents for support. My father is the only family member who earns a salary, earning only R20 000.00 per month. I will afford bail in the amount of R500.00. The said amount is fair and reasonable for someone in my situation, and I cannot afford to lose it.

THEREFORE, I pray that the honourable court finds that the facts articulated above cumulatively prove on the balance of probabilities that the interests of justice weigh exceptionally heavily in favour of my release on bail rather than being kept in custody until my trial is finalised.

I understand the content of this affidavit; I have no objection to taking the prescribed oath, and I consider it as binding in my conscience.

____

SIGNATURE OF THE DEPONENT

I hereby certify that the Deponent has acknowledged that he knows and understands the contents of this Affidavit, which was signed and sworn before me at Brits on 19 August 2024, the regulations contained in Government Notice No 1258 of 21 July 1972, as amended, and Government Notice No R1648 of 19 August 1977, as amended, having been complied with.

____

COMMISSIONER OF OATHS

NAME: SIMPHIWE MAHLANGU

RANK: CST

PLACE: BRITS

8.5.2 *Opposed Schedule 5 or 6 bail application*

In an opposed bail application, it is desirable to place persuasive evidence before the court by reading affidavits into the record and subjecting the accused to cross-examination, as discussed in paragraph 8.2.3, or by leading viva voce evidence. In *S v Pretorius*,[390] the court emphasised this position when it stated that "it is clear from *Mathebula v S* … that an applicant for bail can only be found to have discharged his onus if he opened himself to cross-examination". While this position may be unavoidable in cases where affidavit evidence presented by the accused is contradicted by viva voce evidence led by the prosecution, it cannot mean that an accused who was not subjected to cross-examination, or who did not present oral evidence, will in all cases be refused bail merely because they relied on affidavit evidence alone. This should be understood as emphasising the quality of the evidence required to satisfy the court that the accused ought to be granted bail.

In *Mfeketho and Others v S*,[391] while the court acknowledged that affidavit evidence is generally less persuasive, it rejected the proposition that such

[390] *Pretorius v S* (CC91/2003) [2011] ZAGPPHC 65 (29 April 2011) para 24.
[391] *Mfeketho v S* (CA&R193/2014) [2014] ZAECGHC 67(21 July 2014) para 20.

evidence is incapable of enabling an accused to discharge the onus or that it should be accorded little or no weight. In that matter, the evidence was uncontroverted and, to some extent, confirmed by the prosecution.[392] The court is therefore required to consider affidavit evidence and to accord it due weight when assessing whether the applicant should be released on bail.[393]

In *Sinqu v S,*[394] the court, following *Mfeketho*, rejected the magistrate's finding that no weight should be attached to evidence led by affidavit alone, particularly where such evidence was uncontroverted or uncontested by the prosecution. An accused may discharge the onus by leading evidence by way of affidavit only, and although such evidence may be less persuasive, it does not follow that it should be disregarded.[395] However, where the prosecution leads *viva voce* evidence from the investigating officer which contradicts the accused's affidavit, the accused, relying solely on less persuasive evidence, is unlikely to be granted bail.

In *Killian v S,*[396] the court highlighted the difficulties that arise when both parties present their evidence by affidavit, without the accused being subjected to cross-examination, particularly where there are clear factual disputes on paper. The court adopted the approach that, "if the facts are to be determined on paper, the State's version must be accepted where there is a conflict, unless that version is improbable".[397] Attempting to discharge the onus applicable under Section 60(11) by way of affidavit alone, even where it is anticipated that the State will also rely on affidavit evidence, is fraught with risk, as it may result in disputed allegations not being properly resolved.[398]

While bail is urgent, it is not advisable to proceed with an opposed bail application if the necessary evidence supporting the accused's release is not yet available. It must never be overlooked that personal liberty is a precious right.[399] In preparing for a bail application, it is crucial to anticipate the grounds upon which the State is likely to oppose bail. Where applicable, travel documents should be surrendered, and this fact should be expressly recorded in the affidavit in support of bail. Where witnesses are neighbours or family members, consideration should be given to proposing an alternative address. Care must be taken to ensure that such an address is easily verifiable by providing the contact details of the person at that address and affording the

---

[392] *Mfeketho v S* (CA&R193/2014) [2014] ZAECGHC 67(21 July 2014) para 21.
[393] Ibid.
[394] *Sinqu v S* (CA&R31/2016) [2016] ZAECBHC 14 (21 December 2016) para 9.
[395] *Sinqu v S [supra]* para 10.
[396] *Killian v S* [2021] ZAWCHC 100 (24 May 2021) para 11. See also *Kara and Others v S* (A 218/22; F563/2022) [2022] ZAWCHC 258 (1 December 2022) para 5 and 9, and *Barendse and Another v S* (A01/2023) [2023] ZAWCHC 125 (22 May 2023) para 118.
[397] *Killian v S [supra]* para 13.
[398] *Kara and Others v S* (A 218/22; F563/2022) [2022] ZAWCHC 258 (1 December 2022) para 9.
[399] Check what happened at *Nel and Others v S* (A508/2017) [2017] ZAGPJHC 296; 1018 (1) SACR 576 (GJ) (17 October 2017) para 6-9.

investigating officer an opportunity to confirm it. Should the investigating officer fail to do so, the owner of the alternative address may depose to a confirmatory affidavit or give viva voce evidence confirming ownership of the address, the nature of the relationship with the accused, and their consent to the accused residing there until finalisation of the matter. Where the accused voluntarily surrendered themself at a police station, this fact should likewise be recorded in the bail affidavit.

The issue of bail conditions should be highlighted to demonstrate how they may mitigate the infringement of the factors listed in Section 60(4).[400] When dealing with factors mentioned in Section 60(4), you must not just make a bare denial of them but substantiate why there is no likelihood that the accused will infringe such factors.[401] In *Mathebula v S*, the court emphasised that the mere parroting of Section 60(4) (a) to (e) of the CPA does not, on its own, establish the absence of a likelihood that these factors will be infringed, without the addition of facts that lend weight to the accused's assertions.[402] Where documentary proof exists in support of averments contained in an affidavit, it should be attached as an annexure. All relevant witnesses should be called, as temporary deprivation of liberty may expose the accused to a range of adverse consequences, "such as the loss of his or her employment or home, health problems and disconnection from his or her family and community".[403] It should also be borne in mind that, although hearsay evidence is admissible in bail applications, it generally carries less weight.[404]

Since the accused testifies first, it is important to remember that an application may be made to reopen their case where this is justifiable. The phrase "reasonable opportunity", as used in Section 60(11) (a), (b), and (c) of the CPA, requires the court to afford the bail applicant a fair chance to present their case.[405] A fair opportunity may, in appropriate circumstances, include

---

[400] *Sibeko v S* (BA17/2020) ZAMPMHC 13 (30 May 2020) para 23.

[401] *S v Botha en 'n Ander* [2001] ZASCA 146 (30 November 2001); [2002] 2 All SA 577 (A); 2002 (1) SACR 222 (SCA) para 18. See also *S v Dikhusooka* (18/2002) [2002] ZANWHC 25 (20 June 2002) para 7; *S v Conradie* (A248/2020) [2020] ZAWCHC 177 (11 December 2020) para 18; and *Motsi v S* (A37/22) [2022] ZAWCHC 151; 2023 (1) SACR 218 (WCC) (15 August 2022) para 27 and 28.

[402] *S v Mathebula* (431/2009) [2009] ZASCA 91; 2010 (1) SACR 575 (SCA); [2010] 1 All SA 121 (SCA) (11 September 2009) at para 10. See also *Kula v S* (CAB 02/2023) ZANWHC 35; 2023 (2) SACR 52 (NWM) (4 April 2023) para 59.

[403] Ballard C "Research Report on Remand Detention in South Africa: An Overview of the Current Law and Proposals for Reform" 2011 *Civil Society Prison Reform Initiative* https://dullahomarinstitute.org.za/acjr/resource-centre/South%20Africa%20Ballard.pdf accessed 25 July 2024.

[404] *Kula v S* (CAB 02/2023) ZANWHC 35; 2023 (2) SACR 52 (NWM) (4 April 2023) para 66.

[405] *S v Dlamini, S v Dladla and Others; S v Joubert; S v Schietekat* (CCT21/98, CCT22/98, CCT2/99, CCT4/99) [1999] ZACC 8; 1999 (4) 623; 1999 (7) BCLR 771 (3 June 1999) para 80, as read together with Section 60(11) of the CPA as amended by the Criminal and Related Matters Amendment Act 12 of 2021. See also *Mafe v S* (A49/22) [2022] ZAWCHC 108 (31 May 2022) para 69-71.

requesting the prosecutor to outline the facts of the case before the defence begins leading evidence, particularly where the accused does not fully understand the circumstances underlying the charge.[406]

8.6 Affordability of bail as a separate inquiry

In terms of Section 60(2B) of the CPA, once the court finds that the release of the accused on bail is in the interests of justice, it must conduct a separate inquiry to determine whether the accused can afford to pay the bail amount.[407] As stated in *S v Fhetani,*[408] courts should not set a high bail amount in cases involving an indigent accused, as this is tantamount to a refusal of bail. The accused's financial resources must therefore be taken into account when determining the bail amount. Although legal practitioners may be relieved once bail has been granted, it is important to remember that the affordability inquiry is critical to preventing excessive bail. A proper inquiry at this stage also reduces the likelihood of subsequent applications to reduce the bail amount.

As intended by the legislature, this inquiry should be conducted after the court has decided to grant bail, as it is difficult to meaningfully address bail affordability while the bail question remains undecided. To avoid advancing an uncertain position, a practitioner may prepare two separate affidavits: one dealing with the merits of bail, and another addressing the affordability of the bail amount. Alternatively, both issues may be addressed in a single affidavit, provided that the question of affordability is fully canvassed towards the end.[409] It is important to guide the court to this separate inquiry.

(a) Separate affidavits

Defence:
Your Worship, before reading the affidavit in support of bail, may it be noted that a further affidavit has been prepared dealing specifically with the affordability of the bail amount in

[406] *S v Dlamini, S v Dladla and Others; S v Joubert; S v Schietekat* (CCT21/98, CCT22/98, CCT2/99, CCT4/99) [1999] ZACC 8; 1999 (4) 623; 1999 (7) BCLR 771 (3 June 1999) para 80, as read together with Section 60(11) of the CPA as amended by the Criminal and Related Matters Amendment Act 12 of 2021. See also *Mafe v S* (A49/22) [2022] ZAWCHC 108 (31 May 2022) para 69-71.

[407] Joubert *Applied Law for Police Officials* 5th Ed 327. Also see Mokwena UCA and Lubaale EC "Decolonising Prisons in South Africa: The need for effective bail affordability inquiries" December 2018 *South African Crime Quarterly* https://doi.org/10.17159/2413-3108/2018/i66a5634, accessed on 24 June 2023. De Ruter N and Hardy K "Study on the use of bail in South Africa" May 2018 *African Policing Civilian Oversight Forum Research Paper* http://apcof.org/wp-content/uploads/023-apcof-research-study-on-the-use-of-bail-in-south-africa-nicola-de-ruiter-and-kathleen-hardy-.pdf, accessed on 03 July 2023 para 9.

[408] *S v Fhetani* (158/2007) [2007] ZASCA 113; [2007] SCA 113 (RSA) (21 September 2007) para 10 and 11.

[409] The evidence supporting that the accused cannot afford the bail amount should be attached, e.g. the pay slip of the accused or proof of registration showing that they are a student, etc.

terms of Section 60(2B) of the CPA. With the leave of this court, may the issue of bail be dealt with first. Should the court decide to grant bail, the inquiry into the affordability of the bail amount may then be entertained.

(b) Single affidavit

Defence:
Your Worship, I have prepared a single affidavit addressing both the issue of bail and the affordability thereof. With the leave of this honourable court, I will first address the issue of bail. If bail is granted, I will then address the court on the affordability of the bail amount, as provided for in Section 60(2B) of the CPA.

In an informal Schedule I bail application, the issue of affordability should still be fully addressed, and all information necessary to enable the court to decide the issue should be placed before it. Where the accused is unable to afford any monetary payment, the court should consider release on conditions that do not involve the payment of money, such as a warning or release on a guarantee. In terms of Section 60(13) of the CPA, the accused may be released on a guarantee to pay the bail amount. ``One of the cases where the accused was released on a guarantee is in *Majali v S*.[410] In that matter, bail was fixed in the amount of R10 000.00, but the accused was not required to pay the amount in cash.[411] Instead, he was ordered to pledge his premises within seven days of the order as security for the bail amount.[412]

To avoid a conflict of interest, legal practitioners are not permitted to post bail on behalf of their clients.[413] Bail money should therefore not form part of the legal fees payable to the legal practitioner, and the bail receipt should not reflect the name of the legal practitioner as the depositor.[414]

---

410 *Majali v S* (41210/2010) [2011] ZAGPJHC 74 (19 July 2011).
411 *Majali v S* [*supra*] para 37.
412 Ibid.
413 *Code of Conduct for all Legal Practitioners, Candidate Legal Practitioners and Juristic Entities* GN 162 in GG 42337 29 March 2019 para 58.2. See also *Brown and Another v S* (CC 18/2017) [2018] ZAECPEHC 76; 2019 (1) SACR 691 (ECP) (14 December 2018) para 30.
414 Ibid.

CHAPTER 9

AMENDMENT OF BAIL CONDITIONS

9.1 General amendment of bail conditions

In terms of Section 63 of the CPA, the court may increase or reduce the amount of bail set, or amend or supplement any bail condition imposed in terms of Section 60 or 62 of the CPA, upon application by the accused or the prosecution.[415] Even though the reduction of bail money falls under the general amendment of bail conditions, it is the most common application in practice. Therefore, it is dealt with separately in subparagraph 9.1.1.

Where the conditions upon which the accused was released are no longer suitable to their circumstances, a formal or informal application may be brought before the court. If the application is likely to be opposed, it is better to bring a formal application on affidavit and make the accused available for cross-examination,[416] or lead *viva voce* evidence. Since the accused was initially released on conditions that were necessary in the interest of justice,[417] the amendment of such conditions should also be in the interest of justice.[418] The application for amendment of bail conditions is suitable where circumstances have changed, and it is necessary that appropriate amendments be made to the conditions initially imposed. [419] Various circumstances may necessitate the amendment of bail conditions. For example:

1. Where the accused is released on bail subject to a condition requiring them to reside at an alternative address far from the complainant's residence, they may apply for the relaxation of that condition to visit their original address to attend a family member's funeral.
2. Where an accused person, initially unemployed and released on bail subject to a condition requiring them to report to a police station every Monday and Friday between 06:00 am and 06:00 pm, subsequently secures employment that renders compliance with this condition impractical, they

---

[415] *Brown and Another v S* (CC 18/2017) [2018] ZAECPEHC 76; 2019 (1) SACR 691 (ECP) (14 December 2018) para 24.

[416] Paragraph 8.2.2 explains how the use of an affidavit and subjecting the accused to cross-examination can be done.

[417] Section 60(12) (a) of the CPA.

[418] *Savoi v S* (722/11) [2011] ZASCA 335; 2012 (1) SACR 438 (SCA) (1 December 2011) para 48.

[419] *Brown and Another v S* [*supra*] para 22.

may apply for the condition to be amended to permit reporting on weekends.

3. Where the accused has surrendered their passport to the investigating officer as a condition of bail, they may apply for the condition to be amended to allow the temporary release of the passport—whether for renewal purposes, to travel for business, or to attend a family member's funeral outside the Republic of South Africa.[420]

An application to supplement bail conditions or to increase the bail amount will, in practice, ordinarily be brought by the prosecution. As with an application to amend bail conditions or to reduce the bail amount, such an application may be appropriate where there has been a change in circumstances warranting either the supplementation of bail conditions or an increase in the bail amount. Where an application to supplement bail conditions is brought, whether to oppose it will depend on the nature of the proposed supplement. However, an application to increase the bail amount has the practical effect of denying bail where the accused is unable to afford the increased amount. Applications to increase bail are rare in practice. Decisions to supplement bail conditions or to increase the bail amount are appealable in terms of Section 65(1) of the CPA.

9.1.1 Reduction of bail amount

Where bail has been set, but the accused is unable to afford the stipulated amount, an application for bail reduction must be brought under Section 63 of the CPA at the accused's next court appearance following the bail determination. In such an application, the accused may also be released on a guarantee to pay the bail amount should it be forfeited.[421] While an application for the reduction of bail may be brought informally, without affidavit or oral evidence, it must nevertheless be properly motivated. As a first step, the prosecutor should be informed in advance and their views obtained. Where the application is not opposed, it may be pursued informally as follows:

1. *Your Worship, the defence brings an application for the reduction of the bail amount in terms of Section 63 of the CPA.*
2. The accused's bail was fixed in the amount of R3 000.00 approximately 30 days ago.
3. Since then, the accused has attempted to obtain financial assistance from family members, but they are unable to assist with the said amount.

---

[420] In *Savoi v S* (722/11) [2011] ZASCA 335; 2012 (1) SACR 438 (SCA) (1 December 2011), the bail conditions were relaxed to permit the accused to travel for business purposes.
[421] Section 60(13) of the CPA.

4. As stated during the bail application, the accused owned and operated a car wash business before his arrest. As a result of his continued detention, the business is no longer operating, and the accused is presently unemployed.
5. The accused can afford bail in the amount of R1 000.00. His brother, who is present in court, has the said amount available.
6. The fact that the accused remains in custody 30 days after bail was granted is a clear indication that the bail amount is beyond his financial means. The application is therefore that the bail amount be reduced accordingly. As the court pleases.

Although an informal inquiry is permissible, a formal application supported by an affidavit—together with making the accused available for cross-examination—or the leading of viva voce evidence, may be preferable. Where the accused places an affidavit before the court, it will not merely stand against the ipse dixit of the prosecutor and, for that reason, may carry greater evidential weight.

In terms of section 64 of the CPA, such proceedings must be fully recorded and are appealable in terms of section 65 of the Act.

CHAPTER 10

FAILURE TO APPEAR IN COURT WHILE RELEASED ON BAIL OR WARNING

10.1 Failure to appear in court in general

Once the accused is released on bail or warning, they must continue to appear before the court until the matter is concluded.[422] For various reasons, the accused may be absent from court at certain times. The consequences of failing to appear differ depending on whether the accused was released on a warning or on bail. The various consequences are discussed in the subparagraphs that follow.

10.1.1 Failure to appear while released on warning by the police or the court

Where an accused who has been released on warning—whether by the police or by the court—fails to appear in court, Section 72(4) of the CPA applies. This provision specifically regulates cases of release on warning and prescribes the consequences for non-compliance. In addition, the court may rely on Section 170 of the CPA, a more general provision applicable to any accused who is not in custody, was not released on bail, and fails to appear after a court adjournment. Section 170 thus provides a broader framework for dealing with failures to appear.[423] Whether the court proceeds under either of these provisions, or a combination thereof, a warrant of arrest will be issued, and the accused may be liable to a fine not exceeding R300.00 or to imprisonment for a period not exceeding three months.[424] It must, however, be noted that Section 1(2) of the Adjustment of Fines Act 101 of 1991 applies.[425] Accordingly, the fine may be adjusted in accordance with the period of

[422] Section 58 of the CPA.

[423] *Dludla v S* (R210/2018) [2018] ZAFSHC 137 (13 September 2018) para 8.

[424] Section 72(4) or Section 170(2) of the CPA.

[425] *Cooper v District Magistrate, Cape Town* (WCC) (1699/2017) [2017] ZAWCHC 140; 2018 (1) SACR 369 (WCC) (24 November 2017) para 21.

imprisonment, such that a term of three months' imprisonment is currently equivalent to a fine of R10 000.00.[426]

Sometimes, the client may inform you a day before or on the morning of their expected appearance that they will not be able to attend court. You then have to inform the court of the reasons that led to the client's failure to appear. Where the court accepts the reasons, a warrant of arrest will usually be issued but will be held over. If the warrant has been held over and the accused later appears, it is usually unnecessary for the court to hold an inquiry, but it should cancel the warrant.[427]

Where the client was sick, a medical certificate dated to the relevant date should be sufficient to show that the failure to appear was not due to the client's fault. The accused only bears an evidential burden of satisfying the court that there is a reasonable possibility that the failure to appear was not due to their fault.[428] However, there are presiding officers who are unnecessarily sceptical of medical certificates. They seemingly require more details about the client's ailment, which might end up compromising the client's right to privacy.[429] The medical practitioner's certificate should be enough to state that on the specific date, the client was examined, and in the opinion of the medical practitioner, they were unfit to work or attend court due to a medical problem, and they will remain unfit until a specific date. If the date on which the client failed to appear coincides with the date stated on the medical certificate, that should be the end of the inquiry. The court's views on the contents of the medical certificate or on whether the client was sick are not enough to contradict the findings of the medical practitioner, because the court is a lay person in medicine; therefore, those views can at best be speculative.[430] If the court has "any reservations as to the veracity or authenticity of the medical certificate presented in court", the best thing is to call the medical practitioner to testify and "clarify any aspects for the benefit of the court to enable the court to formulate an appropriate finding which would ultimately be in the interest of justice and in accordance with justice".[431]

Where no explanation for the failure to appear has been furnished by the client or where the court rejects the explanation you give and consequently

---

[426] On calculation of the ratio applicable in the Adjustments of Fines Act 101 of 1991, see *S v Tseko* (04/2022) ZANWHC 195; 208 (NWM) (25 October 2023) para 15-17 and *S v Permall* (171172) [2017] ZAWCHC 143; 2018 (2) SACR 206 (WCC) (8 December 2017) para 9-11. See also E-MANTSHI Issue 18 July 2007, http://www.justiceforum.co.za/JET/JET-LTN/e-Mantshi%20issue%2018%20July%202007.pdf accessed on 17 July 2024.

[427] *Cooper v District Magistrate, Cape Town* [*supra*] para 12-13.

[428] *S v Porritt* (A202/2018) [2018] ZAGPJHC 698 (10 December 2018) para 18, 19, and 32.

[429] See what happened in *Cooper v District Magistrate, Cape Town* (WCC) (1699/2017) [2017] ZAWCHC 140; 2018 (1) SACR 369 (WCC) (24 November 2017) para 14.

[430] *Mafe v S* (A49/22) [2022] ZAWCHC 108 (31 May 2022) para 46.

[431] *Cooper v District Magistrate, Cape Town* [*supra*] para 19.

the warrant is authorised and not held over, on the client's appearance, a summary inquiry will be held to determine whether they can be blamed for such failure to appear.[432] You should consult thoroughly with the accused to ascertain the reasons for the failure to appear, as the onus rests on the accused to satisfy the court that the default was not wilful.[433] You must also establish whether the accused disputes having been duly warned.[434] Where this is not disputed, you should proceed to place before the court the reasons for the failure to appear.[435] The accused or any other relevant witness may be called to testify.[436] It is important to note that the court is required to conduct this inquiry fairly and impartially.[437]

10.1.2 Failure to appear while released on bail by the police, the prosecutor, or the court

Where an accused fails to appear in court after having been released on bail, the bail will be provisionally cancelled, the bail money provisionally forfeited to the State, and a warrant of arrest issued.[438] The matter will then be postponed for 14 days. If the accused does not appear within those 14 days and no satisfactory explanation is provided for the failure to appear, the bail will be cancelled and the bail money finally forfeited to the State.[439]

Even where the accused appears within the 14 days, the court must be satisfied that the failure to appear was not due to fault on the part of the accused.[440] Failing such satisfaction, the court will cancel the bail and order the bail money to be forfeited to the State.[441] As Section 67(2) of the CPA refers to "days" and not "court days", weekends and public holidays are included in the calculation of the 14 days.[442] Where the accused has a valid reason for the non-appearance—such as illness or injury—this should be communicated to the court on the day of the non-appearance. In such circumstances, the court may hold the warrant over for 14 days. If the accused does not appear within that

---

[432] Section 72(4) of the CPA.
[433] *Dludla v S* (R210/2018) [2018] ZAFSHC 137 (13 September 2018) para 9.
[434] *Dludla v S* [*supra*] para 10.
[435] Ibid.
[436] *Cooper v District Magistrate, Cape Town* [*supra*] para 8.
[437] *Dludla v S* [*supra*] para 10.
[438] Section 67(2) of the CPA.
[439] Ibid.
[440] Section 67(2) of the CPA.
[441] Ibid.
[442] *S v Mashego* (R24/2021; A360/2020) [2021] ZAMPMBHC 36; 2021 (2) SACR 520 (MM) (10 August 2021) footnote 1.

period but the explanation remains valid, the court may hold the warrant over again, as circumstances require.[443]
Since *S v Lerumo and Others,*[444] the practice of holding over a warrant of arrest in respect of an accused released on bail has become a contentious issue. In *Lerumo*, the court held that the practice of staying the execution of a warrant of arrest does not comply with Section 67 of the CPA and should be discontinued.[445] This strict interpretation of Section 67(1) proved difficult to follow in practice, as it carries serious implications for the constitutional right not to be deprived of freedom arbitrarily or without just cause.[446] In *Sulani v Mathiya and Another,*[447] the court declined to follow *Lerumo*, holding that Section 67(1) (b) of the CPA "merely makes provision for the issuing of a warrant of arrest but does not provide that it has to be executed immediately". The *Lerumo* judgment has also been criticised for failing to recognise that Section 67 of the CPA cannot be read in isolation from Section 168 of the CPA, which empowers the court to postpone a matter on such terms as it may deem appropriate.[448]

An inquiry into a failure to appear in court is ordinarily conducted only where it appears that the accused was in wilful default. As confirmed by the full bench in *S v Porritt,*[449] the onus rests on the accused to satisfy the court that there is a reasonable possibility that the failure to appear was not due to their fault. This inquiry involves an evidential burden on the accused but not a full onus.[450] The court may receive any evidence it considers necessary.[451] The accused may, either personally or through a legal representative, satisfy the court that he or she was not in wilful default.[452] The application can be informally made by the legal representative addressing the court,[453] or the accused may testify, and even other witnesses may be called.[454] If the court finds that the default was wilful, the accused's bail must be finally cancelled and the bail money finally forfeited.[455] This inquiry cannot result in the accused being found guilty of an offence arising from the failure to appear while released

---

[443] *Sulani v Mathiya and Another* (9246/2016) [2018] ZAECPEHC 2; 2018 (2) SACR 157 (ECP) (2 February 2018) para 3.3, 3.4, 3.7, and 3.25.
[444] *S v Lerumo and Others* (08/2017) [2017] ZANWHC 63; 2018 (1) SACR 202 (NWM) (10 August 2017).
[445] *S v Lerumo and Others* [*supra*] para 17.
[446] Section 12(1) (a) of the Constitution.
[447] *Sulani v Mathiya and Another* [*supra*] para 3.3.
[448] Paizes A and van der Merwe S July 2018 *Criminal Justice Review* p15.
[449] *S v Porritt* (A202/2018) [2018] ZAGPJHC 698 (10 December 2018) para 18, 19, and 32.
[450] Ibid.
[451] Section 67(3) of the CPA.
[452] *Terry v Botes and Another* (1868/2002) ZAWCHC 22; [2002] 3 All SA 798 (C); 2003 (1) SACR 206 (C) (30 April 2002) p5.
[453] Ibid.
[454] *Cooper v District Magistrate, Cape Town* (WCC) (1699/2017) [2017] ZAWCHC 140; 2018 (1) SACR 369 (WCC) (24 November 2017) para 8.
[455] *S v Porritt* [*supra*] para 16.

on bail.[456] Although Section 67A of the CPA criminalises a failure to appear in court, any prosecution on that basis must proceed by way of a formal trial.[457]

Where the accused has no bail because the court, in their presence, ordered the forfeiture of bail—or where they appear after the bail has already been finally cancelled and the money has been forfeited to the State—an inquiry into their status should follow.[458] In the case of an accused whose bail was forfeited in absentia, the reasons for their failure to appear are irrelevant. The bail has already been cancelled and the money forfeited to the State; accordingly, the accused is no longer on bail.[459] Since the accused has no bail, the provisions of Section 50 of the CPA become applicable once again.[460] Therefore, the accused is entitled to apply for bail, and if they are remanded in custody, they must be informed of the reasons for further detention.[461] The courts cannot overlook this inquiry and merely remand the accused in custody because their bail has been forfeited.

For remission of bail money in terms of Section 70 of the CPA, the court is obliged in the interests of justice to determine whether the final order of cancellation and forfeiture should stand.[462] The court may order that all or part of the bail money be paid back to the depositor if there were good reasons for the accused's failure to appear in court.[463]
When representing a client who appears after their bail has been cancelled and finally forfeited to the state, you should obtain more information from the client as to why they failed to appear, and you must use the only remedy available, which is to apply for a fresh bail application.[464] In applying for the release of the client on bail or warning, it is very important to deal with the question of why they failed to appear before the bail money was finally forfeited to the State. The more convincing the reasons are that it was not their fault, the better the chances of their release. Immediately after a successful fresh bail application and while the facts explaining that there was no wilful default are still in the mind of the prosecutor and the magistrate, you should apply for the remission of the bail money, which was finally

---

[456] See *S v Luzil* (18294) [2018] ZAWCHC 75; 2018 (2) SACR 278 (WCC) (19 June 2018) para 9; *S v Edipute* (CA&R45/2018, 20180024) [2018] ZAECGHC 13 (22 February 2018) para 3; and *S v Ngete* (25/2023) [2023] ZAWCHC 116 (19 May 2023) para 5.

[457] See *S v Edipute* [*supra*] para 3. See also *S v Luzil* [*supra*] para 13; *S v Mashego* (R24/2021; A360/2020) [2021] ZAMPMBHC 36; 2021 (2) SACR 520 (MM) (10 August 2021) para 19; *S v Kondile* (11/2020) [2021] ZAECBHC 3 (12 February 2021) para 6; and *S v Ngete* [*supra*] para 5.

[458] *S v Luzil* [*supra*] para 14 and *S v Kondile* [supra] para 5.

[459] Ibid.

[460] *S v Luzil* [*supra*] para 14.

[461] Ibid.

[462] *S v Luzil* [*supra*] para 10-12.

[463] *S v Luzil* [*supra*] para 11.

[464] *S v Luzil* [*supra*] para 14. See also *S v Porritt* [*supra*] para 8 and *S v Kondile* [*supra*] para 5.

forfeited to the State.[465] Where there was no wilful default, fairness to the accused would require that the bail money be remitted.[466] Under Section 65 of the CPA, an appeal can be filed for the final cancellation of bail and forfeiture of bail money.[467]

[465] *S v Luzil* (18294) [2018] ZAWCHC 75; 2018 (2) SACR 278 (WCC) (19 June 2018) para 12.
[466] Ibid.
[467] *S v Porritt* (A202/2018) [2018] ZAGPJHC 698 (10 December 2018) para 33.

CHAPTER 11

CANCELLATION OF BAIL OR WARNING (OTHER THAN FAILURE TO APPEAR)

11.1 Lapse of release on bail or warning

Once bail is granted by a police officer in terms of Section 59, by a prosecutor in terms of Section 59A,[468] or by a court in terms of Section 60 of the CPA, it remains in effect until the verdict, unless it is prematurely terminated.[469] However, where sentence is not imposed immediately after conviction, the court may extend bail until the sentencing proceedings are concluded.[470] Therefore, it is important to apply for the extension of bail once a postponement is proposed after conviction.

Where the accused is convicted of a Schedule 5 or 6 offence, the court is obliged to apply the stringent requirements of Section 60(11) (a) or (b) of the CPA when considering whether to extend bail.[471] The court must take into account that the accused has been convicted and must also consider whether the likely sentence to be imposed for such an offence may motivate the accused to abscond.[472] Such an application is usually made informally by way of an address from the bar. It is important to point out that the accused has never absconded. In respect of Schedule 5 or 6 offences, the fact that the accused has pleaded guilty despite knowledge of the minimum sentence may be a relevant factor. For Schedule 1 offences, the courts usually extend bail; however, for Schedule 5 or 6 offences, bail is rarely extended. If the court does not extend bail after conviction but before sentencing, the order is appealable.[473] However, such an appeal may be a waste of time, since sentencing usually follows within a few days or weeks after conviction, and the appeal cannot halt the continuation of the sentencing stage.

---

[468] The prosecutors' bail remains in effect until the first court appearance. However, after court scrutiny, it may be extended on the same terms, amended, or extended on different terms. See Section 59A(4) of the CPA.

[469] Section 58 of the CPA.

[470] Ibid.

[471] Ibid.

[472] Ibid.

[473] *Doorewaard and Another v S* (CAB33/2018) [2018] ZANWHC 87 (6 December 2018) para 20.

The accused's release on warning is not affected by Section 58 of the CPA; therefore, it remains in effect until sentence proceedings are completed. Section 72 of the CPA, which governs warnings, contains no provision identical to Section 58. For that reason, it appears you are not expected to address the court to seek an extension of the release on warning when the matter is postponed for sentencing proceedings. Nonetheless, it seems that Section 168 of the CPA, which allows postponements "on terms which to the court may seem proper and which are not inconsistent with" the CPA, may find application. Therefore, you might be invited to address the court where it intends to rely on this section. Please wait for such an invitation should this section be invoked. Section 168 is too broad; therefore, it is submitted that a court acting judiciously will first invite you before relying on it to cancel the release on warning.

11.2 General cancellation of bail or warning other than because of failure to appear

Release on bail or warning is only granted if it is in the interest of justice to do so. The same applies to its cancellation.[474] The cancellation of release, other than the accused failing to appear in court, takes place under the following circumstances, namely:

1. **In terms of Section 68A of the CPA**, the accused applies for the cancellation of bail, for example, where the accused has been denied bail in another matter or is serving a sentence in another case.

2. **In terms of Section 66 of the CPA**, the State applies for the cancellation of bail on the ground that the accused has breached one or more bail conditions.

3. **In terms of Section 68 of the CPA**, the State applies for the cancellation of bail or a warning because the interests of justice no longer permit the accused's release.

Failure to comply with specific conditions while released on warning constitutes a criminal offence.[475] However, the State is also permitted to apply, in general terms, for the termination of release on warning where it is in the interests of justice to do so, in terms of Section 68 of the CPA. The provisions

---

[474] *S v Rabele* (76/2014) [2016] ZAFSHC 178 (29 September 2016) para 16. See also *Ranana v S* (CA&R15/ 2017) [2017] ZAECPEHC 48 (10 October 2017) para 2.

[475] Section 72(4) of the CPA.

of Section 68, by virtue of Section 72A of the CPA, are likewise applicable to the cancellation of an accused's release on warning.[476]

Where the accused applies for bail cancellation, this ordinarily presents no difficulty. Accordingly, the discussion in the following subparagraphs is confined to the cancellation of bail at the request of the prosecution under Section 66 and 68 of the CPA.

11.3 Cancellation of bail due to failure to observe bail conditions in terms of Section 66

Section 66 of the CPA provides for the cancellation of bail due to failure to observe the conditions imposed for the accused's release on bail. When the accused is released on bail with conditions, it is because the court finds that it is in the interest of justice to do so.[477] Therefore, the accused's qualification for bail is subject to those conditions. Once the accused breaches such conditions, it means their release on conditions was just a futile exercise. Therefore, the court, depending on the seriousness of the breach or reasons advanced, is justified in cancelling it.

The onus is on the State to prove on the balance of probabilities that the accused has breached the conditions.[478] The state must prove that the accused intentionally breached the condition or was at least negligent.[479] The accused may deny ever breaching the bail conditions, deny that the failure to comply was their fault, or admit that they failed to comply with the conditions.[480] Where it is clear that the breach was caused by the fault of the accused, the court has discretion on whether to cancel the bail.[481] Where the court cancels the bail, it should ordinarily be forfeited to the State.[482]

Where the client is alleged to have breached the bail conditions, you should not approach the matter casually because the courts implement conditions for a reason and expect the client to observe them. The application to cancel bail is always formal in that the State has to provide evidence that convinces the court that the bail conditions have been breached.[483] The evidence on affidavit

---

[476] *S v Rabele* (76/2014) [2016] ZAFSHC 178 (29 September 2016) para 19.
[477] Section 60(12) (a) of the CPA.
[478] Section 66(1) of the CPA. See also *S v Packham* (CC50/2018) [2018] ZAWCHC 183 (20 December 2018) para 13 and *S v S K* (Reasons: Cancellation of Bail) (CC21/2023) [2024] ZANWHC 152 (3 June 2024) para 7.
[479] *S v Packham [supra]* para 13 *and S v S K (Reasons: Cancellation of Bail) [supra]* para 7.
[480] Section 66(2) and (3) of the CPA.
[481] Section 66(3) of the CPA; *S v S K* [*supra*] para 42 and 49; and *S v Packham* [*supra*] para 27.
[482] Section 66(3) of the CPA and *S v Packham* [*supra*] para 50.
[483] Section 66(1) of the CPA.

or *viva voce* from the investigating officer or the complainant is usually led. The reply to the State's application must also be formal. Therefore, it is advisable to put the accused on the witness stand for cross-examination. If there are any witnesses to be called, they should be called. If there are any witnesses to be called, they should be called.

11.4 Cancellation of bail or warning in the interest of justice in terms of Section 68

As already stated, the granting and cancellation of bail or a warning are determined in accordance with the interests of justice principle.[484] Bail or warning can be cancelled in terms of Section 68 of the CPA if there is information under oath.[485] The court cannot cancel bail or a warning without an application under oath from the State.[486] When an application for cancellation of bail or warning is considered, the accused must also be allowed to answer the application.[487] The information placed by the State under oath must relate to one or more of the following grounds:[488]

1. The accused is about to evade justice.
2. The accused has interfered with, threatened, or attempted to interfere with witnesses.
3. The accused has defeated or attempted to defeat the ends of justice.
4. The accused has contravened any prohibition, condition, obligation, or order imposed by a protection order issued in terms of any law for the protection of the complainant.
5. The accused poses a threat to the safety of the public, the complainant, or any other particular person.
6. The accused failed to disclose, or failed to correctly disclose, all previous convictions during the bail proceedings.
7. The accused failed to disclose that a protection order had been issued against them in terms of any law for the protection of the complainant.
8. The accused failed to disclose that, at the time the offence was allegedly committed, they were a sentenced offender placed under correctional supervision, day parole, parole, or medical parole.

---

[484] *S v Rabele* (76/2014) [2016] ZAFSHC 178 (29 September 2016) para 16. See also *Ranana v S* (CA&R15/ 2017) [2017] ZAECPEHC 48 (10 October 2017) para 2.

[485] Section 68(1) of the CPA. It should also be noted that by virtue of Section 72A of the CPA, the provisions of Section 68 are applicable even on release on warning.

[486] *Matiwane v Regional Court President & Another* (CA20/2017) [2017] ZANWHC 71; 2018 (1) SACR 209 (NWM) 23 November 2017) para 12.

[487] *Matiwane* v *Regional Court President & Another* [*supra*] para 13.

[488] Section 68(1) of the CPA, as amended by the Criminal and Related Matters Amendment Act 12 of 2021.

9. Further evidence has become available indicating that the accused furnished false information during the bail proceedings, which may have affected the decision to grant bail or release on warning.
10. It is in the interests of justice to cancel the accused's bail or release on warning.

The onus is on the State to satisfy the court on a balance of probabilities that there are sufficient grounds or information on oath for the cancellation of bail or warning.[489] Even where the accused appears to have contravened any of the listed factors, e.g., they committed an offence while released on bail or warning, or they did not disclose their previous conviction, it must still be proved that such justifies the cancellation of bail in the interest of justice.[490] In essence, when the client faces cancellation of bail or a warning in terms of this Section, you have to remember that the application is formal. Therefore, there must be information under oath from the State.[491] It is always a choice whether to lead evidence by affidavit or *viva voce* in an attempt to refute the State evidence, but it should always be a calculated risk. In this instance, the onus is on the State. If the State uses an affidavit, you may do the same, but the stronger the reason for cancellation, the more the client might need to take the witness stand.

---

[489] *S v Rabele* (76/2014) [2016] ZAFSHC 178 (29 September 2016) para 21.

[490] *Ranana v S* (CA&R15/ 2017) [2017] ZAECPEHC 48 (10 October 2017) para 2. See also *S v Rabele* [*supra*] para 32-36.

[491] Section 68(1) of the CPA. *Minister of Justice and Constitutional Development and Another v Zealand* (387/06) [2007] ZASCA 92; 2007 (2) SACR 401 (SCA) (20 June 2007) para 15.

CHAPTER 12

WHEN BAIL HAS BEEN DENIED

12.1 Bail denial in general

This chapter is concerned not only with bail that was formally denied, but also with bail that has been postponed on first appearance to another date while the accused remains in custody. As already discussed in detail in paragraph 8.1, the accused has a procedural right to a quick bail decision.[492] Where the issue of bail is not dealt with at the first appearance and is postponed for any reason, this is tantamount to a temporary refusal of bail.

While an accused whose bail has been formally refused may apply for bail on new facts or lodge an appeal in terms of Section 65 of the CPA, an accused whose bail hearing has been postponed may likewise apply for an urgent review of the decision postponing the bail hearing. There are few, if any, accused persons who would willingly remain in custody, and dissatisfaction with a refusal or postponement of bail is therefore understandable. Nonetheless, the reality is that some bail applications are justifiably refused or postponed, while others are not.

It is therefore essential to advise clients correctly on whether to pursue an urgent bail review, a bail appeal, or an application for bail on new facts. Where you did not conduct the original bail proceedings, it is crucial to listen to the court record, or to apply immediately for the transcribed record and study it carefully before deciding on the appropriate course of action. Although a client's instructions are important, they remain a layperson and must be properly advised after a consideration of the record or transcripts.

In a bail application on new facts, the transcripts do not need to be available before the matter is heard, as the same magistrate usually presides over the application, unless that magistrate is incapacitated, deceased, or has recused themselves.[493] For bail appeals, the transcribed record must be available before the matter may be set down for hearing.[494] In bail reviews or Section 50(6) postponement reviews, transcripts are essential—particularly where bail

---

[492] *Matshikwe NO v M* [also known as *Magistrate Stutterheim v Mashiya*] (102/2002) [2003] ZASCA 54; [2003] 3 All SA 11 (SCA) (30 May 2003) para 16.

[493] See *Namlela and Another v S (Bail Appeal)* (CA&R 16/2024) [2024] ZAECGHC 25 (7 March 2024) para 9 and 10, where the court stated that where the magistrate who dealt with bail is unavailable another magistrate may deal with the bail on new facts.

[494] See para 8.4 of Gauteng Division [Pretoria and Johannesburg]; para 23 of KwaZulu-Natal Provincial Division; and para 8.4 of Limpopo Division Practice Manuals.

proceedings have already commenced or where the parties have addressed the court before the postponement. However, where postponements were not mechanically recorded, the information captured on the charge sheet (the appearances page) will generally suffice.

12.2 Application for transcribed record

You should apply for the transcribed record (transcripts) from the clerk of the court where the bail was denied, in terms of Rule 66(4) of the Magistrates' Courts Rules. The application for transcripts entails approaching the court clerk (the stenographer) who recorded the specific matter and informing them that you are requesting a typed record of the proceedings. Alternatively, go to the clerk of the court in the appeal section and request transcripts of the case for purposes of bail on new facts, appeal, or review. The date the case was recorded and the case number are always important, but if you are unsure of the date, the clerk of the court can obtain it from the charge sheet or the recording machine. The transcripts are not free unless a Legal Aid practitioner represents the accused. The payment methods will be explained by the court clerk in the appeal section.

Where a transcript request is entrusted to the clerk of the court, it is preferable to make the application in writing so you can easily follow up while you have proof of such an application. It is also common that, instead of the clerk of the court making an application to the transcribers, they give you the information about the service provider who provides transcripts to the Department of Justice. Then you arrange the payment to the service provider directly. A copy is sent to your email, and the other copy is sent to the court clerk. This has proven to be the best method for getting the transcripts, as you can quickly make arrangements and follow up if they take too long.

12.3 Bail on new facts

When bail has been refused, the accused may apply for bail on new facts if the circumstances have changed since the bail refusal. Bail on new facts is governed by Section 65(2) of the CPA. The bail application on new facts is one of the most abused court processes, as most legal practitioners treat it as a second chance to correct shortcomings in earlier bail applications.[495] If you did not handle the bail refusal, you have to arrange with the court clerk to listen to the record or to apply for transcripts of the bail refusal. After analysing all the facts on record and the judgment, you should be satisfied that the facts you intend to bring are new, relevant, and solid enough to persuade the court in

---

[495] See *S v Yanta* (CC44/2021) [2023] ZAWCHC 23 (1 March 2023) para 1.

light of the old facts already on record.[496] As stated in *S v Petersen*, if the facts are not new and relevant but merely a polishing and reshuffling of old facts, the court will refuse bail.[497] Therefore, "the purpose of bail on new facts is not to address problems uncounted in the previous application or to fill gaps in the previously presented evidence".[498]

When preparing for the first bail application, you should thoroughly consult and place all relevant evidence on record, because if the evidence was available during the refused bail application but was not revealed for whatever reason, it cannot later be used as a new fact.[499] However, if the evidence existed but was not accessible to the accused during the initial bail application, it may still constitute a new fact.[500] New facts will vary depending on the specific circumstances of each case. In one instance, the accused may have been denied bail due to a pending case that has since been withdrawn. In another, the accused may have been in good health during the initial bail application but is now gravely ill. It may also be that a significant amount of time has passed in custody since bail was first refused, with the trial still not finalised.[501] All in all, you have to look at the new facts and decide whether, in light of the old facts, these new facts are relevant or at least persuasive enough to warrant a reconsideration of bail.

Bail on new facts must be brought either on affidavit or *viva voce*; failing to present the accused for cross-examination might be catastrophic.[502] The court will consider the new facts alongside the old facts and, depending on the bail schedule, decide whether the release on bail is justified.[503] Therefore, when drafting the affidavit for new facts, there is no need to repeat the old facts–only the old facts which are now affected by the new facts. An example of an application for bail on new facts can look as follows:

---

[496] *S v Yanta* (CC44/2021) [2023] ZAWCHC 23 (1 March 2023) para 15.

[497] *S v Petersen* (A717/07) [2008] ZAWCHC 11; [2008] 3 All SA 301 (C); 2008 (2) SACR 355 (C) (27 February 2008) para 57. Also see *Khumalo v S* (A262/2016) [2016] ZAGPPHC 685 (11 August 2016) para 9.

[498] Ibid. Also see *Davis and Another v S* (2888/2015) [2015] ZAKZDHC 41 (18 May 2015) para 2, *Skhosana v S* (BA16/2020) [2020] ZAMPMHC 10 (27 May 2020) para 11-13 and *Omotoso v S* (CC15/2018) [2020] ZAECPEHC 43 (4 November 2020) para 11 and 12.

[499] *S v Petersen* [*supra*] para 58. See also *Munsamy v S* (A34/2022) [2023] ZAGPJHC 972 (29 August 2023) para 10-12; *S v Yanta* [*supra*] para 15.5; and *Terblanche v S* (CA&R 05/2022) [2022] ZAECQBHC 36 (4 October 2022) para 6e.

[500] *Terblanche v S* [*supra*] para 6e read together with para 11.

[501] *Mququ v S* (CA&R78/2019) [2019] ZAECGHC 55 and 2019 (2) SACR 207 (ECG) (14 May 2019) para 16-17.

[502] The importance of presenting the accused for cross-examination is emphasised in para 8.2.3 and 8.5.2. See also *Khumalo v S* (A262/2016) [2016] ZAGPPHC 685 (11 August 2016) para 4 and *Pretorius v S* (CC91/2003) [2011] ZAGPPHC 65 (29 April 2011) para 23.

[503] *S v Petersen* [*supra*] para 58.

IN THE MAGISTRATES' COURT FOR THE MAGISTERIAL DISTRICT OF CAPE TOWN

[HELD AT FEZEKA]

CASE NO: B84/2020

In the matter between:

RAYMOND REDDINGTON APPLICANT

And

THE STATE RESPONDENT

AFFIDAVIT IN SUPPORT OF BAIL ON NEW FACTS

I, the undersigned **Raymond Reddington**, do hereby make **oath** and say:

1. I am the Accused in this matter and the Applicant in this bail application on the grounds of new facts. I am making this declaration freely and voluntarily without undue influence. The facts herein contained, save where expressly stated to the contrary, are within my personal knowledge and belief, and they are both true and correct. Where I make legal submissions, I have been duly advised by my legal representative and accept them as correct.
2. I am the Accused in this matter and the Applicant in this bail application on the grounds of new facts. I am making this declaration freely and voluntarily without undue influence. The facts herein contained, save where expressly stated to the contrary, are within my personal knowledge and belief, and they are both true and correct. Where I make legal submissions, I have been duly advised by my legal representative and accept them as correct.
3. On 12 May 2021, my previous bail application was denied, in part because I had a pending robbery with aggravating circumstances at Bellville Magistrates' Court. The same matter was withdrawn against me on 24 June 2021. Attached herein is the certified copy of the charge sheet [Annexure A]. Furthermore, when the court denied me bail, my wife was still employed. She has since lost her employment, which means my family is now seriously struggling to support itself in my absence.
4. I plead with this honourable court to find that the above-mentioned circumstances are new, relevant, and worthy enough to warrant a reconsideration of the previous decision on my bail, and it is in the interest of justice that I should be released on bail.

I understand the content of this affidavit; I have no objection to taking the prescribed oath, and I consider it binding in my conscience.

SIGNATURE OF DEPONENT

THUS SIGNED AND SWORN TO ON 18 JULY 2021, THE DEPONENT HAVING ACKNOWLEDGED THAT HE KNOWS AND UNDERSTANDS THE CONTENTS OF THIS AFFIDAVIT, THAT IT IS BOTH TRUE AND CORRECT TO THE BEST OF HIS KNOWLEDGE AND BELIEF, THAT HE HAS NO OBJECTION TO TAKING THE PRESCRIBED OATH, AND THAT THE PRESCRIBED OATH WILL BE BINDING ON HIS CONSCIENCE.

COMMISSIONER OF OATHS

RANK: Sergeant

NAME: Tshepo Kalakgosi

PLACE: Gugulethu Magistrates' Court

12.4 Bail appeal to the High Court

A bail appeal is appropriate when the results of the bail proceedings are challenged, rather than the procedure followed.[504] A bail appeal to the High Court is governed by Section 65 of the CPA. It is trite, as stated in *S v Barber,*[505] that the court of appeal must be persuaded that the magistrate exercised their discretion incorrectly before it intervenes.[506] Even if the court of appeal has a different view, it should not replace the magistrate's decision with its own because that would amount to interference with the magistrate's exercise of their discretion.[507] In other words, it does not matter what the appeal court's

[504] *S v Block* (1897/10) [2010] ZANCHC 56; 2011 (1) SACR 622 (NCK) (12 November 2010) para 14.
[505] *S v Barber* 1979 (4) SA 218 (D) at 220 E-H. See Section 65(4) of the CPA; *Namlela and Another v S (Bail Appeal)* (CA&R 16/2024) [2024] ZAECGHC 25 (7 March 2024) para 12; and *Alehi v S* (A173/2021) [2021] ZAGPPHC 492; 2022 (1) SACR 271 (GP) (10 August 2021) para 9.
[506] Ibid.
[507] Ibid.

view is. "[T]he real question is whether it can be said that the magistrate who had the discretion to grant bail exercised that discretion wrongly".[508]

The court of appeal should approach the bail appeal on the basis that the decision to refuse bail is correct until the appellant satisfies the court that it was wrong.[509] The court of appeal may interfere with the lower court's discretion and deal with the bail afresh where the lower court has "misdirected itself materially on the facts and the legal principles".[510] It may also interfere where the magistrate has ignored some important aspects in deciding to refuse bail.[511]

Still, in *S v Porthen and Others*,[512] the court found that a line should be drawn between discretion in the wide and narrow sense. Schedule 1 and 5 bail applications are governed by clear principles on when the interests of justice permit or do not permit the accused's release on bail, as guided by Section 60(4)-(9) of the CPA.[513] Therefore, the court in Schedule 1 and 5 bail is exercising discretion in the narrow sense.[514] Under the discretion in the narrow sense, the principle developed in *S v Barber* above is applicable. However, the exceptional circumstances requirement in Schedule 6 bail does not provide the court with a range of equally permissible options. The court examines the facts of the case and decides whether exceptional circumstances exist.[515] Even though the court must still consider the factors listed in Section 60(4)–(9) of the CPA, those factors are not conclusive. Therefore, the court is exercising discretion in the wide sense.[516] In a Schedule 6 bail appeal, the court of appeal is entitled to prefer and apply its view and reject that of a magistrate.[517] In short, the court of appeal is entitled to a fresh assessment of whether exceptional circumstances exist, and if they do, the appeal must succeed.

---

[508] *S v Barber* 1979 (4) SA 218 (D) at 220 E-H. See Section 65(4) of the CPA; *Namlela and Another v S* (Bail Appeal) (CA&R 16/2024) [2024] ZAECGHC 25 (7 March 2024) para 12; and *Alehi v S* (A173/2021) [2021] ZAGPPHC 492; 2022 (1) SACR 271 (GP) (10 August 2021) para 9.

[509] *S v Mbele and Another* 1996 (1) SACR 212 (W) at 221F-222B.

[510] *Alehi v S* [*supra*] para 21 and *Sedi v S* (A35/2024) [2024] ZAFSHC 90 (15 April 2024) para 15.

[511] *Ramasia v S* (A24/2012) [2012] ZAFSHC 88 (3 May 2012) para 29 and *Namlela and Another v S (Bail Appeal)* [*supra*] para 13.

[512] *S v Porthern and Others* (A736/2003) [2003] ZAWCHC 36 (21 August 2003) para 8. See also *Sesing v S* (A11/2019) [2019] ZAFSHC 9 (25 January 2019) para 8; *Zondi v S* (SS15/2017) ZAGPJHC 82; 2020 (2) SACR 436 (GJ) (8 April 2020) para 11-14; and *Killian v S* [2021] ZAWCHC 100 (24 May 2021) para 8.

[513] *S v Porthern and Others* [*supra*] para 12 and 14

[514] Ibid.

[515] See *Tafeni v S* (A282/2015) ZAWCHC 150; 2016 (2) SACR 720 (WCC) (16 October 2015) para 4 (although this case deals with finding substantial and compelling circumstances where minimum sentence is applicable, the situation is clearly the same when the court deals with exceptional circumstances on Schedule 6 bail).

[516] *S v Porthern and Others* [*supra*] para 14.

[517] *S v Porthern and Others* [*supra*] para 15 and 16.

The Magistrates' Court Rules of 2010 are silent on bail appeals, as Rule 67 deals only with appeals on conviction and sentence. There is no practice directive at the magistrates' court level which provides any assistance in this regard. Although the high courts' practice directives aim to regulate bail appeals, they are more concerned with protecting themselves from the unready bail appeal cases being placed on their court rolls.[518] Therefore, the issue of bail appeal can only be understood by reading Section 65 of the CPA and by asking the clerk of the court in the appeal section about what is still outstanding. Once the transcripts are available, you must read them and try to find the grounds for the appeal. The appeal will only be decided on the material appearing on the record, including the reasons given during the judgment or furnished later in terms of Section 65(3) of the CPA.[519] Finding the grounds of appeal will mean that you are already aware of who bears the onus of proof on that specific bail schedule, you revisited Section 60(4)-(9) of the CPA, and you have read previous cases affecting the bail appeal in question (particularly what constitutes exceptional circumstances or how to determine whether the interests of justice permit). t is imperative to examine the important facts placed on record but ignored in the reasons for judgment, and, lastly, to consider whether the bail conditions could have helped.

The grounds of appeal in a notice of appeal must be stated plainly and concisely, enabling the presiding judge and the opposing party to fully understand the case being presented and what must be addressed in response.[520] For ease of reference, an example of a bail appeal notice is provided below. After all, every legal practitioner is free to draft in their own style. What the judge wants is enough information about the case and the grounds for the appeal.

IN THE HIGH COURT OF SOUTH AFRICA
(GAUTENG DIVISION, PRETORIA)

APPEAL CASE NO: ________________

PRETORIA NORTH MAGISTRATES' COURT CASE NO: **C45/19**

In the matter between:

MPIYAKHE ZUNGU **APPELLANT**
and
THE STATE **RESPONDENT**

---

[518] See para 8.4 of Gauteng Division [Pretoria and Johannesburg], para 23 of KwaZulu-Natal Provincial Division and para 8.4 of Limpopo Division.

[519] *Namlela and Another v S (Bail Appeal)* (CA&R 16/2024) [2024] ZAECGHC 25 (7 March 2024) para 6.

[520] *Doorewaard and Another v S* (CC33/2017) [2019] ZANWHC 25 (23 May 2019) para 3. See also *Songono v Minister of Law and Order* 1996 (4) SA 384 (E).

NOTICE OF BAIL APPEAL

KINDLY TAKE NOTICE THAT the above-mentioned Appellant hereby notes an appeal in terms of Section 65 (1) of the Criminal Procedure Act 51 of 1977 to the High Court of South Africa (Gauteng Division, Pretoria) against the judgment refusing bail delivered by Learned Magistrate, Mr Chauke, on 23 March 2018 in the Magistrates' Court for the District of Tshwane North, held at Pretoria North under case number: **C45/19**.

1. The learned magistrate erred in finding that the Appellant failed to prove that there are exceptional circumstances which, in the interests of justice, permit his release on bail, even though the Appellant:
   1.1 has no previous or pending cases;
   1.2 has a stable address;
   1.3 has handed himself to the investigating officer after he became aware that the police were looking for him; and
   1.4 is a second-year business management student at Tshwane University of Technology;
2. The learned magistrate misdirected himself by failing to consider and apply the factors mentioned in Section 60(4) of the Criminal Procedure Act;
3. The learned magistrate misdirected himself by failing to weigh the interest of justice against the right of the Appellant to personal freedom and the prejudice he was likely to suffer when detained, more specifically, his tertiary education;
4. The learned magistrate erred in finding that there is a likelihood that the Appellant, if released on bail, will endanger the safety of the complainants, when one considers that:
   4.1 the Appellant was arrested at least ten days after the alleged commission of the offences, yet no complaint was lodged regarding threats to witnesses; and
   4.2 the Appellant handed himself to the police, which was a sign of co-operation.
5. The learned magistrate erred in overemphasising the strength of the State's case as the primary factor indicating that there are no exceptional circumstances which, in the interests of justice, permit the accused's release on bail.

KINDLY URGENTLY ENROLL THE MATTER ACCORDINGLY.

DATED AND SIGNED AT PRETORIA NORTH ON 07 FEBRUARY 2020

____

MORUWE ATTORNEYS

(ATTORNEYS FOR THE APPELLANT)

TO: THE CLERK OF THE COURT: APPEAL SECTION

PRETORIA NORTH MAGISTRATES' COURT

AND TO: DIRECTOR OF PUBLIC PROSECUTIONS PRETORIA

AND TO: REGISTRAR OF THE ABOVE-MENTIONED COURT

Once the notice of appeal is complete, you must give it together with the power of attorney to the clerk of the court in the appeal section of the Magistrates' Court where bail was denied. The clerk will copy the complete record and send it to the magistrate who denied bail to provide reasons. The reasons for denying bail often delay proceedings, despite Section 65(3) of the CPA requiring that they be granted without delay. This leads to a delay in the bail appeal hearing since it cannot be enrolled until the reasons for denying bail are filed.[521]

After the reasons have been given to the clerk, the matter will be served on the DPP and the High Court with jurisdiction. The matter will then be set down for hearing. In a busy court like the Gauteng Division, it is common not to hear anything for up to a month, or even longer. It is always advisable to expect short notice of the hearing date. Typically, it is two or three days' notice. The reasons for the magistrate's judgment are hardly ever served to the legal practitioners of the appellant. Therefore, you should request the clerk of the court to keep a copy of the magistrate's reasons for denying bail, and constantly check its availability. Once the reasons are received, it is time to draft the heads of argument.

Heads of argument are not compulsory in a bail appeal. However, a litigant may be directed by the judge hearing the matter to submit them, sometimes on short notice. In certain instances, the litigant may be directed to provide a statement of the main points to be argued without elaboration. It is not always easy to formulate such main points without comment. It is submitted that few judges will object if a brief elaboration is provided. Ultimately, the purpose is not merely to comply with the directive but to persuade the judge to grant the appeal.
The heads of argument provide the judge and the opposing party with the direction and scope of the argument. They must be served at the DPP's office.

[521] *Sedi v S* (A35/2024) [2024] ZAFSHC 90 (15 April 2024) para 7.

The State advocate typically prepares heads of argument if directed to do so by the judge. Where the State advocate has prepared heads of argument, a copy will also be served on the appellant. On the date of the hearing, an oral argument will be presented to persuade the court to grant the appeal.

12.5 Bail appeal to the Supreme Court of Appeal

Section 65 of the CPA deals with bail appeals from the Magistrates' Court to the High Court, but ceases to apply once the appeal is dismissed.[522] A further bail appeal for the accused is not regulated by any section of the CPA. Therefore, it falls under Section 16(1) (b) of the Superior Courts Act 10 of 2013.[523] The accused must apply to the Supreme Court of Appeal (SCA) for special leave to appeal as soon as possible, but not later than one month after the High Court's judgment dismissing the appeal. Otherwise, they must apply for condonation.[524] The application for special leave to appeal must be on a notice of motion as annexed to the Supreme Court of Appeal Rules (SCA Rules).[525] The notice of motion must be accompanied by an affidavit in support of the application.[526] The notice of motion and the affidavit should address the application as a *special* leave to appeal, not a leave to appeal.[527] It is important to distinguish between an application for leave to appeal and a special leave to appeal because, in addition to the reasonable prospects of success requirement, an applicant for special leave to appeal must show that special circumstances merit a further appeal to the SCA.[528] This occurs when two judges hearing an application for special leave believe that:[529]

1. the appeal raises a substantial point of law;
2. the matter is of very great importance to the parties or the public; and
3. the prospects of success are so strong that refusing leave to appeal would probably result in a manifest denial of justice.

---

[522] *Banger v S* (195/2015) [2015] ZASCA 79; 2016 (1) SACR 115 (SCA) (28 May 2015) para 10 and *Cikolo v S* (CA55/2023) [2024] ZAECMKHC 21 (14 February 2024) para 7.

[523] *Cikolo v S* [*supra*] para 9 and *Banger v S* [*supra*] para 9-10.

[524] Section 16(1) (b) read with Section 17(3) of the Superior Court Act 10 of 2013. See *Cikolo v S* [*supra*] para 11.

[525] SCA Rule 1(1). An example of a notice of motion is attached to the SCA Rules as Form 1. See also Sechaba Mohapi S "Revised checklist for leave to appeal to the SCA" De Rebus 1 April 2015 https://www.derebus.org.za/revised-checklist-for-leave-to-appeal-to-the-sca/ accessed 02 August 2024.

[526] Ibid.

[527] *Savannah Country Estate Homeowners Association v Zero Plus Trading 194 (Pty) Ltd and Others* (773/2022) [2024] ZASCA 40 (4 April 2024) para 17-22.

[528] *Van Wyk v S, Galela v S* (20273/2014, 20448/2014) [2014] ZASCA 152; [2014] 4 All SA 708 (SCA); 2015 (1) SACR 584 (SCA) (29 September 2014) para 21.

[529] SCA Rule 6 (1) and (2).

The application must briefly explain where the High Court allegedly erred, and "the judgment must be subjected to a critical analysis, either as to the findings of fact or as to the exposition and application of the law".[530] "A generalised attack on the findings of the High Court is insufficient, as is reliance on the notice of appeal, or a recitation of the grounds of appeal".[531] The reasons why a special leave is justified, and the special circumstances relied upon, must be clearly and succinctly set out in the affidavit.[532] "If these specific requirements are not adhered to, the application may be rejected by the Registrar."[533] It is submitted that where there are prospects of success and the liberty of the accused is at stake, that should be a special circumstance justifying the special leave to appeal to be granted. The liberty of the person is one of the fundamental rights which in a free society should be jealously guarded at all times, and there is a duty on our courts to protect this right from infringement.[534] Furthermore, freedom is of great importance to the accused since they also face "other range of negative effects, such as the loss of [their] employment or home, health problems and disconnection from [their] family and community" while they are not yet found guilty of the crimes they are incarcerated for.[535]

The SCA Rule 6, which governs applications for leave to appeal, must be strictly followed.[536] Therefore, the application should: [537]

1. be made in triplicate;
2. be accompanied by:
   (a) a copy of the order of the court appealed against; and
   (b) a copy of the judgment delivered by the court a quo.

If the documents cannot be lodged within one month due to the unavailability of the transcribed record, the applicant may file the other available documents and submit a written request to the registrar for an extension (up to one additional month) to file the copy of the judgment.[538] The registrar may accept applications for special leave to appeal without the certified copy of the order

---

530 *Van Wyk v S, Galela v S* (20273/2014, 20448/2014) [2014] ZASCA 152; [2014] 4 All SA 708 (SCA); 2015 (1) SACR 584 (SCA) (29 September 2014) para 22.
531 Ibid.
532 *Van Wyk v S, Galela v S* [*supra*] para 23.
533 Ibid.
534 *Thandani v Minister of Law and Order* 1991 (1) SA 702 (E) 707A-B and *Mahlangu and Another v Minister of Police* (CCT 88/20) [2021] ZACC 10; 2021 (7) BCLR 698 (CC); 2021 (2) SACR 595 (CC) (14 May 2021) para 27.
535 Ballard C "Research Report on Remand Detention in South Africa: An Overview of the Current Law and Proposals for Reform" 2011 *Civil Society Prison Reform Initiative* https://dullahomarinstitute.org.za/acjr/resource-centre/South%20Africa%20Ballard.pdf accessed 25 July 2024.
536 *Van Wyk v S, Galela v S* [*supra*] para 22.d.
537 SCA Rule 6 (1) and (2).
538 SCA Rule 6 (2).

if a letter from the High Court Registrar certifies the date of the order.[539] As soon as possible (but not later than 10 court days) after an answering affidavit has been received, the applicant may lodge an affidavit in reply dealing with new matters raised in the DPP's answering affidavit only.[540] The founding and replying affidavits must:[541]

1. be clear and succinct;
2. furnish all necessary information to help the court decide the application;
3. deal with the merits of the case only insofar as necessary to explain and support the particular grounds upon which special leave to appeal is sought;
4. be properly and separately paginated; and
5. not—
   (a) be accompanied by the record;
   (b) deal with irrelevant matters;
   (c) exceed 30 pages for the founding affidavit and 10 pages for the replying affidavit; or
   (d) request further documents.

Documents longer than 10 pages must be printed double-sided.[542] Lodging documents with the registrar requires a correspondence attorney practising in Bloemfontein.[543] The *dies non* (16 December-5 January) are not included in the calculation of court days applicable in the SCA Rules.[544] The office of the registrar opens during court days between 08.30 am and 01.00 pm and between 02.00 pm and 03.30 pm.[545] Nevertheless, no documents can be lodged after 03.00 pm unless under exceptional circumstances as directed by the judge.[546] The registrar may refuse to accept documents for lodging if they do not comply with the SCA Rules. However, if the rejected documents are submitted again within 10 court days after such rejection, they will be deemed to have been brought within the prescribed time limits.[547] The application will be given a reference number.[548] After that, all documents filed must be marked with the reference number; otherwise, the registrar may reject such documents until they are referenced.[549] There is no need to file a power of attorney unless the authority to act on behalf of the client is disputed.[550]

---

[539] Para 1 of Supreme Court of Appeal Practice Directive 2014 [SCA Practice Directive 2014].
[540] SCA Rule 6(4) read with Rule 1 (2) (a).
[541] SCA Rule 6(5).
[542] Para 3 (a) of the SCA Practice Directive 2014.
[543] SCA Rule 1(1).
[544] SCA Rule 1(2).
[545] SCA Rule 3(1).
[546] SCA Rule 3(1) and (2).
[547] SCA Rule 4(1) (a).
[548] SCA Rule 4(2) (a).
[549] Ibid.
[550] SCA Rule 5(1).

An example of a notice of motion in compliance with Form 1 of the SCA Rules is below:

IN THE SUPREME COURT OF APPEAL OF SOUTH AFRICA

Case no.__________

In the matter between

JABU MZOLO **APPLICANT**

and

STATE **RESPONDENT**

APPLICATION FOR SPECIAL LEAVE TO APPEAL

KINDLY TAKE NOTICE THAT Jabu Mzolo (hereinafter called the Applicant) hereby applies to this Court for an order in the following terms:

1. Special leave to appeal against the judgment of Mojapelo J sitting as a court of appeal at the High Court of South Africa (Northern Cape Division, Kimberley), refusing a bail appeal on 23 March 2024 under case number: 100/2024.
2. The accompanying affidavit of the Applicant is annexed in support of the application.
3. If you intend to oppose this application, you are required to lodge your affidavit in support of your opposition, after prior service upon the Applicant, with the registrar of this court within one month after service of this application upon you.

DATED AT **BLOEMFONTEIN** THIS **24TH** DAY OF **JUNE 2024**

____

Makula Attorneys

APPLICANT ATTORNEYS

14 Mariam Makeba Street

BLOEMFONTEIN

9301

TO: **DIRECTOR OF PUBLIC PROSECUTIONS NORTHERN CAPE**

Wilcon House

22 Fabricia Road

KIMBERLEY

8301

AND TO: **REGISTRAR OF THE COURT, BLOEMFONTEIN**

As soon as possible (but not later than six weeks) after the record has been lodged with the registrar of the SCA, you must lodge six copies of the heads of argument.[551] The heads of argument must comply with the format and form prescribed in SCA Rule 10(4)-(5). The heads of argument must be accompanied by a practice note complying with SCA Rule 10A. The special leave to appeal may be disposed of without hearing an oral argument.[552]

Once the special leave to appeal to the SCA is granted, a notice of appeal must be lodged with the registrar as soon as possible (but no later than 1 month) after the special leave is granted.[553] The issue of bail is always urgent; therefore, the notice of appeal should be accompanied by a letter to the registrar for the attention of the SCA judge president to enrol the bail appeal urgently.[554] The heads of argument on appeal must be filed as soon as possible, but not later than six weeks.[555] They must also comply with the format and form prescribed in SCA Rule 10(4)-(5). The appeal may be disposed of without hearing an oral argument.[556]

12.6 Bail review

Bail review is applicable when the methods or procedures that were followed are being challenged.[557] The effect of Section 50(6) (d) of the CPA on postponements is that the bail hearing is postponed. Therefore, the bail review shall also include this Section. The bail may be reviewed in light of Section 22 of the Superior Courts Act 10 of 2013, where:

1. The court lacked jurisdiction to hear the bail application.
2. The court's decision was influenced by—
   a. an interest in the cause;
   b. malice;

[551] SCA Rule 10(1).
[552] Section 17(2) (d) of the Superior Courts Act.
[553] SCA Rule 7(1).
[554] Para 2 of the SCA Practice Directive 2014.
[555] SCA Rule 10(1).
[556] Section 19 (a) of the Superior Courts Act.
[557] *S v Block* (1897/10) [2010] ZANCHC 56; 2011 (1) SACR 622 (NCK) (12 November 2010) para 14.

   c. bias; or
   d. corruption.
3. There was a gross irregularity in the bail proceedings.
4. Inadmissible or incompetent evidence was admitted, or competent or admissible evidence was rejected.

However, Section 22 of the Superior Courts Act is not the only source of law on which the grounds for review may be based. The decision may be reviewed under the common law and the High Court's inherent power, as confirmed by Section 173 of the Constitution.

Unless reliance is placed on Section 22 of the Superior Courts Act 10 of 2013, it would be in rare cases that the concluded bail application would be taken for review instead of an appeal, simply because the procedure is hardly a problem in the bail application. In the end, the complaint is usually that the court misdirected itself on the facts and/or the law, and that constitutes a ground for appeal, but not for review.[558]

In practice, it is unconcluded bail applications that are taken for review. The High Court's power to intervene in unconcluded bail proceedings in the Magistrates' Courts is founded in common law. It is based on the High Court's supervisory power over the conduct of the proceedings in the Magistrates' Courts.[559] This power is only exercised in exceptional cases "where grave injustice threatens, and where intervention is necessary to attain justice".[560] The Constitution gives a flexible approach that requires the determination of the fairness of the proceedings.[561] The primary ground for reviewing an unconcluded bail application is the court's failure to afford the accused a prompt bail determination, in violation of the procedural rights already discussed.[562] Where 'grave injustice threatens' because of the unnecessary postponement of a bail hearing or a bail decision, the High Court may be approached to review the decision.

Since the bail issue is urgent, the application for review should proceed under Rule 6(12) rather than under Rule 53 of the Uniform Rules of Court. In *Cuniff v Tshite and Others,*[563] the court held that the applicant in review has a choice between initiating proceedings in terms of Rule 6 or 53 of the Uniform Rules of Court. The main purpose of Rule 53 is to enable access to records of the proceedings of the challenged decision. Therefore, a litigant who chooses to

---

[558] *S v Block* (1897/10) [2010] ZANCHC 56; 2011 (1) SACR 622 (NCK) (12 November 2010) para 15.

[559] *Matshikwe NO v M* [also known as *Magistrate Stutterheim v Mashiya*] (102/2002) [2003] ZASCA 54; [2003] 3 All SA 11 (SCA) (30 May 2003) para 13. See also *Majali v S* (41210/2010) [2011] ZAGPJHC 74 (19 July 2011) para 14 and *Setwaba and Others v De Souza NO and Others* (M90/16) [2016] ZANWHC 30 (3 March 2016) para 4.

[560] Ibid.

[561] *S v Block* [*supra*] para 17.

[562] See para 8.1 in this book.

[563] *Cuniff v Tshite and Others* (2000) 3 All SA 554 (T) at 556.

bring a review under Rule 6 loses this opportunity.[564] Since the record of the proceedings is usually not a problem, the applicant may stick to Rule 6. The matter is enrolled in the urgent motion roll. The notice of motion supported by a founding affidavit is required to start the urgent review proceeding.[565] The notice of motion must set out the relief that the applicant seeks and give directions to the respondent as to when and where the application will be heard.[566] The founding affidavit must clearly state the reason for urgency and why the remedy cannot be effective if normal rules are observed.[567] The founding affidavit also has to set out facts upon which the applicant relies for the relief sought.[568]

Bail applications are, as a rule, urgent.[569] During the hearing, the court will deal with the matter in a way that complies with Rule 6 as practically as possible and as it deems fit.[570] Rule 6(12) must always be read with the practice directives of the specific high court on which review takes place. Urgent applications are among the most abused procedures in the High Court. For this reason, all High Court practice directives regulate urgency in detail, and strict compliance with those directives is required. See the guidelines set out in cases such as *Republikeinse Publikasies (Edms) Bpk v Afrikaanse Pers Publikasies (Edms) Bpk,*[571] *Luna Meubel Vervaardigers (Edms) Bpk v Makinand Another (t/a Makins Furniture Manufacturers),*[572] and *Sikwe v SA Mutual Fire & General Insurance.*[573] "Urgency mainly involves the abridgment of times prescribed by the rules and secondarily the departure from established filing and sitting times".[574]

In essence, the urgent application does not entail total ignorance of the rules but means that the rules are followed as they are, only relaxed as justified by the urgency of the situation. While deprivation of freedom is a matter which,

---

[564] *Cuniff v Tshite and Others* (2000) 3 All SA 554 (T) at 556. See also *Mwelase v Minister of Social Development and Others* (CA74/16) [2018] ZAECMHC 16 (22 March 2018) para 33.

[565] Rule 6(1) of the Uniform Rules of Court.

[566] Van Blerk *Legal Drafting: Civil Proceedings* (2015) para 12.1.

[567] Rule 6(12) (b) of the Uniform Rules of the Court.

[568] Rule 6(1) of the Uniform Rules of the Court.

[569] *Setwaba and Others v De Souza NO and Others* (M90/16) [2016] ZANWHC 30 (3 March 2016) para 3.

[570] Rule 6(12) (a) of the Uniform Rules of Court.

[571] *Republikeinse Publikasies (Edms) Bpk v Afrikaanse Pers Publikasies (Edms) Bpk* 1972 (1) SA 773 (A) 782A-G.

[572] *Luna Meubel Vervaardigers (Edms) Bpk v Makinand Another (t/a Makins Furniture Manufacturers)* 1977 (4) SA 135 (W) 137A-E.

[573] *Sikwe v SA Mutual Fire & General Insurance* 1977 (3) SA 438 (W) at 440G-441A.

[574] *Luna Meubel Vervaardigers (Edms) Bpk v Makinand Another (t/a Makins Furniture Manufacturers)* [*supra*] 137A-E. See also the Memorandum to Practitioners regarding Procedure in the Pretoria Urgent Motion Court Roll (also as Annexure A, in Practice Manual of Gauteng Division, Pretoria). See Van Loggerenberg *Erasmus Superior Court Practice* (2015)at D1-84-85.

by its nature, is urgent,[575] the facts of each case should be carefully analysed to determine how far it would be necessary to depart from the ordinary rules of court practice.[576] The diversion from the rules should be justified on the facts of the case.[577] "An applicant must make out a case in the founding affidavit to justify the particular extent of the departure from the norm, which is involved in the time and day for which the matter is set down".[578] An example of an urgent bail postponement review application is below:

IN THE HIGH COURT OF SOUTH AFRICA

(GAUTENG LOCAL DIVISION, JOHANNESBURG)

BAIL REVIEW CASE NO: ____________

PROTEA MAGISTRATES' COURT CASE NO: **A101/20**

In the matter between:

GIFT MALULEKA APPLICANT

and

CHAUKE N.O. 1st RESPONDENT

DPP, JOHANNESBURG 2nd RESPONDENT

NOTICE OF MOTION

PLEASE TAKE NOTICE that the Applicant intends to make an application to this honourable court on **26 May 2020** at **11.30 am** or so soon thereafter as the matter may be heard for orders in the following terms:

1. Declaring the application to be a matter of urgency and dispensing in so far as is necessary in terms of Rule 6(12) with the usual forms and services provided for in the Uniform Rules of Court;
2. Reviewing and setting aside the order of the First Respondent in Case Number A101/20, postponing the bail application of the Applicant to **01 June 2020**; and

---

575 *Majali v S* (41210/2010) [2011] ZAGPJHC 74 (19 July 2011) para 18. Also see *Setwaba and Others v De Souza NO and Others* (M90/16) [2016] ZANWHC 30 (3 March 2016) para 3.

576 *Luna Meubel Vervaardigers (Edms) Bpk v Makinand Another (t/a Makins Furniture Manufacturers)* 1977 (4) SA 135 (W) 137A-E. See also the Memorandum to Practitioners regarding Procedure in the Pretoria Urgent Motion Court Roll (also as Annexure A, in Practice Manual of Gauteng Division, Pretoria). See Van Loggerenberg *Erasmus Superior Court Practice* (2015) at D1-84-85.

577 Ibid.

578 Ibid.

3. Considering the bail application of the Applicant and releasing the Applicant on bail on conditions that the court deems fit.

TAKE NOTICE FURTHER that the affidavit of the Applicant will be used in support of this application.

TAKE NOTICE FURTHER that the Applicant has appointed this email address (**info@mogaleattorneys.co.za**) of his attorneys as the address at which it will receive notices and service of all processes in this matter.

TAKE NOTICE FURTHER that if you intend to oppose this application, you are required to notify the Applicant's attorneys as soon as possible via email at **info@mogaleattorneys.co.za** and further that you may file your answering affidavit, not later than **10.00 am** on **26 May 2020** at **info@mogaleattorneys.co.za**.

KINDLY ENROLL THE MATTER FOR HEARING ON **26 MAY 2020**.

DATED AND SIGNED AT **JOHANNESBURG** ON **25 MAY 2020**.

____

Mogale Attorneys

APPLICANT'S ATTORNEYS

TO: **THE REGISTRAR OF THE ABOVE COURT**

AND TO: **MAGISTRATE LUUS**

AND TO: **THE DIRECTOR OF PUBLIC PROSECUTIONS, JOHANNESBURG**

CHAPTER 13

DEALING WITH UNREASONABLE DELAY

13.1 Application for postponement

In *S v Acheson,*[579] it was held that a postponement in criminal cases is not granted merely for the asking; it must be properly motivated on the grounds that it is either reasonably necessary in the circumstances or expedient—that is, appropriate or suitable to the case—as contemplated in Section 168 of the CPA.

You should always oppose unsubstantiated postponements sought based on "further investigation". The phrase "further investigation" is inherently vague, as it provides no indication of how long the State will take to finalise its investigations. Where the court is informed, for example, that outstanding witness statements, fingerprint results, or DNA reports are still awaited, experience shows that a one-month postponement is often inadequate; two or even three months may be required. You should therefore approach such postponement applications strategically by opposing those that are not properly motivated. Insist that the State is not entitled to a postponement merely upon request.

A postponement constitutes an application that must be both legally and factually justified. Emphasise that the court exercises a discretion not only in deciding whether to grant or refuse the postponement, but also in determining the appropriate duration of the postponement, should it find that a postponement is proper or suitable in the circumstances of the case. Accordingly, the facts upon which the application is based—and on which the court will rely in exercising its discretion—must be clearly and fully articulated. A properly substantiated application for further investigation assists both the defence and the court in assessing whether additional postponements are justified.

When *Acheson* was decided, Section 342A of the CPA had not yet been enacted. However, the introduction of Section 342A did not amend or qualify Section 168 of the CPA in any way. The effect of Section 168 remains that only postponements that are reasonably necessary or suitable should be granted.

---

[579] *S v Acheson* 1991 (2) SA 805 (NM) at 811D-F.

This provision therefore serves to prevent unreasonable delays in criminal proceedings. Rather than waiting for delays to materialise and then relying on Section 342A, practitioners should invoke Section 168 proactively to prevent future delays in the matter. Where the prosecutor applies for a postponement pending DNA results, it is essential to require a proper explanation, including whether material suitable for DNA extraction is available; whether a DNA sample has been taken from the accused for comparison; whether the relevant exhibits have been submitted to the laboratory for analysis; and whether a formal request for the results has been made. Similarly, in matters involving drugs, drunken driving, or firearms, it is important to establish whether the exhibits have been sent for analysis and whether the necessary requests for results have been lodged. Although laboratory analyses often take time, delays are frequently caused by the late submission of exhibits or by a failure to request results that are already available. The 'B' section of the docket should therefore always contain proof, in the form of receipts, that the exhibits were timeously dispatched for analysis.[580]

Nothing prevents you from opposing the State's application for a postponement by pointing out that it seeks an indulgence from the court while failing to place the necessary supporting documentation before it. This includes, for example, the receipts ordinarily contained in section 'B' of the docket, which would demonstrate that exhibits were in fact dispatched for analysis and that the request is properly motivated. Owing to heavy workloads, personnel changes, or simple inefficiency, prosecutors sometimes seek postponements without properly considering the contents of the docket. In such circumstances, the absence of documentary proof may be decisive in resisting an unjustified postponement.[581] If what was outstanding on the previous appearance is still outstanding, the prosecutor should explain what was done to try to finalise the investigation. If no such explanation is provided—or if the explanation is unconvincing—you should oppose any further application for postponement by the prosecutor. This approach seems to have also found acceptance in the *orbiter dictum* of Ndita J, in *S v Ndibe*,[582] where the following was stated:

> It can be accepted that judicial officers to a large extent, and as they should, proactively recognise the forms of prejudice an accused can suffer due to [the] slow grinding wheels of justice. To this end, they sometimes tailor the postponement in such a way that the harsh impact of the delay is mitigated, or grant relief as may be appropriate in the circumstances of a particular case.

---

[580] To properly understand sections of the docket, please see paragraph 14.1.2. in this book.

[581] See what happened in Katlehong Magistrates' Court where the prosecutor dealt with a bail application without reading the docket as discussed by Combrinck H "'He's out again': The role of the prosecutor in bail for persons accused of sexual offences" 2001 *Law, Democracy & Development* p31-32 https://journals.co.za/doi/pdf/10.10520/EJC162740 accessed 18 July 2024.

[582] *S v Ndibe* (14/544/2010) [2012] ZAWCHC 245 (14 December 2012) para 6.

As a legal practitioner, you will also apply for postponements for various reasons. Section 168 is also applicable to your application for postponement. It is a known fact that some legal practitioners may offer various excuses to delay the commencement of a trial. Sometimes, the accused delays the matter by being absent until the warrant is issued and witnesses are excused, only to appear immediately thereafter and make various excuses for being late. Most presiding officers are aware of these tactics, and they often refuse to postpone cases until all surrounding circumstances have been investigated. Nothing prohibits the presiding officer from issuing the warrant of arrest with immediate effect and ordering the investigating officer to execute it and locate the accused while other matters are proceeding.

Courts may, at times, decline to grant postponements due to legitimate concerns such as delays, congested court rolls, or potential procedural misuse—even when the circumstances might otherwise justify a postponement. The problem is that, regardless of circumstances, sometimes legal practitioners ask for a postponement instead of applying for one. When an application is made and properly motivated, the court recognises that it has discretion that should be applied judiciously by balancing fairness to the accused with the need to avoid unnecessary delays and abuse of process. This application is usually informal, but nothing prohibits it from being formal.[583] A strong application should always be made, especially where the accused cannot be properly represented if such a postponement is not secured. As was stated in *Ramonyathi v S,*[584] the accused has a right to effective legal representation.

When applying for a postponement, it is sometimes wise to open with style and brevity, drawing on the techniques of the best orators. Borrowing from the case of *Lelaka v S,*[585] the following was quoted at the beginning of the judgment: "while there is truth that justice delayed is justice denied, in many it is true that hurried justice is not justice at all, in many more that it is not justice done sufficiently, and still more that it is not justice done manifestly". When applying for a postponement, you should clearly set out the facts that justify it. You should also explain the possible consequences if the court refuses the application, especially in light of the interests of justice and the accused's right to a fair trial.

13.2 Application against unreasonable delay

When you encounter an unreasonable delay, it is important to remember that an accused has the right to have their trial begin and conclude without unreasonable

[583] The difference between formal and informal applications is discussed in paragraph 5.3 in this book.
[584] *Ramonyathi v S* (A470/2014) [2014] ZAGPPHC 915 (23 October 2014) para 5.
[585] *Lelaka v S* (CAF10/2014) [2014] ZANWHC 34 (10 October 2014) para 1.

delay.[586] This right applies to every accused person, regardless of whether the accused is in custody or has been released on bail.[587] Section 342A(1) of the CPA requires the court before which criminal proceedings are pending to investigate any unreasonable delay that may cause substantial prejudice to the accused, a legal practitioner, the prosecution, the State, or witnesses.[588] In determining whether proceedings are being unreasonably delayed, the court should, at the very least, conduct an informal inquiry.[589] This inquiry, whether conducted formally or informally, generally involves the following three stages:[590]

1. The court investigates the reason for the delay, considering the factors listed in Section 342A(2) (a)-(i).[591]
2. The court makes a ruling on whether the delay is reasonable or not.
3. If the delay is unreasonable, the court must apply any suitable remedy to stop such delay, including remedies stated in Section 342A(3),[592] such as:
   (a) refusing further postponement;
   (b) granting postponement on suitable conditions; or
   (c) if it is before plea, striking the matter off the roll and not re-enrolling it without DDP's approval.

---

[586] Section 35(3) (d) of the Constitution.
[587] Ibid.
[588] *Omotoso v S* (CC15/2018) [2020] ZAECPEHC 43 (4 November 2020) para 6-7.
[589] *S v Ndibe* (14/544/2010) [2012] ZAWCHC 245 (14 December 2012) para 6.
[590] Ibid. See also *Ramabele v S; Msimango v S* (CCT 232/17; CCT 207/18) [2020] ZACC 22; 2020 (11) BCLR 1312 (CC); 2020 (2) SACR 604 (CC) (16 September 2020) para 62.
[591] ... the court shall consider the following factors:

(a) The duration of the delay;
(b) the reasons advanced for the delay;
(c) whether any person can be blamed for the delay;
(d) the effect of the delay on the personal circumstances of the accused and witnesses;
(e) the seriousness, extent or complexity of the charge or charges;
(f) actual or potential prejudice caused to the State or the defence by the delay, including a weakening of the quality of evidence, the possible death or disappearance or non-availability of witnesses, the loss of evidence, problems regarding the gathering of evidence and considerations of cost;
(g) the effect of the delay on the administration of justice;
(h) the adverse effect on the interests of the public or the victims in the event of the prosecution being stopped or discontinued;
(i) any other factor, which in the opinion of the court, ought to be considered.

[592] Only three remedies are referred to out of the six, because it is not within the scope of this book to deal with delays during trial. Furthermore, the order as to costs has not yet been put into effect, and the order for administrative investigation further delays the proceedings.

It has been held that an order for a permanent stay of prosecution is a competent remedy in terms of Section 342A (3) of the CPA, provided that the unreasonable delay occurs after the case has been enrolled.[593] However, in *Van Der Walt and Another v Director of Public Prosecutions and Another,*[594] Jolwana J rejected this interpretation of Section 342A and found that a permanent stay order is not a competent remedy because it does not eliminate delays in the proceedings. It is a prohibitory interdict which terminates the same proceedings, rather than eliminating delays therein.[595] Taking into account the purpose of the Section 342A enquiry, which is to eliminate delays in criminal proceedings, "it cannot be correct that an order for a permanent stay of prosecution eliminates a delay on any possible interpretation of the word".[596] In continuing to emphasise this valid point, the court stated that "[s]uch a relief is so far-reaching in its width that it cannot be incidental to any other power which a lower court may exercise".[597] It is indeed inconceivable that the legislature would, without express legislative intention, introduce a remedy that is "radical, both philosophically and socio-politically"—in that it bars the prosecution from presenting society's complaint against an alleged transgressor of its rules of conduct—without first determining the actual effect of the delay on the outcome of the case.[598] Accepting this decision as correct, it appears that the accused who wants to apply for a permanent stay of prosecution must approach the High Court with jurisdiction. Such an accused cannot rely on Section 342A of the CPA, since "an order for a permanent stay of prosecution does not eliminate a delay in pending criminal proceedings, [but] it brings such proceedings to an abrupt end".[599]

The practical effects of the different remedies in terms of Section 342A(3) of the CPA are the following:

1. As a starting point, the court may craft any suitable remedy to eliminate the delay and the prejudice arising from the delay, or to prevent further delay or prejudice in the proceedings which are before

---

[593] See *Naidoo v S* (A 293/2011) [2011] ZAWCHC 448; 2012 (2) SACR 126 (WCC) (6 December 2011) para 18 and *Naidoo v Regional Magistrate for Durban Magistrates Court, Mr M Maharaj and Another* (AR769/14) [2017] ZAKZPHC 19; 2017 (2) SACR 244 (KZP) (23 May 2017) para 22.

[594] *Van Der Walt and Another v Director of Public Prosecutions and Another* (1281/2019) [2021] ZAECGHC 64; [2021] 4 All SA 251 (ECG); 2022 (1) SACR 320 (ECG) (13 July 2021) para 8-10.

[595] Ibid.

[596] *Van Der Walt and Another v Director of Public Prosecutions and Another* [*supra*] para 9.

[597] *Van Der Walt and Another v Director of Public Prosecutions and Another* [*supra*] para 8-10.

[598] *Sanderson v Attorney-General, Eastern Cape* (CCT10/97) [1997] ZACC 18; 1997 (12) BCLR1675; 1998 (2) SA 38 (2 December 1997) para 38.

[599] *Van Der Walt and Another v Director of Public Prosecutions and Another* para 8.

it.[600] These broad powers are permissible as long as they are relevant to eliminating or preventing the delay or prejudice emanating from the delay. Therefore, the court may remove the matter from the roll with or without crafting conditions for its re-enrolment.

2. Where the court has refused a postponement for further investigation, it means that the State should withdraw the matter or apply to have it postponed for other purposes, e.g., disclosure. If the prosecution insists on its application for postponement, the court may remove the matter from the roll with or without conditions.

3. Where the court has granted a postponement on condition, e.g. where the matter is postponed finally for further investigation, such a condition is binding. If investigations are still incomplete on the subsequent date, the State must decide whether to withdraw the matter or continue with the prosecution in the absence of such outstanding evidence. If the prosecution insists on its application for postponement, the court may remove the matter from the roll with or without conditions.

4. Where the court has struck the matter off the roll and ordered that prosecution cannot be reinstituted without the Director of Public Prosecutions' (DPP) written approval, the Director of Public Prosecutions, as a higher authority, must decide whether to reinstitute the prosecution or not.[601] Therefore, one should not accept the written approval at face value merely because the letterhead bears the designation "the DPP". It should be clear that the DPP has signed the certificate. Note that the Deputy Director of Public Prosecutions (DDPP) has the authority to sign this certificate.[602] This remedy should be applied only in exceptional cases, since the prosecutor cannot reinstitute prosecution at will.[603]

---

[600] Section 342A(3) of the CPA.

[601] *Naidoo and Others v National Director of Public Prosecutions and Others* (06/2004) [2005] ZASCA 23 (29 March 2005) para 38 and 41.

[602] Section 24(9) of the National Prosecuting Authority Act 32 of 1998 provides that "(a) [...] a Deputy Director [...] has all the powers, duties and functions of a Director; (b) [a] power, duty and function which is exercised, carried out or performed by a Deputy Director is construed, for purposes of this Act, to have been exercised, carried out or performed by the Director concerned". As a result of this Section, it appears that even though the SCA refused to rule on the issue in the *Naidoo* case [*supra*], the Deputy DPP is a higher authority which may issue a Section 342A certificate to reinstitute the prosecution.

[603] *Naidoo and Others v National Director of Public Prosecutions and Others* [*supra*] para 46.

CHAPTER 14

PROCEDURES CLARIFYING ISSUES BEFORE TRIAL

14.1 Pre-trial disclosure

14.1.1 Pre-trial disclosure in general

Pre-trial disclosure is a fundamental component of a fair trial, as it enables the accused to understand the nature of the State's case and the evidence the prosecution intends to rely upon in support of the charges. The history of disclosure is a regrettable one. Accused persons facing trial in the High Court were comparatively better placed, as their matters were initially subjected to a preparatory examination in the Magistrates' Court. During this process, most of the witnesses who were expected to testify in the High Court would give evidence beforehand, thereby affording the defence valuable insight into the State's case.[604]

In stark contrast, no equivalent safeguard was available in matters tried in the lower courts, even though the Regional Courts have long been seized with serious criminal matters.[605] This disparity was eventually resolved—not by extending procedural safeguards to the lower courts, but by withdrawing them from High Court proceedings. Legislative amendments to the CPA introduced the summary trial procedure, thereby abolishing the compulsory requirement of preparatory examinations before a matter could be referred to the High Court.[606]

---

[604] *Shabalala v Attorney-General of the Transvaal and Another* (CCT23/94) [1995] ZACC 12; 1995 (12) BCLR 1593; 1996 (1) SA 725 (29 November 1995) para 18.

[605] Ibid.

[606] *Shabalala v Attorney-General of the Transvaal and Another* [*supra*] para 18. Also see *S v Fani and Others* 1994 (1) BCLR 43 (E) at 46B-H; 1994 (3) SA 619 (E) at 621J-622H.

South African criminal procedure historically mirrored the English common law tradition, which held that no party was entitled to inspect their adversary's brief—a doctrine known as litigation privilege.[607] In criminal proceedings, the case docket was regarded as the prosecutor's brief, and accused persons were thus denied access to its contents.[608] This position inevitably resulted in a troubling reality: defence counsel often had to prepare their case blindly, without knowledge of the evidence to be presented. Such practices fundamentally undermined the fairness of criminal proceedings and, in some cases, almost certainly contributed to the wrongful conviction of innocent individuals.

However, since the Constitution became the supreme law, the litigation privilege relating to the contents of the case docket exists only in a limited form.[609] At present, obtaining copies of the docket is no longer a significant problem, as a result of the decision in *Shabalala v Attorney-General of the Transvaal and another.*[610] The current principles regarding disclosure, as imported from the Canadian Supreme Court decision of *R v Stinchcombe*, have been summarised as follows:[611]

1. "Justice is better served by the elimination of surprise."
2. The fruits of the investigation in the possession of the prosecution "are not the property of the prosecution but of the public, to ensure that justice is done".
3. The defence is entitled to be adversarial; therefore, it has no obligation to disclose or assist the prosecution.
4. The search for the truth is advanced by requiring the prosecution to disclose all relevant material.

---

[607] *National Director of Public Prosecutions v King* (86/09) [2010] ZASCA 8; 2010 (2) SACR 146 (SCA); 2010 (7) BCLR 656 (SCA); [2010] 3 All SA 304 (SCA) (8 March 2010) para 1.

[608] Ibid.

[609] *National Director of Public Prosecutions v King* [*supra*] para 2.

[610] *Shabalala v Attorney-General of the Transvaal and Another* (CCT23/94) [1995] ZACC 12; 1995(12) BCLR 1593; 1996 (1) SA 725 (29 November 1995).

[611] The SCA, in *Du Toit v The Magistrate and Others* (733/2015) [2016] ZASCA 15;[2016] 2All SA 328 (SCA);2016 (2) SACR 112 (SCA) (11 March 2016) para 8,quoted this principle from the Canadian Supreme Court decision of *R v Stinchcombe* [1991] 3 SCR 326; 18 CRR (2d) 210; 68 CCC (3d) 1 (SCC).

5. However, the prosecution must retain a degree of discretion regarding what must be disclosed.
6. Nonetheless, the exercise of the prosecution's discretion to grant disclosure is reviewable by the court.
7. Moreover, disclosure is not supposed to be refused "if there is a reasonable possibility that failure to disclose may impede or impair the accused's right to make full answer and defence, which is a principle of fundamental justice protected under the Constitution".
8. Ultimately, each case must be determined based on its unique set of facts.

14.1.2 The content of the docket

For trial preparation, the prosecution must disclose the content of the case docket and the charges preferred against the accused. The docket is divided into three sections: the 'A' section, the 'B' section, and the 'C' section.[612] The 'A' section contains witness statements, expert reports, and other documentary evidence.[613] Accordingly, this is the most important section for trial purposes. The 'B' section is sometimes empty, but its purpose is to contain internal reports and memoranda (e.g. proof that exhibits have been sent for analysis to the forensic laboratory, instructions from the SPP or the DPP, etc.) [614] On the question of unreasonable delays, particularly in forensic laboratories, the prosecution should examine this section to determine when the exhibits were sent, as receipts are contained therein. The 'C' section refers to the investigation diary (SAPS 5), which contains instructions from senior police officers and public prosecutors directed to the investigating officer, who is expected to act in accordance with those instructions.[615]

When the defence receives copies of the docket, it should be noted that the first statement, documentary evidence, or expert report in the docket will be marked 'A1'. All subsequent statements will follow the same order as A2, A3,

---

[612] *National Director of Public Prosecutions v King* (86/09) [2010] ZASCA 8; 2010 (2) SACR 146 (SCA); 2010 (7) BCLR 656 (SCA); [2010] 3 All SA 304 (SCA) (8 March 2010) para 1. Also see *Panayiotou v S and Others* (CC26/2016) [2016] ZAECPEHC 50; 2017 (1) SACR 354 (ECP) (20 September 2016) para 20.

[613] Ibid.

[614] Ibid.

[615] Ibid.

A4, and so forth until the end. The same order applies to the 'B' section and the 'C' section.[616] Unlike an inquest docket, the statements in a standard criminal docket are not necessarily arranged in a sequence that narrates the events from beginning to end. Instead, they typically follow the chronological order of the witness statements, up to the last recorded statement. It is common to find that the documents are not arranged in the order listed; however, since each statement is usually marked or numbered, it should not be difficult to compile them in accordance with the official docket structure. Where a witness has provided more than one statement, the subsequent entry will be marked as an 'additional statement'.

In practice, given that prosecutors are human and fallible, there may be instances where certain statements are not disclosed, whether inadvertently or, on rare occasions, deliberately. If the copies are assembled following A1, A2, A3, and so forth until all statements are accounted for, any outstanding statements will become apparent. The document that is most likely to be missing from the disclosure is a 'notice of rights' (SAPS 14A). This is not because the document is concealed, but simply because it is smaller than A4. The paper is too soft, causing paper jams in photocopiers. Additionally, the accused was given the original when they were detained. Where other statements are not contained in the disclosure, the defence should approach the prosecutor dealing with the matter. If no assistance is forthcoming, the issue may be raised during the judicial pre-trial conference in Regional Court matters,[617] or an application for better disclosure may be brought before the court.

14.1.3 What the accused is entitled to in the docket

The question of disclosure is concerned with a fair trial rather than with access to information.[618] The general rule is that the accused is entitled to all copies

---

[616] In the B section, the receipts will be marked as B1, B2, B3, and so forth, while in the C section, the pages are marked as C1, C2, C3, and so on until the end; however, instructions and replies are noted according to the dates rather than page numbers.

[617] Pre-trial conference is not held in district court matters.

[618] *Du Toit v The Magistrate and Others* (733/2015) [2016] ZASCA 15; [2016] 2 All SA 328 (SCA); 2016 (2) SACR 112 (SCA) (11 March 2016) para 9.

of the case docket that are relevant for the purpose of exercising the accused's right to a fair trial.[619] Documents that are "incriminating, exculpatory or prima facie likely to be helpful to the defence" ought to be disclosed.[620] Disclosure "is not restricted to statements of witnesses or exhibits but [extends] to all documents that might be 'important for an accused to properly adduce and challenge evidence' to ensure a fair trial".[621]

Accordingly, although it is standard practice to disclose the 'A' section of the docket only, the 'B' or the 'C' sections may also be disclosed if, based on the particular facts of the case, they are relevant and important for the accused to adduce and challenge evidence to ensure a fair trial.[622] Where an application is made for the disclosure of the contents of the 'B' or the 'C' sections, it must be shown that the specific correspondence or receipt contained in the 'B' section, or the specific instruction or reply contained in the 'C' section, is relevant for purposes of the accused's right to a fair trial.[623]

While "entitlement to disclosure is a matter of constitutional right", it is subject to the limitation clause.[624] The prosecution may refuse to grant disclosure if the requested information is not in its possession or is irrelevant.[625] Where the information is relevant for the purpose of exercising the right to a fair trial, but there is a reasonable risk that disclosure might expose the identity of informers or state secrets, or might lead to the intimidation of witnesses or obstruction of the proper ends of justice, the

---

[619] *National Director of Public Prosecutions v King* (86/09) [2010] ZASCA 8; 2010 (2) SACR 146 (SCA); 2010 (7) BCLR 656 (SCA); [2010] 3 All SA 304 (SCA) (8 March 2010) para 1.

[620] Ibid.

[621] Ibid.

[622] *National Director of Public Prosecutions v King* [*supra*] para 12 and 48. Also see *Panayiotou v S and Others* (CC26/2016) [2016] ZAECPEHC 50; 2017 (1) SACR 354 (ECP) (20 September 2016) para 21.

[623] *Panayiotou v S and Others* [*supra*] para 26, 32 and 34.

[624] Ibid. See also *Shabalala v Attorney-General of the Transvaal and Another* (CCT23/94) [1995] ZACC 12; 1995 (12) BCLR 1593; 1996 (1) SA725 (29 November 1995) para 55 g.

[625] 627 *Du Toit v The Magistrate and Others* (733/2015) [2016] ZASCA 15; [2016] 2 All SA 328 (SCA); 2016 (2) SACR 112 (SCA) (11 March 2016) para 9.

prosecution may be justified in refusing disclosure.[626] However, the refusal by the prosecution to grant disclosure is reviewable by the trial court.[627]

Where the prosecution refuses to grant disclosure, an application may be made to the trial court to compel disclosure. Even where the court finds that disclosure is likely to infringe upon the interests the prosecution seeks to protect, this does not mean that disclosure should always be denied, particularly where there is a clear risk that the accused would not receive a fair trial.[628] The court is required to exercise a proper discretion "by balancing the degree of risk involved in attracting the consequences sought to be avoided by the prosecution (if access is permitted) against the degree of the risk that a fair trial might not ensue (if such access is denied)".[629] The court may permit disclosure of certain parts of the docket or allow disclosure at a particular stage of the trial.[630] Each case must be determined on its own facts.[631] The court in *Du Toit v The Magistrate and Others*[632] ruled that it was sufficient for the defence to receive access through a private viewing of the child pornography images, rather than reproducing the images and providing copies to the defence.

14.1.4 Application for disclosure

Once police investigations have been completed, trial preparation begins. The defence should apply for copies of the docket and the charge, which is annexed to the charge sheet (J15 or J175). A copy of the charge is as essential as the docket itself, as it informs the defence of the particulars of the charge and the alleged applicable statutory provision(s) upon which the State will rely in proving the charge. The defence is entitled to peruse the

---

[626] *Shabalala v Attorney-General of the Transvaal and Another* (CCT23/94) [1995] ZACC 12; 1995 (12) BCLR 1593; 1996 (1) SA 725 (29 November 1995) para 51 read with para 40 and 72 [5].

[627] *Du Toit v The Magistrate and Others* (733/2015) [2016] ZASCA 15; [2016] 2 All SA 328 (SCA); 2016 (2) SACR 112 (SCA) (11 March 2016) para 8.

[628] *Shabalala v Attorney-General of the Transvaal and Another* [*supra*] para 52.

[629] *Shabalala v Attorney-General of the Transvaal and Another* [*supra*] para 55g.

[630] *Shabalala v Attorney-General of the Transvaal and Another* [*supra*] para 56.

[631] *Shabalala v Attorney-General of the Transvaal and Another* [*supra*] para 36.

[632] *Du Toit v The Magistrate and Others* [*supra*] para 16.

charge sheet on request. This enables thorough preparation and allows the defence to advise the accused properly on the charges and the applicable penalty provisions. Before the court session, the defence may request the original charge sheet from the court clerk and take a photograph or digital image, rather than requesting a copy from the prosecutor, who is not the custodian of the original document.

It is essential to note that the charge sheet is not final until the prosecutor confirms it during the pre-trial conference. In the District Courts matters, where no pre-trial conference takes place, the defence should, after receiving disclosure and before confirming the trial date, obtain an undertaking from the prosecutor in court that the charge has been reviewed in light of the evidence and is considered final. The charges in the charge sheet are often hastily prepared by the control prosecutor or another prosecutor assigned to screen the docket. Consequently, the charges are not final, as they are prepared before further investigations are completed and often by a prosecutor who will not be responsible for conducting the trial.

In most cases, when a matter is postponed for trial, the defence receives a provisional charge on the basis of which trial preparation is undertaken. For example, the defence may draft a Section 115(1) plea explanation or Section 220 admissions based on a provisional charge of theft, only to be confronted with a fraud charge on the day of trial. This may be acceptable where the change arises from new circumstances or from consultation with witnesses that necessitates an amendment of the charge. In practice, however, such changes often occur because the prosecutor, under workload pressures, has not had an opportunity to properly consider the contents of the docket at the disclosure stage.

Requiring such an undertaking gives effect to the accused's constitutional rights "to be informed of the charge with sufficient detail to answer it",[633] "to have adequate time [...] to prepare a defence",[634] "to adduce and challenge evidence",[635] and to a trial that begins and concludes without

[633] Section 35(3)(a) of the Constitution guarantees the right to be informed of the charge with sufficient detail. Consultations and trial preparations are conducted on the basis of a particular charge, and a sudden change to the charge on the date of trial is unfair. Such a change usually leads to a postponement that ought to have been avoided and results in additional legal costs to the prejudice of a legally represented accused.

[634] Section 35(3) (b) of the Constitution.

[635] Section 35(3) (i) of the Constitution.

unreasonable delay.[636] Disclosure is ordinarily given after investigations have been completed.[637] The rationale for this practice is to avoid prejudice to the State that may arise from disclosing investigative material before investigations are finalised.[638]

The procedure for applying for disclosure varies from court to court. In certain courts, the defence must make a written application and submit it to the prosecutor. Once copies have been made, a form has been completed, and the number of copies has been calculated, payment is made to the court clerk. This is the most common method. The application may be drafted by hand and submitted to the prosecutor immediately after confirmation that investigations have been completed. In other courts, the matter is simply postponed for disclosure, and on the next date, the prosecutor hands the disclosure to the defence in court, without payment of a fee. In some courts, the defence is required to bring photocopies of documents equivalent to those disclosed. It is therefore advisable to enquire about the practice followed in a particular court, especially when appearing there for the first time. If the prosecutor is unavailable, the interpreter or court clerk may be consulted, as they are usually well acquainted with the court's practice.

The following is an example of an application for disclosure:

IN THE MAGISTRATES' COURT FOR THE MAGISTERIAL DISTRICT OF MORETELE

[HELD AT TEMBA]

Case No. A12/21

In the matter of

THE STATE

and

DEMBE ZUMA ACCUSED

APPLICATION FOR DISCLOSURE

---

1. The Accused hereby applies for the contents of the docket relevant for the purpose of exercising the Accused's right to a fair trial, irrespective of whether such contents are contained in sections A, B,

[636] Section 35(3) (d) of the Constitution.

[637] *S v Dlamini, S v Dladla and Others; S v Joubert; S v Schietekat* (CCT21/98, CCT22/98, CCT2/99, CCT4/99) [199] ZACC 8; 1999 (4) 623; 1999 (7) BCLR 771 (3 June 1999) para 81-82.

[638] Ibid.

or C of the docket.

2. The Accused further applies for a copy of the final charges preferred against him as appearing in the charge sheet.

SIGNED AND DATED AT **TEMBA** ON **24 JUNE 2020.**

____

Adv. Mthimunye

Counsel for the Accused

Where an accused person is unable to afford the cost of obtaining copies of the docket and charge sheet, this should not constitute a barrier to disclosure. The inability to pay must be clearly stated in the application for disclosure. If the prosecutor refuses to provide the copies on this basis, an application may be brought before the court to compel the State to provide disclosure at its own expense. Legal Aid practitioners receive disclosure at State expense; accordingly, there is no justification for denying the same benefit to an accused represented by a private legal practitioner on a pro bono basis.

14.2 Request for further particulars

14.2.1 When to request further particulars

This is another procedure that may be utilised to clarify the State's case against the accused. It is well established that the "heart and soul" of a charge lies in informing the accused of the case that the prosecution intends to advance against them.[639] In terms of Section 84 of the CPA, a charge must reasonably set out two essential elements: the nature of the offence and its particulars, such as the time, place, person, or property involved.[640]

[639] *Sithole and Others v S* (25/2016) [2017] ZAFSHC 160 (12 September 2017) para 23.
[640] *Sithole and Others v S* (25/2016) [2017] ZAFSHC 160 (12 September 2017) para 23.

Where it appears that the charge lacks either the heart, the soul, or both, a written request must be addressed to the prosecution, at any stage before evidence is led on the charge, requesting particulars or further particulars of any matter alleged.[641] The "primary determination in such an application is whether the charge sufficiently informs [the accused] of what case [they have] to meet".[642] If the trial court finds that the charge lacks sufficient particularity, it may, *mero motu* and before evidence is led, direct that particulars or further particulars be furnished to the accused.[643]

The accused's statutory right, in terms of Section 87 of the CPA, to details of what is outstanding in the charge, or to further particulars of what is alleged, is linked to the recognition of the accused's common-law right to be properly informed of the case that the State intends to prove, so as to enable proper trial preparation.[644] This right is firmly protected under the fair-trial guarantees contained in Section 35(3)(a) of the Constitution, which provides for the right "to be informed of the charge with sufficient detail to answer it".[645]

A written request for further particulars must be served on the prosecutor handling the matter, who is expected to respond in writing. An application for further particulars is ordinarily made after disclosure but before the pre-trial conference in the Regional Court matters.[646] Although the CPA permits a request for particulars to be made at any time before evidence is led on a specific charge, Regional Court practice requires that this issue be addressed during the pre-trial conference. The purpose of the pre-trial conference is to ensure that, once a trial date is allocated, the trial proceeds to finality without the need to resolve preliminary issues.[647]

---

[641] Section 87(1) of the CPA.

[642] *African Paper Products (Pty) Ltd and Another v Director of Public Prosecutions: Eastern Cape and Another* (250/2020) [2022] ZAECMKHC 90 (31 October 2022) para 58. Also see *Levenstein v S* (890/12) [2013] 4 All SA 528 (SCA) (1 October 2013) para 98.

[643] Section 87(1) of the CPA.

[644] *S v Levenstein* (317/04) [2006] ZAGPHC 108 (20 December 2006) para3.1.

[645] *Sithole and Others[supra]* para 23.

[646] Pre-trial conferences in the Magistrates' Courts are held only in Regional Courts.

[647] *Sithole and Others v S v S* (25/2016) [2017] ZAFSHC 160 (12 September 2017) para 14.

There are numerous instances in which charges are not properly drafted, rendering a request for further particulars necessary for effective trial preparation. For example, some pro forma murder charges fail to specify how the deceased was killed by the accused, such as by stabbing with a sharp object, shooting with a firearm, hacking with a panga, or striking with a blunt object. In such circumstances, a request for particulars is justified, particularly where the disclosed docket does not provide clarity. If the instrument used is unknown, the prosecution must state this explicitly.

Similar difficulties arise in rape cases where the charge fails to specify the manner of sexual penetration. Some charges merely allege that the accused had "sexual intercourse without consent", without clarifying how penetration was effected. The difficulty is compounded where the first report contradicts the complainant's statement, is silent on a material issue, or where a J88 confirms anal penetration that was not mentioned by the complainant. Such inconsistencies impede proper trial preparation and give rise to uncertainty regarding the essential elements of the offence.[648] The charge should clearly specify the object or body part allegedly used to effect penetration, as well as the part of the complainant's body that was penetrated.[649] Where words were used to commit the offence, such as insults or threats, the precise words must be pleaded. Failing this, further particulars should be requested.[650]

Difficulties also frequently arise in matters involving multiple accused charged with the same or related offences, where reliance is placed on the doctrine of common purpose, whether based on prior agreement or active association, but this doctrine is inadequately pleaded.[651] In such cases, it is often unclear where and when the agreement was reached, or how, when,

[648] *African Paper Products (Pty) Ltd and Another v Director of Public Prosecutions: Eastern Cape and Another* (250/2020) [2022] ZAECMKHC 90 (31 October 2022) para 56. See also *Levenstein v S* (890/12) [2013] 4 All SA 528 (SCA) (1 October 2013) para 98. While these cases were not decided in the context of rape, they are clear authority for the proposition that a charge which leaves the accused to speculate about the elements of the offence is impermissible.

[649] Ibid.

[650] E Du Toit et al *Commentary on the Criminal Procedure Act* (2023 RS 70) 14–26.

[651] *Mkolo and Others v Jacobs and Another* (1831/2015) [2017] ZAECGHC 46 (11 April 2017).

and where a particular accused is alleged to have participated.[652] While some of this information may be gleaned from the docket, this is not always the case. A request for further particulars in these circumstances is therefore justified. An example of a request for further particulars is provided below:

IN THE REGIONAL COURT FOR THE REGIONAL DIVISION OF LIMPOPO

[HELD AT GIYANI]

Case No. RC G23/23

In the matter between

THE STATE

and

NHLAMULO MALULEKE ACCUSED

ACCUSED'S REQUEST FOR FURTHER PARTICULARS

KINDLY TAKE NOTICE that the Accused, after perusing the charge and the disclosure granted, in terms of Section 87 of the Criminal Procedure Act 51 of 1977, hereby requests the following further particulars in respect of the charge against the Accused:

1. Precisely on which day in October 2022 does the State allege that the Accused committed the offence?
2. Precisely which part of the body of the victim was allegedly sexually penetrated?
3. Precisely what instrument was allegedly used to sexually penetrate the victim?
4. Precisely how old was the victim at the time of the alleged commission of the offence?

SIGNED AND DATED AT **GIYANI** ON **22 FEBRUARY 2023**.

____

ADV. RIKHOTSO

Counsel for the Accused

---

[652] *S v Mpetha* 1981 (3) SA 803 (C) at 809H-810H.

Since a request for further particulars is made in writing to the prosecutor, the response—whether providing particulars or further particulars—will likewise be delivered in writing to the defence. These particulars are placed on record and form part of the charge.[653] The prosecution is "bound by them and must prove them".[654]

14.2.2 Request for further particulars as an abuse of court process

This application is one of the most misunderstood, or, more accurately, deliberately abused procedures in our courts. It is not uncommon to encounter purported requests for further particulars consisting of 30 to 60 pages, together with annexures, even in relatively straightforward matters involving three counts of rape or murder. This procedure is not intended to serve as a mechanism to contest the State's case on paper or to delay the commencement of the trial.

A legal practitioner is expected to refrain from and not to permit any abuse of court processes, as the practitioner's role demands conduct that upholds and promotes the integrity, fairness, and effectiveness of the legal system.[655] It is submitted that this responsibility extends beyond the practitioner's personal conduct to encompass the actions of clients, witnesses, and colleagues acting under the practitioner's guidance. Vigilance against procedural manipulation, frivolous applications, or unethical tactics is essential to maintaining public confidence in the legal process and the broader justice system.

In *Sithole and Others v S*,[656] the court reiterated what had been stated in *S v Chao*,[657] namely that "the courts must guard against the abuse of s 87 where the accused's aim is not to advance the proper administration of justice, but rather to obfuscate the issues".

While a legal practitioner is required to represent a client to the best of

---

[653] Section 87(2) of the CPA. Also see E Du Toit et al *Commentary on the Criminal Procedure Act* (2023 RS 70) 14–26.

[654] *S v Boekhoud* (2011 (2) SACR 124 (SCA)) [2011] ZASCA 48; 522/10 (30 March 2011) para 60.

[655] *The Code of Conduct for all Legal Practitioners, Candidate Legal Practitioners and Juristic Entities* GN 162 in GG 42337 (29 March 2019) para 60.1.

[656] *Sithole and Others v S* (25/2016) [2017] ZAFSHC 160 (12 September 2017) para 27.

[657] *S v Chao and Others* 2009 (1) SACR 479 (C) para 31.

their ability, there exists a primary duty to assist the court in arriving "at a proper and just decision at all times and not to endeavour or use strategies which shall set the court up for failure".[658] The courts depend heavily on the manner in which legal practitioners discharge their duties in order to function effectively and administer justice properly.[659]

The purpose of this application is not to grant a special permit to search for possible loopholes or defences unrelated to the facts or instructions provided by the accused.[660] Where the State's case is properly pleaded in the charge sheet, and disclosure of the witness statements and all documents upon which the charge is founded has been granted, there is no need to bring an application for further particulars. The accused is not entitled to be informed of every detail of the case against them.[661] After all, the prosecution cannot be expected to provide further particulars that it does not possess.[662]

14.2.3 What happens when the State fails to answer further particulars sufficiently

Where the prosecution fails to respond to a request for further particulars, or where the responses provided are unsatisfactory, two procedural options are available. Section 87 of the CPA empowers the court to direct the prosecution to furnish further particulars. Accordingly, the first option is to bring an application to compel the furnishing of further particulars in terms of Section 87 of the CPA.

In essence, such an application invites the court to exercise its statutory powers to direct the prosecution to provide further particulars to the accused. This application also finds its constitutional foundation in Section 35(3)(a) of the Constitution. The court will be required to assess whether sufficient

---

[658] *Omotoso and Others v S* (CC 15/2018) [2018] ZAECPEHC 81 (30 October 2018) para 7. Also see the *Code of Conduct for all Legal Practitioners, Candidate Legal Practitioners and Juristic Entities* [*supra*] para 3.3.

[659] *Goane Jack Montshiwa (Ex Parte Application)* (672/2021) [2023] ZASCA 19 (3 March 2023) para 36.

[660] *Sithole and Others v S* (25/2016) [2017] ZAFSHC 160 (12 September 2017) para 28.

[661] *National Director of Public Prosecutions v King* (86/09) [2010] ZASCA 8; 2010 (2) SACR 146 (SCA); 2010 (7) BCLR 656 (SCA); [2010] 3 All SA 304 (SCA) (8 March 2010) para 5. Also see *Van der Westhuizen v S* (CC 11 of 2018) [2018] NAHCMD (28 September 2018) para 12.

[662] *Van der Westhuizen v S* [*supra*] para 13.

information has been provided to the defence, and in doing so, it will consider the following:[663]

1. whether the information is necessary to answer the charge;
2. whether the refusal to furnish the particulars will prejudice the accused;
3. the relevance of the particulars where the request is made after the plea; and
4. what the interests of justice dictate.

The second option, where the prosecution fails to provide sufficient information, is to deliver a notice of objection to the charge in terms of Section 85 of the CPA, setting out the grounds of objection. The grounds for objecting to a charge that may be relevant to an application for further particulars in terms of Section 85 of the CPA include the following:

1. the charge fails to set out, with reasonable clarity, the relevant offence and the particulars relating to time, place, person, or property;
2. the charge does not set out the essential elements of the offence; and
3. the charge does not contain sufficient information regarding any matter alleged therein.

Where the court is satisfied that the application is well-founded, it may order that the particulars be furnished to the defence.[664] Should the prosecutor fail to furnish the particulars as directed, an application for the quashing of the charge may be brought.[665]

---

[663] *Van der Westhuizen v S* (CC 11 of 2018) [2018] NAHCMD (28 September 2018) para 27. Also see A Kruger *Hiemstra's Criminal Procedure, Criminal Procedure,* (2016) p14-24.

[664] Section 85(2) (a) of the CPA. Also see *Rodrigues v National Director of Public Prosecutions and Others* (1186/2019) [2021] ZASCA 87; [2021] 3 All SA 775 (SCA); 2021 (2) SACR 333 (SCA) (21 June 2021) para 59.

[665] Section 85(2) (b) of the CPA. Also see *Rodrigues v National Director of Public Prosecutions and Others* [*supra*] para 59.

CHAPTER 15

PROCEDURES WHICH CURTAIL ISSUES BEFORE TRIAL

15.2 Notices in terms of Section 212B of the CPA

Some prosecutors use a notice under Section 212B of the CPA to ensure that facts not in dispute are agreed upon in advance, thereby eliminating the need to prove them at trial.[666] This mechanism serves to streamline proceedings and to avoid the unnecessary proof of uncontested facts.

This notice sets out the facts the prosecutor expects to prove in support of the charge against the accused, but which the prosecutor considers uncontested.[667] Where any of the facts contained in the notice are disputed, the defence is expected to consult with the accused and to respond accordingly. Unless the defence gives notice disputing any fact, those facts will be deemed to have been proved at trial.[668]

A notice in terms of Section 212B must be delivered either by hand or by electronic means at least 14 days before the commencement of the trial, or within a shorter period if such period is condoned by the court or agreed upon by the parties.[669] Where the defence intends to place any fact mentioned in the notice in dispute, a notice in terms of Section 212B(3) of the CPA must be delivered to the clerk of the court at least five days before the trial, or within a shorter period if condoned by the court or agreed upon with the prosecutor.[670]

Where the notice has been delivered by electronic means, the written response may, as a matter of practice, be transmitted directly to the

[666] Section 212B(1) of the CPA.
[667] Ibid.
[668] Ibid.
[669] Section 212B(2) of the CPA.
[670] Section 212B(3) of the CPA.

prosecutor. As an officer of the court, the prosecutor cannot, in good faith, deny receipt of such a response if it was indeed received. This approach promotes efficiency and is consistent with the section's purpose. Where a shorter period has been agreed upon with the prosecutor, or where condonation is sought from the court, notice to that effect must be given to the clerk of the court—either in writing or orally—for proper recording.[671]

In Regional Court matters, this notice is usually issued before the judicial pre-trial conference. Given that it is uncommon for the parties to conduct a pre-trial conference among themselves in Regional Court proceedings, the use of this notice helps narrow the issues before the judicial pre-trial conference.

A notice in terms of Section 212B is not confined to the period before the commencement of the trial and may be issued by the prosecutor at any stage of the proceedings, provided that it remains practical to do so.[672] The prosecutor will inform the court of the notice issued and the defence's response.[673] The court must satisfy itself that the accused understands their rights and the implications of the procedure, and that they confirm they do not dispute the facts identified in the notice.[674]

The court may deem the undisputed facts to have been sufficiently proved by the State and, therefore, unnecessary to be proved by evidence during the trial.[675] Notwithstanding this, the court may, mero motu or upon application by the accused, direct that evidence be led to prove any fact contained in the notice.[676]

An example of a Section 212B(1) notice issued by the prosecutor appears below:

---

671 Section 212B(3) of the CPA.
672 Section 212B(1) of the CPA.
673 Section 212B(5) of the CPA.
674 Ibid.
675 Section 212B(4) of the CPA.
676 Section 212B(6) of the CPA.

IN THE REGIONAL COURT FOR THE REGIONAL DIVISION OF GAUTENG

HELD AT SOSHANGUVE

Case No: RC2: 47/2023

In the matter between:

THE STATE

and

SIGEGETHE MAGADUZELA ACCUSED

NOTICE IN TERMS OF SECTION 212B (1) OF ACT 51 OF 1977

KINDLY TAKE NOTICE that, in accordance with the provisions of Section 212B(1) of the Criminal Procedure Act 51 of 1977 (CPA), this Notice is hereby delivered, and I, the undersigned, Benito Smith, hereby confirm that:

1. I am the prosecutor in this matter;
2. the proceedings in this matter have commenced in accordance with Section 76 of the CPA;
3. the accused has appointed a legal representative; and
4. the following facts appear to me not to be in dispute for purposes of proving the charge of attempted murder against the accused at trial:

   4.1. Sigegethe Magaduzela (hereinafter referred to as "the accused") is a 39-year-old South African male, with identity number 840624 6535 080, residing at 2121 Aubrey Matlala Street, Block L, Soshanguve, Gauteng Province.

   4.2. Nomasonto Molefe (hereinafter referred to as "the victim") is a 30-year-old South African female, with identity number 930520 4535 081, residing at 2120 Aubrey Matlala Street, Block L, Soshanguve, Gauteng Province.

   4.3. The incident giving rise to the present case occurred on 20 February 2023 at approximately 20h00.

   4.4. The incident occurred at or near Short-Right Pub, Block L, Soshanguve.

4.5. At the time of the incident, the accused and the victim were involved in a romantic relationship.

4.6. As a result of the incident, the victim sustained two stab wounds.

4.7. Both stab wounds were located in the left hypochondrium.

4.8. The victim was initially medically examined at Clinic 3, Block BB, Soshanguve.

4.9. The victim was examined by Dr Chauke on 20 February 2023.

4.10. A J88 medico-legal report, dated 20 February 2023, was completed by Dr Chauke.

4.11. The victim was transferred to Dr George Mukhari Hospital on 20 February 2023.

4.12. The victim was discharged from the hospital on 15 March 2023.

KINDLY TAKE NOTICE FURTHER that any fact set out in paragraph 4 of this Notice shall be deemed to have been proved at trial unless a Notice in terms of Section 212B(3) of the CPA is delivered indicating which fact is placed in issue.

KINDLY TAKE NOTICE FURTHER that, in terms of Section 212B(3) of the CPA, where it is intended to place any fact mentioned in paragraph 4 of this Notice in issue during the trial, a notice to that effect must be delivered to the clerk of the court at least five days before the trial date, or within such shorter period as may be condoned by the court or agreed upon with the prosecutor. Such notice may be delivered in writing or communicated orally to the clerk of the court, in which event the clerk shall record the notice accordingly.

DATED AND SIGNED AT **SOSHANGUVE** ON **23 JUNE 2023**

____

Adv B Smith

REGIONAL COURT PROSECUTOR, MAGISTRATES' COURT SOSHANGUVE

E-mail: advX@justice.gov.za Tel: 012 73**0 1000**

TO: Adv Kgomo

COUNSEL FOR THE ACCUSED

An example of a replying notice in terms of Section 212B(3) is below:

IN THE REGIONAL COURT FOR THE REGIONAL DIVISION OF KWAZULU-NATAL

HELD AT UMZIMKHULU

Case No: RC:40/2023

In the matter between:

THE STATE

and

ATHENKOSI DLAMINI ACCUSED

NOTICE IN TERMS OF SECTION 212B (3) OF ACT 51 OF 1977

KINDLY TAKE NOTICE that the accused, in accordance with the provisions of Section 212B(3) of the Criminal Procedure Act 51 of 1977, hereby gives notice placing certain facts in issue. This Notice is delivered to the prosecutor, and the following facts are placed in dispute:

1. that, as a result of the incident, the victim suffered two stab wounds;
2. that both wounds were located in the left hypochondrium;
3. that the victim was first medically examined at the Sihleza Clinic, Mvolozana; and
4. that the victim was discharged from the hospital on 15 March 2023.

DATED AND SIGNED AT **UMZIMKHULU** ON **27 JULY 2023**

____

ADV MOAGI
Counsel for the Accused
E-mail: moagi@law.co.za

TO: THE CLERK OF THE COURT
UMZIMKHULU MAGISTRATES' COURT

AND TO: THE REGIONAL COURT PROSECUTOR
ADV SK MBANJWA
UMZIMKHULU MAGISTRATES' COURT

15.3 Pre-trial conference

Once disclosure has been obtained and it becomes apparent that a matter will proceed to trial, the next procedural stage is ordinarily a pre-trial conference. It is important to note, however, that in District Courts, pre-trial conferences are generally not held. Instead, once disclosure has been granted, the matter is simply postponed for trial. This practice may be attributed to the nature of cases ordinarily heard in District Courts, which predominantly involve less serious offences that do not usually attract sentences exceeding three years' imprisonment.[677]

The purpose of a pre-trial conference is to ensure that all preliminary issues are resolved so that, once a matter is allocated for trial, it may commence and be finalised without the need to address *in limine* or other preliminary issues.[678] It therefore follows that where the accused intends to plead guilty, or to enter into a plea and sentence agreement in terms of Section 105A of the CPA, a pre-trial conference will ordinarily not be held. Even where a judicial pre-trial conference has been conducted, the accused is not precluded from subsequently changing the plea and pleading guilty.

A pre-trial conference between the parties—namely, the prosecutor and the defence—ordinarily takes place before the judicial pre-trial conference. The purpose of this engagement is to ensure that the matter is trial-ready and to explore whether the anticipated duration of the trial may be reduced. Issues

[677] The maximum sentence of three years' imprisonment applies only to common-law offences. Statutory offences regulate their own penalty provisions and, accordingly, even where a matter is justiciable in the district court, the prescribed maximum sentence may exceed three years' imprisonment.

[678] *Sithole and Others v S* (25/2016) [2017] ZAFSHC 160 (12 September 2017) para 14.

that are common causes and those that remain in dispute are identified to avoid unnecessary witness testimony. The possibility of a plea to a lesser charge, or the negotiation of a plea and sentence agreement, is also considered at this stage. Trial proceedings are not always predictable. In appropriate circumstances, the prosecution may be willing to accept a plea to a lesser count of murder, which ordinarily attracts a minimum sentence of 15 years' imprisonment, instead of a charge of premeditated murder, which typically attracts a sentence of life imprisonment. Where the accused is inclined to plead guilty, but the likely sentence is unduly severe, it may be appropriate to attempt to negotiate a reduced sentence by way of a plea and sentence agreement in terms of Section 105A of the CPA, where permissible.

Once the parties' engagement has concluded, a judicial pre-trial conference is held before the court. It should be noted that pre-trial conferences between the parties are not regulated by statute, the rules of court, or practice directives, and in practice, they seldom occur. Consequently, the parties' failure to engage meaningfully beforehand often results in the judicial pre-trial conference becoming a forum for unexpected disclosures and strategic ambushes.

A matter is certified as trial-ready only during the judicial pre-trial conference, as provided for in the Criminal Practice Directives for the Regional Court of South Africa, 2023. The judicial pre-trial conference is an informal procedure during which the court poses predetermined questions to satisfy itself that the matter is ready to proceed to trial. The Practice Directives require that the following issues be addressed during the judicial pre-trial conference of a legally represented accused:[679]

1. whether the parties are ready for trial;
2. whether all investigations have been completed;
3. whether the defence has been paid, or whether satisfactory financial arrangements have been made for the determined number of trial dates;
4. whether the defence has received copies of the final charge sheet and the copies of the docket;
5. whether the State has consulted all relevant witnesses and whether there is no outstanding investigation or evidence;
6. whether the defence has consulted with the accused
7. where the defence represents more than one accused, whether there is a potential conflict of interest between the respective versions of the accused;
8. whether the parties have exhausted all possibilities of making representations,

---

[679] Criminal Practice Directives for the Regional Court of South Africa 2023 para

4.2.

engaging in informal mediation, or considering diversion, where applicable;

9. Whether the State intends to present technical evidence, including admissions or confessions, pointings-out, forensic or expert evidence, section 212 statements, or other documentary evidence
10. whether the admissibility of any written statements, pointings-out made by the accused, forensic evidence, or Section 212 statements will be placed in issue.
11. whether applicable minimum sentences and competent verdicts have been explained;
12. whether consideration has been given to pleading guilty or to entering into a plea and sentence agreement;
13. the intended plea;
14. whether admissions will be made, and if so, which admissions will be made in order to avoid subpoenaing unnecessary witnesses;
15. whether the State has delivered any Section 212B and/or Section 213 notices, and whether the defence has responded to such notices.
16. the number of witnesses the parties intend to call;
17. whether any witnesses include children or persons with mental or other disabilities;
18. whether the appointment of an intermediary is necessary and whether appropriate arrangements have been made;
19. whether the use of an intermediary or audiovisual equipment will be required, and arrangements have been made;
20. the language understood by the accused and the witnesses, in order to determine whether the services of a foreign-language interpreter are required;
21. whether the appointment of assessors is necessary;
22. the estimated duration of the trial; and
23. the proposed trial dates.

If any of the above issues remain unresolved, the presiding officer may postpone the matter for a further pre-trial hearing and issue appropriate directions.[680] Before a trial date is allocated, you should ensure that your witnesses are available. If the matter cannot proceed for any reason—including the unavailability of witnesses—you should inform the prosecutor and the court as early as possible.[681]

---

[680] Criminal Practice Directives for the Regional Court of South Africa 2023 para 4.5.

[681] Criminal Practice Directives for the Regional Court of South Africa 2023 para 4.8 and 4.9.

CHAPTER 16

PROCEDURES WHICH FINALISE CASES BEFORE TRIAL

16.1 Representations

In the context of pending criminal proceedings, representations refer to written submissions directed to the Senior Public Prosecutor (SPP), Chief Public Prosecutor (CPP), Director of Public Prosecutions (DPP), or National Director of Public Prosecutions (NDPP), requesting that a matter be withdrawn—such as on the basis of *de minimis non curat lex* or a lack of prospects of success—or that it be dealt with in a particular manner, for example, by combining multiple cases against the accused to be tried in the same court or by referring the matter for diversion.[682]
If the decision to prosecute was made by a lower-court prosecutor and is the subject of the representation, the request for reconsideration should be directed to the SPP.[683] If you are dissatisfied with the SPP's decision, the matter should be escalated to the CPP or DPP.[684] When requesting such a review, it is important to attach the correspondence received from the relevant junior officials.[685] For example, where the NDPP is requested to review the decision of the DPP, the DPP's correspondence should be attached.[686]

Representations may be made at any time before the commencement of the trial, unless the purpose of the representation is to stop the prosecution. It is generally difficult to draft detailed representations seeking the withdrawal of a matter unless disclosure has been granted. It is therefore preferable to await disclosure, after which the practitioner may consult and analyse the evidence disclosed. Where it appears that there are no reasonable prospects of success,

[682] *Sibiya v National Director of Public Prosecutions and Others* (2292/2020) [2021] ZAMPMBHC 41 (8 September 2021) para 10.
[683] Ibid.
[684] Access to Information Manual of the National Prosecuting Authority of South Africa Version 1.06 para 11.3 https://www.npa.gov.za/sites/default/files/uploads/PAIA%20Manual%20for%20NPA%5B1%5D.pdf, accessed on 20 June 2023. *Sibiya v National Director of Public Prosecutions and Others* [*supra*] para 11.
[685] Procedure to follow for the review of a decision in a criminal matter: https://www.npa.gov.za/sites/default/files/Written%20Representations%20&%20Complaints.pdf, accessed on 20 June 2023.
[686] Ibid.

representations may be submitted explaining why, in the practitioner's legal opinion, the prosecution lacks such prospects.
Representations should include all relevant case information, including the name of the court, the case number, the SAPS CAS number, and the name of the accused.[687] When drafting representations, the practitioner ought to be conversant with the applicable Prosecution Policy. The NDPP has, in terms of Section 179(5) of the Constitution, created a Prosecution Policy[688] and issued policy directives[689] which must be observed in the prosecution process. The Prosecution Policy is a public document.[690]
While the NPA treats its policy directives as confidential for internal purposes, the court in *S v Shaik and Others,*[691] held that the NPA Policy Manual, which incorporates those Directives, is a public document. In any event, some of the important directives were disclosed on the NPA website,[692] until recently, and some are quoted in court judgments.[693] Therefore, some of them are in the public domain and no longer confidential.[694]

The decision to prosecute is guided by the Prosecution Policy. Consequently, any challenge to such a decision requires familiarity with the applicable policy framework. The Prosecution Policy is binding on prosecutors and on the NPA as an institution.[695] The policy provisions relevant to the decision to prosecute may be summarised as follows:[696]

1. The decision whether or not to prosecute must be taken with care since it may have serious consequences for victims, witnesses, accused persons, and their

---

[687] Procedure to follow for the review of a decision in a criminal matter: https://www.npa.gov.za/sites/default/files/Written%20Representations%20&%20Complaints.pdf, accessed on 20 June 2023.

[688] NPA Prosecution Policy [Revision Date: June 2013], this copy is available at https://www.opensecrets.org.za/wp-content/uploads/2022/06/Zondo-Commission_NPA-Prosecution-Policy.pdf, accessed on 23 June 2023.

[689] NPA Policy Directives Issued by NDPP 01 June 2014. See also *Van Deventer v National Director of Public Prosecutions NO* (64268/2013) [2015] ZAGPPHC 550 (7 August 2015) para 16.

[690] NPA Prosecution Policy [Revision Date: June 2013] para 2, available at https://www.opensecrets.org.za/wp-content/uploads/2022/06/Zondo-Commission_NPA-Prosecution-Policy.pdf, accessed on 23 June 2023.

[691] *S v Shaik and Others* (CCT 86/06) [2007] ZACC 19; 2008 (2) SA 208 (CC); 2007 (12) BCLR 1360 (CC); 2008 (1) SACR 1 (CC) (2 October 2007) para 33. See also Du Toit and Ferreira "Reasons for Prosecutorial Decision" PELJ vol 18 n.5 Potchefstroom 2015 https://scielo.org.za/pdf/pelj/v18n5/09.pdf, accessed 24 June 2023.

[692] Some of these Policy Directives were always present when visiting https://www.npa.gov.za/content/prosecution-policy-and-policy-directives.

[693] *Van Deventer v National Director of Public Prosecutions NO* (64268/2013) [2015] ZAGPPHC 550 (7 August 2015) para 17.

[694] *Genesis One Lighting v Jamieson and Others* (19/3212) [2019] ZAGPJHC 93 (18 March 2019) para 32.

[695] NPA Prosecution Policy [Revision Date: June 2013] para 1.

[696] NPA Prosecution Policy [*supra*] para 4.

families. "A wrong decision may also undermine the community's confidence in the prosecution system and the criminal justice system."

2. Resources must be reserved for deserving cases and not wasted on unsuitable cases.

3. The "prosecutor must assess whether there is sufficient and admissible evidence" that provides a reasonable prospect of success before instituting criminal proceedings. In the absence of a reasonable prospect of conviction, prosecution should not be commenced or continued. This assessment is usually difficult; therefore, where it is unclear, the prosecutor should consult with witnesses to evaluate their reliability. "The version or defence of an accused person must also be considered before a decision is made."

4. "This test of a reasonable prospect must be applied objectively after careful consideration, to avoid an unjustified prosecution. However, prosecutors should not make unfounded assumptions about the potential credibility of witnesses."

5. "The review of a case is a continuing process" that requires the prosecutor to consider the changing circumstances of the case and fresh facts, which may come to light after an initial decision to prosecute or not to prosecute has been made. This may occur after considering the version of the accused person or representations made on their behalf. The prosecutor may therefore withdraw charges before the accused person has pleaded, despite the initial decision to prosecute.

While the drafting style of representations may vary from one legal practitioner to another, the underlying approach should remain constant: they are instruments of persuasion. Representations challenging the prospects of success should preferably take the form of a structured written argument, even though they are directed to senior officials within the NPA. The purpose is to persuade the senior official that the decision to prosecute was incorrect, or that the initial decision was not properly reconsidered in light of changed circumstances. The material facts should be concisely summarised, and the applicable legal principles carefully applied, in order to demonstrate that the prosecution lacks reasonable prospects of success.

Such representations are made on a "without prejudice" basis and, accordingly, do not constitute a binding version of the accused's case that may be used against them at trial.[697] To ensure that the representations remain a non-binding version of the client, the legal practitioner should be the one signing

[697] Access to Information Manual of the National Prosecuting Authority of South Africa Version 1.06 para 11.4 https://www.npa.gov.za/sites/default/files/uploads/PAIA%20Manual%20for%20NPA%5B1%5D.pdf, accessed on 24 June 2023.

the representations, not the client. Representations to the NDPP are addressed to: repsadmin@npa.gov.za.[698]

16.2 Diversion

In deserving cases, prosecutors should implement the Probation Services Act 116 of 1991, which provides an alternative way of combating crime without invoking the normal criminal court process.[699] The State may refer the matter for diversion instead of prosecuting the accused. Diversion benefits both the accused and society, as it places the accused in appropriate programmes aimed at addressing the underlying causes of their offending behaviour—while also avoiding the imposition of a criminal record. The NPA has developed a policy that guides prosecutors when dealing with diversion, and it can be summarised as follows:[700]

1. Diversion means the exercise of discretion by a prosecutor to finalise a suitable and deserving case in a manner other than through normal court proceedings.
2. Diversion usually entails the provisional withdrawal of the matter on condition that the accused participates in certain programmes and/or makes reparation to the complainant. [Prosecutors are required to submit daily statistics, and a successful diversion reflects positively in these reports, whereas a withdrawal does not. As a result, in practice, the case is often kept on the court roll until the diversion programme is completed, since it cannot be recorded in the prosecutor's daily statistics as a diversion without a completion report].
3. Diversion is preferable to a mere withdrawal of a case since the accused takes responsibility for their actions.
4. Diversion is mostly used in cases involving youthful offenders. However, there are diversion programmes for adults, such as victim–offender mediation and community service, as alternatives to prosecution.
5. Diversion is inappropriate in serious offences.

---

698 Procedure to follow for the review of a decision in a criminal matter: https://www.npa.gov.za/sites/default/files/Written%20Representations%20&%20Complaints.pdf, accessed on 20 June 2023.

699 *S v Frederick; S v Maxhongo* (18531; 18532) [2018] ZAWCHC 89; 2018 (2) SACR 686 (WCC) (11 July 2018) para 11 and *S v Nkuna* (18/2012) [2012] ZAGPJHC 115; 2012 (2) SACR 526 (GSJ) (18 May 2012) para 11.

700 *Van Deventer v National Director of Public Prosecutions NO* (64268/2013) [2015] ZAGPPHC 550 (7 August 2015) para 17.

6. The accused should have no previous convictions and should not have a previous diversion record unless exceptional circumstances exist.

7. When the prosecutor exercises discretion to divert, they must be satisfied that the accused has a fixed address, takes responsibility for the offence, and is prepared to participate in the diversion programme.

8. Once the accused has completed the diversion programme, the social worker submits a report to the prosecutor. If the report indicates that the accused has cooperated with and benefited from the programme, the matter is withdrawn. If not, the prosecution proceeds.

9. A register of all offenders who have been screened for the diversion programme should be kept. The decision to divert or not, and how the matter was eventually finalised, must be recorded.

Where the accused is charged with a less serious offence, and there are cogent reasons why a diversion programme may be appropriate, the defence should approach the prosecutor and request that the matter be referred to a probation officer to investigate the accused's personal circumstances and to compile a *pre-trial report recommending the desirability or otherwise of prosecution.*[701] However, the prosecutor remains *dominus litis*, and the decision whether to continue with the prosecution or to divert the matter lies within the prosecutor's discretion.[702] Where a public prosecutor refuses to divert the matter, representations may be made to the SPP, the CPP, the DPP, or the NDPP.

When exercising the power to divert, prosecutors must act "lawfully, rationally and in good faith".[703] A decision by the NPA's higher authority to refuse diversion is reviewable under the general principle of legality.[704] Despite this, there are many cases in which diversion would be more beneficial than subjecting the accused to the ordinary criminal process, yet such matters are

---

[701] Section 4(1) (i) and (j) of the Probation Services Act 116 of 1991.

[702] *S v C.S* (A74/14, A395/15,06/2014) [2015] ZAGPPHC 520 (11 June 2015) para 16.

[703] See *Van Deventer v National Director of Public Prosecutions NO* (64268/2013) [2015] ZAGPPHC 550 (7 August 2015) para 13 and *S v C.S* (A74/14,A395/15,06/2014) [2015] ZAGPPHC 520 (11 June 2015) para 17.

[704] *Van Deventer v National Director of Public Prosecutions NO* [*supra*] para 12.

not referred for diversion.[705]

One sometimes encounters cases involving tertiary students charged with offences such as shoplifting, malicious injury to property, public violence (where only traffic flow was disturbed), or common assault. Instead of being diverted, these accused often plead guilty and accumulate criminal records, rendering them unemployable. Consequently, rather than becoming productive contributors to society through the skills they have acquired, they become a burden on the State. It is in the interest of a better future for society to invest in youth development and guide them when they go astray, rather than destroying their prospects through criminal records, particularly when diversion would clearly be the more appropriate option.

Diversion is particularly important for accused persons who struggle with substance use. In many instances, such individuals commit offences in order to sustain their addiction.[706] They are often repeatedly charged with petty theft or drug possession. These vulnerable accused are subjected to the conventional criminal process, which does little to address the underlying causes of their offending behaviour. As a result, they may receive increasingly harsh sentences, being perceived as having little or no regard for the law.[707] The standard court process, however, typically fails to confront the root cause of the offending—namely, substance addiction.

The enactment of the Prevention of and Treatment for Substance Abuse Act 70 of 2008 (PATSAA) was a legislative response to the escalating crisis of substance abuse in South Africa.[708] It introduced a comprehensive framework for prevention, early intervention, and treatment. Despite its progressive intent, however, PATSAA presents procedural challenges that limit its effective application in criminal proceedings—particularly where the accused is already before the court under the CPA. A central tension arises from Section 33 of

---

[705] See *S v Frederick; S v Maxhongo* (18531; 18532) [2018] ZAWCHC 89; 2018 (2) SACR 686 (WCC) (11 July 2018); *S v Nkuna* (18/2012) [2012] ZAGPJHC 115; 2012 (2) SACR 526 (GSJ) (18 May 2012); and *S v Jacobs* (E830/20; 192/21; 1/21) [2021] ZAWCHC 111; 2021 (2) SACR 644 (WCC) (31 March 2021).

[706] Regan Jules-Macque "Exploring Substance Use Among South African Adult And Young Offenders" NICRO (2015) para 4, https://nicro.org.za/images/PDFs/Exploring-substance-use- among-adult-and-young-offenders-Revised-Nov-2014.pdf, accessed 15 August 2024. Also see *S v Jacobs* [*supra*] para 8.

[707] See *S v Frederic* [*supra*]*k; S v Maxhongo* [*supra*] ; *S v Nkuna* ; and *S v Jacobs* [*supra*].

[708] Preamble to the Prevention of and Treatment of Substance Abuse Act 70 of 2008.

PATSAA, which requires that any summons or warrant initiating an inquiry be issued in terms of PATSAA itself, rather than under the CPA. This procedural rigidity effectively prevents a court from initiating a Section 35 inquiry—which permits the committal of a person to a treatment centre—once the accused has entered the criminal justice system via Section 38 of the CPA. In such circumstances, although the accused is lawfully before the court, the procedural prerequisites of PATSAA are not satisfied.[709]

The only statutory mechanism presently available to reconcile the procedural tension between the CPA and PATSAA arises later in the trial process—through Section 255 of the CPA, read with Section 37 of PATSAA—which permits the conversion of a criminal trial into an inquiry. This mechanism, however, does not reflect the principle of early intervention envisaged in Section 2(d) of PATSAA, which emphasises the prompt identification and treatment of substance dependence before the criminal process advances too far.

As a result, prosecutors frequently rely on the older, more general—and at times inadequate—provisions of the Probation Services Act, which provide a comparatively flexible basis for early intervention and diversion. While this approach continues to play an important rehabilitative role, it also highlights a significant legislative shortcoming: the statute specifically designed to address substance abuse—PATSAA—is often procedurally inaccessible in precisely those cases where its application would be most appropriate.

Despite the procedural inconvenience that arises once an accused is already before the court, it is submitted that early intervention,[710] as contemplated in Section 2(d) of PATSAA, remains achievable before trial—provided that prosecutors and legal practitioners adopt a proactive and coordinated approach.

The procedural steps that follow outline a viable pathway for initiating a Section 35 inquiry in terms of PATSAA, even where the accused has already entered the criminal justice system through the CPA.

1. **Legal practitioner's submission**

The legal practitioner representing the accused submits a written request to the

---

[709] In *re Vorster* 1997 (1) SACR 269 (O) P271-272. While this case was decided under Section 21 of the Prevention and Treatment of Drug Dependency Act 20 of 1992, which has been repealed, Section 33 of the PATSAA has the same requirements.

[710] While *early intervention* is not defined in the Prevention of and Treatment of Substance Abuse Act 70 of 2008 (PATSAA), the Probation Services Act 116 of 1991 defines it as the "provision of services, diversion programmes and other programmes aimed at preventing the need for a person who is alleged to have committed an offence to be dealt with in terms of the formal court procedure".

prosecutor handling the matter, indicating that:

a) the accused is dependent on substances;

b) the offence was committed to sustain the accused's substance dependence; and

c) the accused should be referred for assessment and treatment in terms of PATSAA.

2. **Affidavit in support of the request**
The prosecutor receives an affidavit from a person closely associated with the accused (such as a family member or caregiver), confirming that the accused:
a) resides within the jurisdiction of the court to which the prosecutor is attached
b) is dependent on substances; and
c) has committed the current offence and/or previous criminal offences to sustain their substance dependence.

3. **Request for a social worker's report**

The prosecutor requests that a social worker investigate the accused's social circumstances and any other relevant factors and compile a report.
Thereafter, the prosecutor applies to the court for the criminal matter to be postponed pending receipt of the social worker's report

4. **Where the accused is not in custody**

If the accused is not in custody and the social worker's report confirms substance dependence, the prosecutor should request the clerk of the court to issue a Section 33 summons. The summons must be served on the accused by a police officer while the accused is present in court. The criminal matter should then be postponed to the date specified in the summons for the Section 35 inquiry.

5. **Where the accused is in custody**

If the accused is in custody, the prosecutor should apply to the magistrate for the issuing of a Section 33 warrant of arrest, which must be executed immediately by a police officer.

6. **Appearance at the Section 35 inquiry**

The accused will appear before the magistrate in terms of the Section 33 summons or warrant of arrest for the purpose of conducting a Section 35 inquiry.

7. **Findings at the Section 35 inquiry**

If the presiding officer finds that:

a) the accused is dependent on substances;
b) the accused is in need of, or is likely to benefit from, treatment and skills development; or
c) it is in the interest of the accused, the accused's dependents, or society that the accused undergo treatment, the presiding officer may make an order that the accused:
   (i) undergo detoxification and be admitted to a treatment centre for a

period not exceeding 12 months.

8. **Withdrawal of criminal charges**

Once an order is made under Section 35, the prosecutor may withdraw the criminal charges against the accused.

16.3 Informal mediation

You will sometimes encounter cases where the client has already repaired the damaged property, offered an apology to the complainant, or where the complainant has forgiven the client and no longer wishes to proceed with the matter. Although the prosecutor remains *dominus litis*, compelling an unwilling complainant to proceed—particularly where there are other complainants eager to have their cases heard—may amount to an inefficient use of prosecutorial and court resources, unless the seriousness or particular circumstances of the case dictate otherwise.

Complainants usually indicate their lack of interest in pursuing a matter by submitting a written *withdrawal statement* to the investigating officer. However, in practice, such statements are not always readily accepted—especially where the investigating officer has invested considerable time and effort in the investigation.

Legal practitioners frequently encounter situations where the complainant privately informs the accused or the accused's family that they no longer wish to proceed with the case. This gives rise to an ethical and procedural dilemma: disclosing the information may raise suspicions of intimidation or undue influence, while withholding it may result in unnecessary delays and unresolved case dynamics. In such circumstances, the practitioner should, in good faith, inform the prosecutor of the complainant's position and clearly place on record that the accused did not influence the complainant's decision. It remains within the prosecutor's discretion to evaluate the disclosure and determine the appropriate course of action. This approach promotes procedural fairness, enables informed prosecutorial decision-making, and avoids unnecessary delays—ultimately contributing to a more efficient and just criminal process.

Where the complainant wishes to withdraw the matter under these circumstances, the outcome is often recorded as an *informal mediation*. This may include a withdrawal subject to conditions, such as the accused paying compensation before a specified date. Should the accused fail to comply with these conditions, the matter may be re-enrolled.

If the prosecutor refuses to withdraw the case despite the complainant's lack of interest, the defence may submit written representations through the prosecutorial hierarchy—beginning with the CPP, escalating to the SPP, then the DPP, and, where necessary, the NDPP.

PART 2:

PROCEDURES AFFECTING A CHILD CLIENT BEFORE THE TRIAL BEGINS

CHAPTER 17

PROCEDURES TO BE FOLLOWED BEFORE A CHILD CLIENT APPEARS IN COURT

17.1 Procedures before a child appears in court generally

When representing a child who allegedly committed an offence, it is essential to have a thorough understanding of the provisions of the Child Justice Act 75 of 2008 (CJA). The provisions of the CJA are not always applied in isolation from those of the CPA. Accordingly, to appreciate fully how the CJA impacts proceedings under the CPA, careful attention must be paid to the guidance provided in Schedule 5 of the CJA.[711]

A police officer may, instead of arresting the child, secure the child's attendance at the preliminary inquiry by issuing a written notice to appear[712] or a summons.[713] However, this does not invariably occur, and the legal practitioner must be prepared to represent a child who has been arrested. Where a child has been arrested and detained, it is imperative to understand the mechanisms by which the child may be released before the preliminary inquiry.

This requires familiarity with Section 21(2)(a), read together with Schedule 1 of the CJA, which provides for the release of a child on written notice into the care of a parent, guardian, or appropriate person. It further requires knowledge of Section 21(2)(b), read with Schedules 1 and 2, which authorises the release of a child on bail granted by a prosecutor. It is important to emphasise from the outset that an arrested child may be released before the preliminary inquiry only through these two statutory mechanisms.

---

[711] Section 4(3) of the CJA.
[712] Section 18 of the CJA.
[713] Section 19 of CJA.

When representing a child, the legal practitioner should "make a concerted effort to ensure that the child's best interests are served" and should "go the extra mile" to ensure that justice is not only done but is manifestly seen to be done.[714] After all, "children are the soul of our society, and if we fail them, then we have failed as a society."[715]

17.2 Written notice to appear at a preliminary inquiry

Arrest is the most extreme and potentially traumatising method of securing the attendance of a child at a preliminary inquiry.[716] To limit the adverse effects of arrest in cases involving less serious offences, Section 18 of the CJA empowers a police official to issue a written notice to appear at a preliminary inquiry to a child who allegedly committed an offence listed in Schedule 1 of the CJA. Section 56 of the CPA remains applicable, but it must be read together with Section 18 of the CJA and applied within the protective framework of child justice. The procedure generally requires that the child be visited at home or that the child be requested to attend the police station in the company of a parent, guardian, or appropriate person.

The written notice to appear must be given to the child in the presence of a parent, guardian, or appropriate person, and it must specify the date, time, and place at which the inquiry will be held.[717] Both the child and the accompanying parent, guardian, or appropriate person must acknowledge receipt of the written notice to appear.[718] In exceptional circumstances, a child may be issued a written notice to appear despite the absence of a parent.[719] Where a written notice has been issued to the child, a copy must be provided to the parent as soon as possible, and both must be warned to appear at the preliminary inquiry.[720] Unlike a written notice issued to an adult accused under the CPA, a written notice issued in terms of the CJA does not contain a provision permitting the payment of an admission of guilt fine.[721] This distinction reinforces the restorative and developmental orientation of the child justice system and prevents the child from acquiring a criminal record through

---

[714] *S v LJ* (346/22) [2023] ZAWCHC 6; 2023 (1) SACR 396 (WCC) (24 January 2023) para 23.
[715] *S v LJ* [supra] para 11.
[716] *Raduvha v Minister of Safety and Security and Another* (CCT151/15) [2016] ZACC 24; 2016 (10) BCLR 1326 (CC); 2016 (2) SACR 540 (CC) (11 August 2016) para 67.
[717] Section 18(3) (a) of the CJA.
[718] Ibid.
[719] Section 18(3) (b) of the CJA.
[720] Ibid.
[721] Section 18(2) of the CJA.

administrative disposal.

Failure by a child to appear at a preliminary inquiry may result in the issuing of a warrant of arrest, or the court may order that the child be served with a summons.[722] If the failure to appear is attributable to the child, the court may release the child on different or more stringent conditions, or it may order that the child be detained.[723] Importantly, in terms of the CJA, it is not a criminal offence for a child to fail to appear at a preliminary inquiry. This approach reflects the Act's commitment to avoiding the unnecessary criminalisation of children. In contrast, a parent, guardian, or appropriate person who fails to attend the preliminary inquiry without reasonable cause commits an offence. Such failure is punishable by a fine not exceeding R10 000.00 or imprisonment for a period not exceeding three months.[724]

17.3 Summons issued in terms of CJA

The arrest and detention of children in conflict with the law are permissible only in limited circumstances, particularly in respect of serious offences listed in Schedule 2 and Schedule 3 of the CJA. Notwithstanding this statutory authority, police officers are generally discouraged by the National Instruction[725] from arresting children unless such action is strictly necessary. These instructions accord with Section 28(1)(g) of the Constitution, which provides that a child may be detained only as a measure of last resort.

In *Raduvha v Minister of Police and Another*,[726] the Constitutional Court interpreted the expression "a measure of last resort" to mean that the detention of a child should occur only when all reasonable alternative measures have been exhausted. Police officers are therefore required to consider less restrictive means of securing the child's attendance at the preliminary inquiry before resorting to arrest and detention.[727] A summons constitutes one such effective mechanism, as it secures the child's attendance while avoiding arrest and detention—measures that have been described as having "traumatic, brutalising, dehumanising and degrading effects on people".[728]

---

[722] Section 46 of the CJA read together with Section 24(7) (a) of the CJA.

[723] Section 46 of the CJA read together with Section 24(7) (d) of the CJA.

[724] Section 46 of the CJA read together with Section 24(7) (e) of the CJA, further read together with Section 1(2) of the Adjustments of Fines Act 101 of 1991, as applied in the context of *Cooper v District Magistrate, Cape Town* (WCC) (1699/2017) [2017] ZAWCHC 140; 2018 (1) SACR 369 (WCC) (24 November 2017) para 21.

[725] National Instruction 2 of 2010: *Children in Conflict with the Law*, para 3(4)(b).

[726] *Raduvha v Minister of Safety and Security and Another* (CCT151/15) [2016] ZACC 24; 2016 (10) BCLR 1326 (CC); 2016 (2) SACR 540 (CC) (11 August 2016) para 67.

[727] Ibid.

[728] Ibid.

Although authorised by the CJA to effect an arrest, a police officer may instead continue the investigation and refer the docket to the prosecutor for a decision on whether to prosecute. [729] Should the prosecutor elect to prosecute, a summons may be issued to secure the child's attendance at a preliminary inquiry.[730] The issuing of a summons is governed by Section 19 of the CJA, read with Section 54 of the CPA. The summons must be served on the child in the presence of a parent, appropriate person, or guardian, and both must acknowledge receipt by signing it.[731] In exceptional circumstances, service may be effected in the absence of such a person, provided that a copy is subsequently served on the parent, appropriate person, or guardian.[732]

The consequences of a failure to appear on a summons are identical to those arising from a failure to appear while released on a written notice, as discussed in paragraph 17.2. Where an inquiry into failure to appear is pending, the proof of service must be scrutinised carefully. This document is submitted to the court as evidence that the child and the parent, appropriate person, or guardian were properly served. It must reflect the date, time, and place of the preliminary inquiry, together with the names and signatures of the signatories.[733] Should any of these elements be absent, this may constitute a complete defence. Section 54(3) of the CPA remains applicable; accordingly, the summons must be served at least 14 days before the date of the preliminary inquiry. Failing compliance with this requirement, no warrant of arrest may be issued.

17.4 Release of an arrested child on written notice

Where a child has been arrested instead of being issued with a written notice to appear in terms of Section 18, or a summons in terms of Section 19 of the CJA, the police officer remains obliged to release the child on a written notice into the care of a parent, appropriate person, or guardian to attend a preliminary inquiry, provided that the alleged offence is a Schedule 1 offence under the CJA.[734] However, the child may not be released where a parent, appropriate person, or guardian cannot be located, or where there is a substantial risk that the child poses a danger to themselves or to others.[735] Where a child has been arrested for a Schedule 1 offence under the CJA and has not been released on a written notice to appear, the police officer must

[729] National Instruction 2 of 2010: *Children in Conflict with the Law* para 3(4)(b).
[730] Ibid.

[731] Section 19(2) of the CJA.
[732] Ibid.

[733] Section 54(1) (a) of the CPA.
[734] Section 21(2) (a) of the CJA.
[735] Section 22(1) of the CJA

submit a written report to the magistrate presiding over the preliminary inquiry (the inquiry magistrate) explaining the reasons for the failure to release the child.[736]

In summary, in respect of Schedule I offences, a police officer who fails to issue a written notice to appear at a preliminary inquiry in terms of Section 18 of the CJA is compelled by Section 21(2)(a) of the same Act to do so after arresting the child. In the event of non-compliance with this obligation, the police officer must submit a report to the inquiry magistrate explaining the reasons for non-compliance. The offences in respect of which a child may be released by the police on a written notice into the care of a parent, appropriate person, or guardian are specifically listed in Schedule I of the CJA. These offences may be summarised as follows:

1. Theft, where the value does not exceed R2 500.00.
2. Receiving stolen property, where the value does not exceed R2 500.00.
3. Theft by false pretence, where the value does not exceed R2 500.00.
4. Fraud, where the amount involved does not exceed R1 500.00.
5. Extortion, where the amount involved does not exceed R1 500.00.
6. Forgery and uttering, where the amount involved does not exceed R1 500.00.
7. An offence referred to in the Prevention and Combating of Corrupt Activities Act, 2004 (Act 12 of 2004), where the amount involved does not exceed R1 500.00.
8. Malicious injury to property, where the amount involved does not exceed R1 500.00.
9. Assault without the infliction of grievous bodily harm (GBH).
10. Perjury.
11. Contempt of court.
12. Crimen iniuria.
13. …[737]
14. Trespass.
15. Public indecency.
16. Engaging the sexual services of persons 18 years or older.
17. Bestiality.
18. Statutory rape (e.g., where a child of 16 years or older engages in consensual sexual penetration with a child who is more than two years younger than that child, and the DPP has authorised the prosecution thereof in writing).
19. Statutory sexual assault (e.g., where a child of 16 years or older engages in consensual sexual violation with a child who is more than two years younger than that child, and the DPP has authorised the prosecution thereof in writing).
20. Any other statutory offence where the maximum penalty does not exceed three months' imprisonment or a fine of R3 000.00.

---

[736] Section 22(2) of the CJA.

[737] Common law defamation has been repealed by Section 34(1) of the Judicial Matters Amendment Act 15 of 2023.

21. Any conspiracy, incitement, or attempt to commit any offence referred to herein.

Failure to appear at a preliminary inquiry after being released on written notice into the care of a parent, an appropriate person, or a guardian will result in the same consequences as failing to appear after being given written notice to appear at the preliminary inquiry by a police officer. A detailed analysis of failure to appear is discussed in paragraph 17.2.

17.5 Release of an arrested child on CJA prosecutor's bail

When representing a child client, the same bail procedure applicable to adult prosecutions is followed. However, the child is released on bail to attend a preliminary inquiry. To understand the prosecutor's bail in the context of a child accused, Section 59A of the CPA must be read together with Section 21(2)(b) of the CJA. Instead of applying Schedule 7 of the CPA to determine whether an offence is suitable for this form of bail, the prosecutor applies Schedule 1 and Schedule 2 of the CJA. Therefore, where a police officer has not released the child on warning, the prosecutor may nevertheless release a child charged with a Schedule 1 offence on the prosecutor's bail. A summary of Schedule 1 of the CJA has already been provided in paragraph 17.4. Schedule 2, which in most cases applies to prosecutor's bail, is summarised below:

1. Theft, where the value exceeds R2 500.00.
2. Receiving stolen property, where the value exceeds R2 500.00.
3. Theft by false pretence, where the value exceeds R2 500.00.
4. Fraud, where the amount involved exceeds R1 500.00.
5. Extortion, where the amount involved exceeds R1 500.00.
6. Forgery and uttering, where the amount involved exceeds R1 500.00.
7. An offence referred to in the Prevention and Combating of Corrupt Activities Act, 2004, where the amount involved exceeds R1 500.00.
8. Malicious injury to property, where the amount involved exceeds R1 500.00.
9. Common robbery.
10. Assault involving the infliction of grievous bodily harm (GBH).
11. Public violence.
12. Culpable homicide.

13. Arson.
14. Housebreaking with intent to commit an offence.
15. Administering a poisonous or noxious substance.
16. Exposing an infant.
17. Abduction.
18. Sexual assault where GBH has not been inflicted.
19. Compelled sexual assault where GBH has not been inflicted.
20. Compelled self-sexual assault where GBH has not been inflicted.
21. Compelling or causing persons 18 years or older to witness sexual offences, sexual acts, or self-masturbation.
22. Exposure or display of, or causing the exposure or display of, child pornography or pornography.
23. Incest.
24. Sexual acts with a corpse.
25. Flashing.
26. Violating a dead body or grave.
27. Defeating or obstructing the course of justice.
28. Intimidation.
29. Any offence relating to criminal gang activities referred to in Chapter 4 of the POCA.
30. Any contravention of Section 2 of the Animals Protection Act, 1962 (Act 71 of 1962).
31. Possession of dependence-producing drugs, where the value of the quantity involved exceeds R500.00 but is less than R5 000.00, and where the maximum penalty applicable is less than five years' imprisonment or a fine not exceeding R50 000.00.
32. Any other statutory offence where the maximum penalty applicable is imprisonment for more than three months but less than five years, or a fine not exceeding R50 000.00.
33. Any conspiracy, incitement, or attempt to commit any offence referred to herein.

Failure to appear in court while released on CJA prosecutor's bail has the same effect as failure to appear while released on CPA prosecutor's bail. Accordingly, Section 67 of the CPA applies.[738] A detailed analysis of failure to appear while released on bail is provided in paragraph 10.1.2.

---

[738] Section 25 of the CJA makes it clear that Chapter 9 of the CPA applies to a child's release on bail. The guidelines on the relationship between the CJA and the CPA contained in Schedule 5 of the CJA also show that Section 67 is applicable.

CHAPTER 18

PROCEDURES TO BE FOLLOWED ON THE FIRST APPEARANCE OF A CHILD CLIENT

18.1 Procedures on the first appearance of a child generally

Children under the age of 12 years lack criminal capacity.[739] Although a police officer may not arrest such a child, the probation officer must be informed.[740] The probation officer will assess the child and determine the appropriate intervention under the circumstances.[741] The focus at this stage is protective and rehabilitative rather than punitive.

Where a child is 12 years old but not yet 14 years old, there exists a rebuttable presumption of criminal incapacity.[742] In deciding whether to prosecute a child older than 12 but younger than 14 years, the prosecutor must take the following factors into account:[743]

1. "the educational level, domestic and environmental circumstances, age, and maturity of the child";
2. the nature and seriousness of the alleged offence;
3. the impact of the offence on the victim;
4. the interests of society;
5. the assessment report of the probation officer;
6. the prospects of proving criminal capacity if the matter were to be referred to the child justice court;
7. "the appropriateness of diversion"; and

---

739 Section 7(1) of the CJA. The age increase from 10 to 12 has been effected by the Child Justice Amendment Act 28 of 2019.

740 Section 9(1) of the CJA.

741 Section 9(2) and (3) of the CJA.

742 Section 7(2) of the CJA as amended by the Child Justice Amendment Act 28 of 2019.

743 Section 10 of the CJA as amended by the Child Justice Amendment Act 28 of 2019. Also see the Child Justice Act (75/2008): Directives by NDPP in terms of Section 97(4), No. R. 252 (31 March 2010) para D2.

8. "any other relevant factor".

These considerations underscore that prosecution of children within this age bracket is not automatic, but must follow a careful and balanced assessment of the child's developmental stage, the surrounding circumstances, and the broader interests of justice.

Where criminal capacity cannot be established, the prosecutor is obliged to refer the child to a probation officer to be dealt with as if the child were under the age of 12 years.[744] In such instances, the matter proceeds within a child-protection framework rather than through the criminal justice system.

18.2 Assessment

The child, accompanied by a parent, guardian, or appropriate person, should arrive early on the day of the preliminary inquiry. This ensures that sufficient time is available for the probation officer to conduct the assessment before the inquiry commences.[745] Unless expressly exempted or excluded by the probation officer, a parent, guardian, or appropriate person must be present during the assessment.[746]

Legal practitioners and prosecutors do not attend the assessment. Notwithstanding their absence, it is essential that the legal practitioner understands the purpose and scope of the assessment in order to properly explain the process to the child and the accompanying adult. A clear explanation of what to expect assists in reducing anxiety, fostering trust in the process, and enabling the child to participate meaningfully. Proper preparation also promotes cooperation and ensures that the assessment proceeds in a manner consistent with the best interests of the child. The principal purposes of the assessment are to:[747]

1. determine whether the child is in need of care and protection;
2. estimate the age of the child, where necessary;
3. establish whether the child has previous convictions, previous diversions, or pending matters;

---

[744] Child Justice Act 75 of 2008, Directives by the NDPP in terms of Section 97(4), No. R. 252 (31 March 2010) para E2.

[745] Sections 34–40 of the CJA regulate the assessment of the child.

[746] Section 38(2) of the CJA.

[747] Section 35 of the CJA.

4. identify appropriate measures where a child under the age of 12 years is alleged to have committed an offence;
5. determine whether an adult may have used or influenced the child to commit the offence; and
6. assess the prospects of diversion.

The assessment, therefore, serves as a foundational step in the child justice process, ensuring that decisions taken at the preliminary inquiry are informed, balanced, and responsive to the child's individual circumstances.

18.3 Diversion by the prosecutor before the preliminary inquiry in Schedule 1 offences

On the morning of the child's first appearance, the legal practitioner should engage the prosecutor to confirm the precise charge preferred against the child. This engagement is not merely procedural; it is strategic. Confirmation of the charge determines whether the matter falls within Schedule 1 of the CJA and, consequently, whether diversion before the preliminary inquiry is competent.

Under the CJA, a prosecutor is empowered to divert a child charged with a Schedule 1 offence before the child appears at a preliminary inquiry.[748] Such a diversion does not take effect automatically; it must be made an order of the court.[749] Furthermore, where diversion occurs at this early stage, only Level 1 diversion options contemplated in Section 53(3) of the CJA may be utilised.[750]

Section 51 of the CJA sets out the objectives of diversion. Diversion is a central mechanism through which the Act gives effect to its restorative, child-centred, and developmentally appropriate philosophy of child justice. The objectives of diversion are to:

1. deal with the child outside the formal criminal justice system in appropriate cases;
2. encourage the child to accept accountability for the harm caused;

---

[748] Section 41 of the CJA.
[749] Section 42 of the CJA.

[750] Section 54(2) of the CJA.

3. address the particular needs and circumstances of the individual child;
4. promote the reintegration of the child into his or her family and community;
5. provide an opportunity for those affected by the harm to express their views regarding its impact;
6. encourage the rendering of some symbolic benefit or compensation to the victim;
7. promote reconciliation between the child and the person or community affected by the offence;
8. prevent stigmatisation and the adverse consequences flowing from formal criminal proceedings;
9. reduce the potential for re-offending;
10. prevent the child from acquiring a criminal record; and
11. promote the dignity, well-being, and self-worth of the child, as well as the child's ability to contribute meaningfully to society.

These objectives underscore the restorative and rehabilitative ethos of the CJA, which prioritises accountability, healing, reintegration, and long-term development over punitive intervention.

Before diverting a child before the preliminary inquiry, the prosecutor must be satisfied that:[751]

1. the child accepts responsibility for the commission of the offence;
2. such acceptance is voluntary and not the result of undue influence;
3. a prima facie case exists against the child; and
4. the child and the parent, appropriate adult, or guardian consent to the diversion.

These safeguards ensure that diversion is informed, voluntary, and supported by a sufficient evidential basis.

Notwithstanding that an offence falls within Schedule 1, the prosecutor may not divert the child before the preliminary inquiry where:[752]

1. the facts or circumstances of the offence are of a serious nature;
2. the child has a previous conviction, a previous diversion, or a pending matter of a similar or more serious nature; or
3. the prosecutor forms the view that the child may be in need of care and protection, including where the child:
   a) has been abandoned or orphaned and lacks visible means of support;
   b) displays behaviour beyond the control of the parent or caregiver;
   c) lives or works on the streets or begs for a living;
   d) is addicted to drugs and lacks support to obtain treatment;
   e) has been exploited or lives in circumstances exposing the child to exploitation;
   f) lives in or is exposed to conditions that may seriously harm the child's physical, mental, or social well-being;

---

[751] Section 52(1) of the CJA

[752] The Child Justice Act (75/2008): Directives by NDPP in terms of Section 97(4), No. R. 252 (31 March 2010) para G6.

g) may be at risk if returned to the custody of a parent or caregiver;
h) is in a state of physical or mental neglect;
i) is being maltreated, abused, deliberately neglected, or degraded by a parent, caregiver, person with parental responsibilities and rights, family member, or any person under whose control the child is;
j) is a victim of child labour;
k) resides in a child-headed household; or
l) engages in conduct rendering the child unsuitable for diversion.

In such circumstances, the matter should proceed to the preliminary inquiry, where broader considerations relating to the child's circumstances and possible protective interventions may be addressed.

In respect of Schedule I offences, consultation with the victim, any person with a direct interest in the victim's affairs, and the investigating officer is encouraged where practicable, but is not mandatory.[753] Although not a jurisdictional requirement, meaningful consultation enhances transparency, supports the restorative objectives of diversion, and strengthens confidence in the process.

18.4 Preliminary inquiry

Where a child has been assessed by a probation officer and the prosecutor elects not to divert the matter in terms of section 42 of the CJA prior to the preliminary inquiry, the child must be brought before a magistrate for the holding of a preliminary inquiry.

The preliminary inquiry is an inquisitorial, informal, and pre-trial procedure established by the CJA. It is presided over by a district magistrate, sitting as an inquiry magistrate, and is ordinarily conducted in chambers. The purpose of the preliminary inquiry is to determine the most appropriate manner in which to deal with a child alleged to have committed an offence, within a child-friendly and non-intimidating environment.[754] It is not a trial, but rather a screening and case-management mechanism designed to give practical effect to the restorative and protective framework of the CJA.

---

[753] See the Child Justice Act (75/2008): Directives by NDPP in terms of Section 97(4), No. R. 252 (31 March 2010) para F9 and G2.

[754] Section 43(1) of the CJA.

The preliminary inquiry constitutes the child's first appearance in court.[755] Consequently, where the child has been arrested and is in detention, the child must be brought before the preliminary inquiry within 48 hours of arrest, in compliance with constitutional and statutory requirements.[756] The persons who must attend the preliminary inquiry are the prosecutor, probation officer, inquiry magistrate, legal practitioner, court support staff (i.e. the interpreter and court clerk), the child, and the child's parent, appropriate person, or guardian.[757] The presence of these role-players ensures that the inquiry is informed, participatory, and responsive to the child's individual circumstances, while safeguarding the child's procedural rights. The main purpose of a preliminary inquiry is to:[758]

1. consider the assessment report, with particular regard to:
   (a) the age estimation of the child, where it is uncertain;
   (b) whether another or more detailed assessment is necessary;
2. determine whether the prosecutor (in Schedule 1 and Schedule 2 offences) or the DPP (in Schedule 3 offences) accedes to diversion before plea;
3. identify a suitable diversion option if the prosecutor or the DPP agrees that the child may be diverted;
4. determine whether the child needs care and protection and should therefore be referred to the children's court;
5. ensure that all available information relevant to the child, the child's personal circumstances, and the offence is considered when a decision on diversion and placement is taken; and
6. determine whether the child should be released or placed in a child and youth care centre pending the preliminary inquiry, an appearance at the child justice court, or the children's court.

During the preliminary inquiry, the inquiry magistrate will ask questions to elicit information relevant to the purpose of the proceedings.[759] The court will ask whether the child acknowledges responsibility for the offence

---

[755] Section 43(3) (c) of the CJA.

[756] Section 43(3) (b) of the CJA.

[757] Section 44(1) and (5) of the CJA.

[758] Section 43(2) of the CJA.

[759] Section 47(1) of the CJA.

committed,[760] and whether the prosecutor or the DPP agrees to diversion.[761] Where necessary, a preliminary inquiry may be postponed under strict time limits.[762] The preliminary inquiry may be postponed for a period not exceeding 48 hours where:[763]

1. the child is detained, and the prosecutor indicates that diversion is being considered; however, an assessment has not been conducted but is necessary;
2. it is necessary to:
   (a) secure the attendance of a person who is important for the conclusion of the inquiry;
   (b) obtain information relevant to the conclusion of the inquiry;
   (c) enable the prosecutor to establish the views of the victim regarding diversion and the option being considered;
   (d) make arrangements regarding diversion options;
   (e) find alternatives to detention; or
   (f) assess the child; and
3. further investigations are necessary.

The inquiry magistrate may postpone the matter again for a period not exceeding 48 hours if the postponement is likely to increase the prospects of diversion.[764] However, where the preliminary inquiry remains unconcluded after a second postponement, it must be closed and the matter must be referred to the child justice court,[765] unless the inquiry magistrate postpones the inquiry for a period not exceeding 14 days on the grounds that:[766]

1. the probation officer, in the assessment report or during the preliminary inquiry, recommends that a more detailed assessment be made and the court is satisfied during the preliminary inquiry that such a request is justified; or
2. the prosecutor seeks to obtain the DPP's written approval for diversion in Schedule 3 offences.

The inquiry magistrate may postpone the preliminary inquiry for a period they deem fit if the child needs medical treatment.[767]

---

[760] Section 47(2) (b) of the CJA.

[761] Section 52 of the CJA.

[762] Section 48(1) of the CJA.

[763] Ibid.

[764] Section 48(2) of the CJA.

[765] Section 48(2) of the CJA.

[766] Section 48(2) read with Section 48 (4) of the CJA.

[767] Section 48(5) of the CJA.

18.5 Diversions which may take place during the preliminary inquiry

Although diversion at the preliminary inquiry stage constitutes diversion by the court, it occurs only upon the recommendation of the prosecutor or, where applicable, the DPP.[768] The inquiry magistrate does not initiate diversion independently but considers and confirms a recommendation placed before the court. A child appearing at the preliminary inquiry may still be diverted, even if the child has a previous diversion or prior conviction, provided that all relevant circumstances indicate that the child should be afforded another opportunity and would clearly benefit from the proposed programmes.[769] The process remains individualised and guided by the best interests of the child, balanced against the interests of justice.

During a preliminary inquiry, diversion may occur in one of three categories, depending on the nature of the offence:

1. Schedule 1 diversion;
2. Schedule 2 diversion; or
3. Schedule 3 diversion.

Each category is governed by distinct statutory requirements and levels of intervention, reflecting the seriousness of the alleged offence and the structured approach adopted by the CJA.

18.5.1 Diversion in Schedule 1 offences during the preliminary inquiry

Where a child has not been diverted by the prosecutor prior to the preliminary inquiry, diversion may still be considered at the preliminary inquiry stage.[770] In such instances, the substantive requirements applicable to diversion in Schedule I offences before the preliminary inquiry (as discussed in paragraph 18.3) apply with equal force. Although the diversion ultimately becomes an order of the court, it is granted upon the recommendation of the prosecutor.

---

[768] Section 47(9) read together with Section 52 of the CJA.

[769] Section 52(1) of the CJA. Also see the Child Justice Act (75/2008): Directives by NDPP in terms of Section 97(4), No.R.252 (31 March 2010) para F8.

[770] Section 52(2) of the CJA.

Only Level 1 diversion options are applicable.[771] For Schedule 1 offences, see paragraph 17.4. The Level 1 diversion options include:

a) an oral or written apology to a specified person, persons, or institution;

b) formal caution, with or without conditions;

c) placement under a supervision and guidance order;

d) placement under a reporting order;

e) a compulsory school attendance order;

f) a family time order;

g) a peer association order;

h) a good behaviour order;

i) an order prohibiting the child from visiting, frequenting, or appearing at a specified place;

j) referral to counselling or therapy;

k) compulsory attendance at a specified centre or place for a specified vocational, educational, or therapeutic purpose;

l) symbolic restitution to a specified person, group of persons, community, charity, welfare organisation, or institution;

m) restitution of a specified object to a specified victim or victims, where the object can be returned or restored;

n) community service under the supervision or control of an organisation, institution, specified person, or group of persons identified by the probation officer;

o) provision of a service or benefit by the child to a specified victim or victims;

p) payment of compensation to a specified person, group of persons, community, charity, welfare organisation, or institution, where the child or the child's family is able to afford it; and

q) where there is no identifiable person or group to whom restitution or compensation may be made, the provision of a service or benefit, or payment of compensation, to a community, charity, welfare organisation, or institution.

---

771 Section 53(3) of the CJA.

These options reflect the restorative orientation of the CJA and are designed to promote accountability, reparation, and reintegration while avoiding the adverse consequences of formal criminal prosecution.

Where a Level I diversion option is selected for a child:

a) under the age of 14 years, the order may not exceed 12 months, where a time period is applicable;[772]

b) Where the child is 14 years of age or older, the diversion order may not, where a time period is applicable, exceed 24 months, unless reasons for a longer period are expressly recorded on the record.[773]

In respect of all diversion options, the court may order a child to appear at a family group conference in terms of Section 61 or at a victim-offender mediation in terms of Section 62, on a specified date and at a specified time and place.[774] In appropriate circumstances, the court may further order any other suitable restorative justice option, either as an alternative to, or in combination with, any of the diversion options.[775] This discretion enables the court to tailor the diversion order to the individual circumstances of the child, the nature and seriousness of the offence, and the interests of the victim and the community, while remaining aligned with the restorative objectives of the CJA.

18.5.2 Diversion on Schedule 2 offences during the preliminary inquiry

In respect of Schedule 2 offences, a child may be diverted at the preliminary inquiry after the inquiry magistrate has considered the factors set out in Section 52(1) of the CJA. The following requirements must be satisfied:

1. The child accepts responsibility for the commission of the alleged offence.
2. The child has not been unduly influenced to accept responsibility.
3. There is sufficient evidence implicating the child in the commission of the alleged offence.
4. The child and the parent, appropriate person, or guardian consent to the diversion.
5. The prosecutor consents to the diversion.

---

[772] Section 53(5) (a) (i) of the CJA.
[773] Section 53(5) (a) (ii) of the CJA.
[774] Section 53(7) of the CJA.
[775] Ibid.

Before consenting to diversion in a Schedule 2 matter, the prosecutor should consider the views of the victim or any person with a direct interest in the victim's affairs, consult the investigating officer, and obtain the necessary authorisation from the Senior Public Prosecutor (SPP).[776] These additional safeguards reflect the increased seriousness of Schedule 2 offences and the need for structured oversight in the diversion decision. Only Level 2 diversion options are applicable.[777] These options are more intensive in nature and are designed to address the underlying causes of the child's offending behaviour through structured intervention. Schedule 2 offences are discussed in paragraph 17.5. The Level 2 diversion options include:

1. the Level 1 diversion options referred to in Subsection (3)(j) to (q) and discussed in paragraph 18.5.1;
2. compulsory attendance at a specified centre or place for a specified vocational, educational, or therapeutic purpose, which may include one or more periods of temporary residence;
3. referral to intensive therapy to treat or manage problems identified as a cause of the child coming into conflict with the law, which may include one or more periods of temporary residence; and
4. placement under the supervision of a probation officer, on conditions that may include restrictions on the child's movement outside the magisterial district in which the child ordinarily resides without the prior written approval of the probation officer.

An order exceeding the time period referred to in paragraph (a) may be granted, provided that the reasons are recorded in the proceedings.

Where a diversion option from Level 2 is selected in respect of a child who is:

a) under the age of 14 years, the order may not exceed 24 months, where a time period is applicable;
b) Where the child is 14 years of age or older, the diversion order may not, where a time period is applicable, exceed 24 months, unless reasons for a longer period are expressly recorded during the proceedings.

---

[776] The Child Justice Act (75/2008): Directives by NDPP in terms of Section 97(4), No. R. 252 (31 March 2010) para H10.

[777] Section 53(2) (b).

18.5.3 Diversion on Schedule 3 during the preliminary inquiry

In respect of Schedule 3 offences under the CJA, diversion is not permissible at the prosecutorial level. However, the Director of Public Prosecutions (DPP) may, where exceptional circumstances exist, issue a written indication that the matter be diverted.[778] Prosecutors are under a duty to identify and bring deserving cases to the attention of the DPP where diversion, notwithstanding the seriousness of the offence, appears to warrant consideration.[779] This obligation reflects the overarching principle that the best interests of the child remain paramount, even in cases involving serious offences.

The exceptional circumstances that may justify the DPP recommending diversion include:[780]

1. the presence of compelling mitigating factors relating to the commission of the offence;
2. the child's limited degree of participation in the offence;
3. the child's relatively minor role in a group or syndicate context;
4. the absence of serious physical harm to the victim;
5. genuine remorse demonstrated by the child and a willingness to accept responsibility;
6. a positive assessment report by the probation officer indicating strong prospects of rehabilitation;
7. the child's age, level of maturity, and developmental profile;
8. the existence of strong parental or community support structures;
9. the victim's attitude, particularly where the victim supports or does not oppose diversion; and
10. any other factor indicating that diversion would better serve the interests of justice than formal prosecution.

It is submitted that the existence of exceptional circumstances must be clearly articulated and supported by the contents of the probation officer's assessment report, together with all other relevant information placed before the Director of Public Prosecutions (DPP). Diversion in Schedule 3 matters is intended to remain the exception and must therefore be justified by compelling and objectively demonstrable considerations.

It is further submitted that the assessment of exceptional circumstances must be undertaken cumulatively and contextually. The proper inquiry is not whether the offence is serious—Schedule 3 offences are inherently serious—but whether, having regard to the particular circumstances of the child and the

---

[778] Section 52(3) of the CJA.

[779] The Child Justice Act (75/2008): Directives by NDPP in terms of Section 97(4), No. R. 252 (31 March 2010) para O3 (c).

[780] The Child JusticeAct (75/2008):Directives by NDPP [*supra*] para J2.

specific facts of the case, diversion would better serve the interests of justice than formal prosecution. In light of the constitutional principle that a child's best interests are paramount,[781] it is submitted that the focus must shift to proportionality, individualisation, and the child's prospects of rehabilitation. Where accountability, restoration, and reintegration can be achieved more effectively through diversion, the seriousness of the offence does not, in itself, constitute an absolute bar to such an outcome.

Before issuing a written indication to divert, the DPP must consult with the investigating officer and consider the views of the victim or any person with a direct interest in the victim's affairs.[782] This consultative requirement ensures that the decision is informed, balanced, and consistent with the restorative objectives of the CJA.

Where diversion appears appropriate in a Schedule 3 matter, the legal practitioner is not required to await prosecutorial initiative.[783] Proactive written representations may be addressed directly to the DPP, setting out the exceptional circumstances relied upon and attaching all relevant supporting documentation, including the probation officer's assessment report. Such representations should be structured, evidence-based, and aligned with the statutory framework governing diversion.

Where a child is diverted in Schedule 3 offences, Level 2 diversion options are applicable.[784] For Level 2 diversion options, see paragraph 18.5.2. Given the seriousness of Schedule 3 offences, Level 2 options—which are more intensive and of longer duration—are considered appropriate to ensure meaningful accountability, structured intervention, and effective rehabilitation. Schedule 3 offences under the CJA are the following:

1. Treason.
2. Sedition.
3. Murder.
4. Extortion with aggravating circumstances.
5. Kidnapping.
6. Robbery with aggravating circumstances.
7. Rape or compelled rape.
8. Sexual assault, compelled sexual assault, or compelled self-sexual assault involving the infliction of GBH.

---

[781] Section 28(2) of the Constitution.

[782] The Child Justice Act (75/2008): Directives by NDPP in terms of Section 97(4), No. R. 252 (31 March 2010) para J3.

[783] The Child Justice Act (75/2008): Directives by NDPP [*supra*] para J4.

[784] Section 53(2) (b) of the CJA.

9. Sexual exploitation of children, sexual grooming of children, and using children for or benefiting from child pornography.
10. Exposure or display of, or causing the exposure or display of, child pornography or pornography to children, if that exposure or display is intended to facilitate or promote:
    (a) the sexual exploitation or sexual grooming of a child; or
    (b) the use of a child for purposes of child pornography or to benefit in any manner from child pornography.
11. Compelling or causing children to witness sexual offences, sexual acts, or self-masturbation.
12. Sexual exploitation or sexual grooming of persons who are mentally disabled; exposure or display of, or causing the exposure or display of, child pornography or pornography to persons who are mentally disabled; or using persons who are mentally disabled for pornographic purposes or for benefiting therefrom.
13. Trafficking in persons for sexual purposes and involvement in the trafficking of persons for sexual purposes.
14. Any offence referred to in Parts 1, 2, and 3 of Chapter 2 of the Protection of Constitutional Democracy against Terrorist and Related Activities Act, 2004.
15. Any offence referred to in the Prevention of Organised Crime Act, 1998, which relates to:
    (a) racketeering activities; or
    (b) the proceeds of unlawful activities.
16. The crimes of genocide, crimes against humanity, and war crimes referred to in the Implementation of the Rome Statute of the International Criminal Court Act, 2002.
17. Any offence under any law relating to:
    (a) the dealing in or smuggling of ammunition, firearms, explosives, or armament; or
    (b) the possession of firearms, explosives, or armament.
18. Any offence referred to in Section 13(f) of the Drugs and Drug Trafficking Act, 1992.
19. Any offence of a serious nature where it is alleged that the offence was committed by a person, group of persons, syndicate, or enterprise acting in the execution or furtherance of a common purpose or conspiracy.
20. Any offence under any law relating to the illicit possession of dependence-producing drugs, where the quantity involved exceeds R5 000.00 in value.
21. Any other statutory offence where the maximum penalty determined by that statute is imprisonment for a period exceeding five years or a fine calculated for that period in accordance with the Adjustment of Fines Act, 1991.
22. Any conspiracy, incitement, or attempt to commit any offence referred to in this Schedule.

18.6 Failure to divert the child

The prosecutor is *dominus litis*; accordingly, the decision whether to prosecute or to divert a matter falls within the prosecutor's discretion. That discretion, however, is not unfettered. It must be exercised rationally, in good faith, and in accordance with the statutory framework of the CJA and the Constitution.[785] In particular, the discretion must "be exercised in the best interests of the child in conformity with the Bill of Rights, which demands that the treatment of children take into account their age and discourages the general and unsystematic incarceration of children, which must occur only as a measure of last resort.[786] The prosecutorial decision must, therefore, reflect a proper balancing of the seriousness of the offence, the interests of society, the rights of victims, and, centrally, the developmental needs and rehabilitative prospects of the child.

Although the CJA does not expressly require the prosecutor to furnish reasons to the child or the legal representative for a decision not to divert, the reasons for such a decision must nevertheless be recorded in the investigation diary of the docket (section C), as required by the directives issued in terms of the CJA.[787] The recording of reasons serves as an important accountability mechanism and ensures that the decision is capable of subsequent scrutiny.

Where a decision refusing diversion is disputed, representations may be directed to the Senior Public Prosecutor (SPP), thereafter to the Director of Public Prosecutions (DPP), and, where appropriate, to the National Director of Public Prosecutions (NDPP). Where representations have been unsuccessful at all levels of prosecutorial authority, an application may be brought to review the decision under the principle of legality.[788]

---

785 S v S (A74/14, A395/15, 06/2014) [ZAGPPHC 520] (11 June 2015) para 17.

786 Ibid.

787 The Child Justice Act (75/2008): Directives by NDPP in terms of Section 97(4), No. R. 252 (31 March 2010) para F4.

788 *Van Deventer v National Director of Public Prosecutions NO* (64268/2013) [2015] ZAGPPHC 550 (7 August 2015),para 12.

18.7 Failure to comply with the diversion order

Where a child fails to comply with a diversion order, the inquiry magistrate or child justice court ("the court") may issue a warrant for the child's arrest or direct that a summons be issued to secure the child's attendance.[789] Upon the child's appearance, the court is required to conduct an inquiry into the reasons for the non-compliance and to determine whether the failure is attributable to the child personally.[790] This inquiry is essential to distinguish between wilful disregard of the diversion conditions and circumstances beyond the child's control, such as lack of parental support, logistical challenges, or institutional shortcomings.

If the failure was not attributable to the child, the court may order that the child continue with the same diversion option, add or substitute another diversion option, or issue an order to ensure compliance with the original diversion conditions.[791] Although non-compliance not attributable to the child does not terminate the diversion, it remains a relevant consideration should the child later be assessed for diversion in another matter.[792]

In terms of Section 58(4) of the CJA, where the court finds that the child is personally responsible for failing to comply with the diversion order, the prosecutor may elect either to proceed with the prosecution of the matter or to request the court to impose a new diversion order that is more onerous. That decision should be informed by the circumstances of the case and, fundamentally, by what serves the best interests of the child while maintaining accountability and the integrity of the diversion process.

18.8 Consequences of the diversion programme

Where a child has completed a diversion programme, no prosecution may be instituted against the child based on the same facts.[793] The completion of diversion, therefore, brings finality to the matter and precludes the State from proceeding with a trial arising from the same incident. Furthermore, a diversion order does not constitute a previous conviction.[794] It does not result in a criminal record and may not be treated as such. This is consistent with the

---

[789] Section 58(1) of the CJA.
[790] Section 58(2) of the CJA
[791] Section 58(3) of the CJA.
[792] Section 58(4) of the CJA.
[793] Section 59(1) (a) of the CJA; S v EA 2014 (1) SACR 183 (NCK) at 186d-e; and *S v C.S* (A74/14, A395/15, 06/2014) [2015] ZAGPPHC 520 (11 June 2015) para 19.
[794] Section 59(1) (b) of the CJA.

restorative and rehabilitative objectives of the CJA, which seek to prevent the long-term stigmatisation of children who have accepted responsibility and complied with corrective interventions. However, the fact that a child has previously completed a diversion programme is a relevant consideration when the child is assessed for diversion in a subsequent matter.[795] While it does not automatically disqualify the child from further diversion,[796] it may inform the decision-maker's assessment of suitability, accountability, and the appropriateness of alternative interventions.

18.9 Release of an arrested child by the court at a preliminary inquiry or child justice court

Where an arrested child has not been released by the police official or the prosecutor before the preliminary inquiry in terms of Section 21(2) of the CJA, the inquiry magistrate or child justice court may order the release of the child if such release is in the interests of justice:[797] The court may release the child in any of the following three ways:[798]

1. in respect of any offence, into the care of a parent, appropriate person, or guardian;
2. in respect of Schedule 1 or Schedule 2 offences, on the child's own recognisance; or
3. where the child is not released in terms of the above, on bail.

When considering whether the interests of justice permit the release of the child—whether into the care of a parent, appropriate person, or guardian (for any offence), or on the child's own recognisance (for Schedule 1 and 2 offences)—the court must consider the probation officer's assessment report together with all relevant factors, including:[799]

1. the best interests of the child;
2. the previous convictions of the child;
3. the presumption of a lack of criminal capacity where the child is 12 years old but younger than 14 years;
4. the interests and safety of the community; and

---

[795] The Child Justice Act (75/2008): Directives by NDPP in terms of Section 97(4), No. R. 252 (31 March 2010) para G6 read with Section 35 of the CJA.

[796] Section 52(1) of the CJA. Also see the Child Justice Act (75/2008): Directives by NDPP in terms of Section 97(4), No. R. 252 (31 March 2010) para F8.

[797] Section 21(3) read together with Section 24(1)-(3) and Section 25(2) of the CJA.

[798] Ibid.

[799] Section 24(3) of the CJA.

5. the seriousness of the offence committed.

Where the court considers releasing the child on bail in terms of Section 25 of the CJA, the provisions of Section 60 of the CPA apply.[800] In determining whether the interests of justice permit the child's release, Section 60(4) and Section 60(9) of the CPA are applicable.[801] Furthermore, Section 50(6) of the CPA governs bail applications that have not yet been finalised.[802]

Once the court is satisfied that the interests of justice permit release on bail, it must conduct a separate inquiry into the child's ability to pay bail.[803] The court may not fix bail without properly considering the child's financial circumstances and those of the parent or caregiver. If no amount is affordable, the court must release the child on alternative conditions that do not involve the payment of money.[804] This ensures that detention does not result solely from poverty and that pre-trial release remains consistent with the child-centred and rights-based framework of the CJA.

18.10 Transfer of a matter to the child justice court

If the child is not diverted and the matter is not withdrawn, the inquiry magistrate must transfer the case to the child justice court for trial.[805] The proceedings thereafter continue in accordance with the ordinary plea and trial procedures prescribed by the CPA, read together with Chapters 9 and 10 of the CJA.[806]

During the preliminary inquiry, where diversion is not contemplated, the inquiry magistrate is obliged to enquire from the prosecutor whether sufficient evidence is available to proceed to trial, or whether there is reason to believe that further investigations are likely to result in the necessary evidence becoming available.[807] The inquiry magistrate must record the prosecutor's response and formally refer the matter to the child justice court.[808]

The CJA imposes strict limitations on the period for which matters may be postponed in the child justice court before the commencement of trial.[809] These limits reflect the constitutional imperative that children be dealt with

---

[800] Section 25(1) of the CJA.
[801] Ibid.
[802] Section 66(3) of the CJA
[803] Section 25(2) (b) of the CJA.
[804] Section 25(2) (c) (i) of the CJA.
[805] Section 47(9) of the CJA.
[806] Section 63(1) (b) of the CJA.
[807] Section 47(9) of the CJA.
[808] Ibid.
[809] Section 66 of the CJA

expeditiously and that detention be used only as a measure of last resort and for the shortest appropriate period. The permissible postponement periods are as follows:

1. Child detained in prison: not more than 14 days at a time before the trial commences.[810]
2. Child detained in a child and youth care centre: not more than 30 days at a time before the trial commences.[811]
3. Child who has been released: not more than 60 days at a time before the trial commences.[812]

These statutory timeframes are per postponement and do not permit open-ended adjournments.

A matter that was not diverted at the preliminary inquiry stage may nevertheless still be diverted in the child justice court at any time before the closure of the State's case.[813] The opportunity for diversion, therefore, remains open during the early stages of the trial process.

In such instances, the same jurisdictional requirements applicable to diversion—determined by the relevant Schedule of the offence—must be satisfied. The availability of diversion at this stage reinforces the flexible, restorative framework of the CJA and ensures that formal prosecution remains a measure of last resort where appropriate.

---

[810] Section 66(2) (a) of the CJA.
[811] Section 66(2) (b) of the CJA.
[812] Section 66(2) (c) of the CJA.
[813] The Child Justice Act (75/2008): Directives by NDPP in terms of Section 97(4), No. R. 252 (31 March 2010) para 11.

BIBLIOGRAPHY

BOOKS

Du Toit E et al *Commentary on the Criminal Procedure Act* (2023 RS 70)

Joubert C *Applied Law for Police Officials* (2018)

Kruger A *Hiemstra's Criminal Procedure* (2016) Van Blerk P *Legal Drafting: Civil Proceedings* (2015)

Van Loggerenberg D.E. *Erasmus Superior Court Practice* (2015)

ARTICLES

Ballard C "Research report on remand detention in South Africa: An overview of the current law and proposals for reform" 2011 *Civil Society Prison Reform Initiative*

Bruce D "The risks of police custody: the potential for independent monitoring of police custody in South Africa" October 2019 *African Policing Civilian Oversight Forum Research Paper*

Combrinck H "'He's out again': the role of the prosecutor in bail for persons accused of sexual offences" 2001 *Law, Democracy & Development*

de Ruter N and Hardy K "Study on the use of bail in South Africa" May 2018 *African Policing Civilian Oversight Forum Research Paper.*

De Villiers, W.P. "The interdictum de homine libero exhibendo and the question whether it is incumbent on a peace officer to consider less invasive means to secure attendance at court before effecting an arrest – National Commissioner of Police v Coetzee" 2014

Dr Curlewis L "Sugar-coating guilt: admission of guilt fines – no easy fix" April 2014 *De Rebus*

Du Toit PG and Ferreira GM "Reasons for prosecutorial decision" 2015 *Potchefstroom Electronic Law Journal*

Jules-Macque R "Exploring substance use among South African adult and young offenders" 2015 *National Institute for Crime Prevention and the Reintegration of Offenders*

King B "Commentary on the Adjustment of Fines Act, 1991 (Act 101 Of 1991)" July 2007

E-Mantshi

Mohapi S "Revised checklist for leave to appeal to the SCA" April 2015 *De Rebus*

Mokoena UCA & Lubaale EC "Decolonising prisons in South Africa: the need for effective bail affordability inquiries" December 2018 *South African Crime Quarterly*

Paizes A and van der Merwe S July 2018 *Criminal Justice Review*

CASES

A

S v Acheson 1991 (2) SA 805 (NM)

African Paper Products (Pty) Ltd and Another v Director of Public Prosecutions: Eastern Cape and Another (250/2020) [2022] ZAECMKHC 90 (31 October 2022)

Alehi v S (A173/2021) [2021] ZAGPPHC 492; 2022 (1) SACR 271 (GP) (10 August 2021)

AmaBhungane Centre for Investigative Journalism NPC and Another v Minister of Justice and Correctional Services and Others; Minister of Police v AmaBhungane Centre for Investigative Journalism NPC and Others (CCT 278/19; CCT 279/19) [2021] ZACC 3; 2021 (4) BCLR 349 (CC); 2021 (3) SA 246 (CC) (4 February 2021)

American Natural Soda Ash Corporation and Another v Competition Commission of South Africa (554/2003) [2005] ZASCA 42; [2005] 1 CPLR 1 (SCA); [2005] 3 All SA 1 (SCA); 2005 (6) SA 158 (SCA); 2005 (9) BCLR 862 (SCA) (13 May 2005)

Areff v Minister van Polisie 1977 (2) SA 900 (A)

B

S v Baleka 1986 (1) SA 361 (T)

Banger v S (195/2015) [2015] ZASCA 79; 2016 (1) SACR 115 (SCA) (28 May 2015)

S v Barber 1979 (4) SA 218 (D)

Barendse and Another v S (A01/2023) [2023] ZAWCHC 125 (22 May 2023)

S v Block (1897/10) [2010] ZANCHC 56; 2011 (1) SACR 622 (NCK) (12 November 2010)

S v Boekhoud (2011) (2) SACR 124 (SCA)) [2011] ZASCA 48; 522/10 (30 March 2011)

S v Botha en 'n Ander [2001] ZASCA 146 (30 November 2001); [2002] 2 All SA 577 (A); 2002 (1) SACR 222 (SCA)

Brown and Another v S (CC 18/2017) [2018] ZAECPEHC 76; 2019 (1) SACR 691 (ECP) (14 December 2018)

S v Bruintjies (676/2002) [2003] [ZASCA 4 (25 February 2003)

C

Carmichele v Minister of Safety and Security (CCT 48/00) (2001) ZACC 22 (16 August 2001)

S v C.S (A74/14, A395/15, 06/2014) [2015] ZAGPPHC 520 (11 June 2015)

S v Chao and Others 2009 (1) SACR 479 (C)

Cikolo v S (CA55/2023) [2024] ZAECMKHC 21 (14 February 2024)

S v Conradie (A248/2020) [2020] ZAWCHC 177 (11 December 2020)

Cooper v District Magistrate, Cape Town (WCC) (1699/2017) [2017] ZAWCHC 140; 2018 (1) SACR 369 (WCC) (24 November 2017)

Crossberg v S (439/2007) [ZASCA] 93 (22 August 2007)

Cuniff v Tshite and Others (2000) 3 All SA 554 (T)

D

S v Dane 157 (2) SA 472 (N)

Davis and Another v S (2888/2015) [2015] ZAKZDHC 41 (18 May 2015)

De Klerk v Minister of Police (329/17) [2018] ZASCA 45 (28 March 2018)

De Klerk v Minister of Police (CCT 95/18) [2019] ZACC 32 (22 August 2019)

Deyi v S (A16/13) [2013] ZAGPPHC 75 (6 March 2013)

S v Diale and Another 2013 (2) SACR 85 (GNP)

S v Dikhusooka (18/2002) [2002] ZANWHC 25 (20 June 2002)

Director of Public Prosecutions, Northern Cape v Brooks and Others (505/19) [2020] ZASCA 80 (2 July 2020)

S v Dlamini, S v Dladla and Others; S v Joubert; S v Schietekat (CCT21/98, CCT22/98, CCT2/99, CCT4/99) [199] ZACC 8; 1999 (4) 623; 1999 (7) BCLR 771 (3 June 1999)

Dludla v S (R210/2018) [2018] ZAFSHC 137 (13 September 2018)

Doorewaard and Another v S (CAB33/2018) [2018] ZANWHC 87 (6 December 2018)

Doorewaard and Another v S (CC33/2017) [2019] ZANWHC 25 (23 May 2019)

Du Toit v The Magistrate and Others (733/2015) [2016] ZASCA 15; [2016] 2 All SA 328 (SCA); 2016 (2) SACR 112 (SCA) (11 March 2016)

E

S v EA 2014 (1) SACR 183 (NCK)

Earl Rensburg v Minister of Police and Another (557/2021) [2022] ZASCA 105 (29 June 2022)

S v Edipute (CA&R45/2018, 20180024) [2018] ZAECGHC 13 (22 February 2018)

S v Elgin (274/21) [2021] ZAWCHC 147; 2022 (1) SACR 325 (WCC) (5 August 2021)

F

Factaprops 164 v Strydom Bouers CC 1977 (4) SA 135 (W)

S v Fani and Others 1994 (1) BCLR 43 (E) at 46B-H; 1994 (3) SA 619 (E)

S v Fhetani (158/2007) [2007] ZASCA 113; [2007] SCA 113 (RSA) (21 September 2007)

Flanagan v Minister of Safety and Security (497/2017) [2018] ZASCA 96 (1 June 2018)

S v Frederick; S v Maxhongo (18531; 18532) [2018] ZAWCHC 89; 2018 (2) SACR 686 (WCC) (11 July 2018)

G

Genesis One Lighting v Jamieson and Others (19/3212) [2019] ZAGPJHC 93 (18 March 2019)

Gininda v Minister of Safety & Security (1322/2016) [2019] ZAECMHC 35 (25 June 2019)

S v Gqoki and Others (CC14/2018) [2020] ZAECMHC 63 (26 February 2020)

Groves N.O. v Minister of Police (CCT 223/22) [2023] ZACC 36; 2024 (1) SACR 286 (CC); 2024 (4) BCLR 503 (CC) (14 November 2023)

Goane Jack Montshiwa (Ex Parte Application) (672/2021) [2023] ZASCA 19 (3 March 2023)

Gombe v S (CA&R 06/2024) [2024] ZAECMHC 22 (2 May 2024)

S v Green and Another (008/06) [2006] ZASCA 3; 2006 (1) SACR 603 (SCA) (3 March 2006)

Gumede v S (A51/2017) [2021] ZAMPMHC 22 (24 May 2021)

Gcwabe v S (CA&R 03/2012 [2012] ZAECPEHC 23 (17 April 2012)

H

S v Hewu and Others (170002) [2017] ZAECGHC 44; 2017 (2) SACR 67 (ECG) (06 April 2017)

S v Hlongwa 1979 (4) SA 112 (D)

S v Houtzamer (B7968969/08) [2015] ZAWCHC 25 (10 March 2015)

I

Isaacs v Minister van Wet en Orde [1995] ZASCA 152; 1996 (1) SACR 314 (A)

In re Vorster 1997 (1) SACR 269 (O)

J

R v Jones 1952 (1) SA 327 E

Jonkers v Minister of Police and Another (10702/2016) [2018] ZAGPJHC 693 (20 December 2018)

Jozela v Minister of Police (2011/05017) [2013] ZAGPJHC 272 (1 November 2013)

K

Kara and Others v S (A 218/22; F563/2022) [2022] ZAWCHC 258 (1 December 2022)

S v Kgogong 1980 (3) SA 600 (A)

Khumalo and Another v Minister of Police (958/2017&959/2017) [2019] ZANWHC 9 (21 February 2019)

Khumalo v S (A262/2016) [2016] ZAGPPHC 685 (11 August 2016)

Killian v S [2021] ZAWCHC 100 (24 May 2021)

S v Kock (670/02) [2003] ZASCA 1; [2003] 1 All SA 551 (SCA); 2003 (2) SACR 5 (SCA) (14 February 2003)

S v Kondile (11/2020) [2021] ZAECBHC 3 (12 February 2021)

Kula v S (CAB 02/2023) [2023] ZANWHC 35; 2023 (2) SACR 52 (NWM) (4 April 2023)

L

Lelaka v S (CAF10/2014) [2014] ZANWHC 34 (10 October 2014)

S v Lerumo and Others (08/2017) [2017] ZANWHC 63; 2018 (1) SACR 202 (NWM) (10 August 2017)

S v LJ (346/22) [2023] ZAWCHC 6; 2023 (1) SACR 396 (WCC) (24 January 2023)

Levenstein v S (890/12) [2013] 4 All SA 528 (SCA) (1 October 2013)

S v Levenstein (317/04) [2006] ZAGPHC 108 (20 December 2006)

Luna Meubel Vervaardigers (Edms) Bpk v Makinand Another (t/a Makins Furniture Manufacturers) 1977 (4) SA 135 (W)

S v Luzil (18294) [2018] ZAWCHC 75; 2018 (2) SACR 278 (WCC) (19 June 2018)

M

S v M (CCT 53/06) [2007] ZACC 18; 2008 (3) SA 232 (CC); 2007 (12) BCLR 1312 (CC) (26 September 2007)

S v Mabena and Another (373/06) [2006] ZASCA 178; [2007] 2 All SA 137 (SCA); 2007 SACR 482 (SCA) (17 October 2006)

Madlala v S (A387/2013) [2014] ZAGPJHC 258; 2015 (2) SACR 247 (GJ) (13 June 2014)

Mafe v Acting Director of Public Prosecutions Western Cape and Another (871/2022) [2022] ZAWCHC 63; 2022 (2) SACR 54 (WCC) (29 April 2022)

Mafe v S (A49/22) [2022] ZAWCHC 108 (31 May 2022)

Magano v Magistrate Johannesburg and Others 1994 (2) 304 (W)

Mahendren v S (SSCC3/2022; A34/2022;10/2/5/2-2022) [2022] ZAGPJHC 251 (25 April 2022)

Mahlangu and Another v Minister of Police (CCT 88/20) [2021] ZACC 10; 2021 (7) BCLR 698 (CC); 2021 (2) SACR 595 (CC) (14 May 2021)

Mahlanza v Minister of Police (EL1326/2017) [2019] ZAECELLC (26 November 2019)

Majali v S (41210/2010) [2011] ZAGPJHC 74 (19 July 2011)

S v Mashego (R24/2021; A360/2020) [2021] ZAMPMBHC 36; 2021 (2) SACR 520 (MM) (10 August 2021)

Mashilo v Prinsloo (576/11) (2012) ZASCA 146 28 September 2012)

Matebese v Minister of Police (2224/2017) [2019] ZAECPEHC 37 (18 June 2019)

S v Mathebula (431/2009) [2009] ZASCA 91; 2010 (1) SACR 575 (SCA); [2010] 1 All SA 121 (SCA) (11 September 2009)

Matiwane v Regional Court President & another (CA20/2017) [2017] ZANWHC 71; SACR 209 (NWM) (23 November 2017)

S v Matross (47/2019) [2019] ZAWCHC 68 (13 June 2019)

Mazibuko and Another v S (8774/09) [2009] ZAKZPHC 61; 2010 (1) SACR 433 (KZP) (19 November 2009)

Mbaleki and Another v S (2853/2011) [2011] ZAKZDHC 68; 2013 (1) SACR 165 (KZD) (1 April 2011)

S v Mbele and Another 1996 (1) SACR 212 (W)

MEC Department Police Roads & Transport, FS Province v Roberts and Another (A116-2019) [2020] ZAFSHC 23; 2020 (3) SA 478 (FB) (13 February 2020)

Mfeketho v S (CA&R193/2014) [2014] ZAECGHC 67 (21 July 2014)

Mgijima v S (CA&R 13/23) [2023] ZANCHC 18 (28 April 2023)

Minister of Justice and Constitutional Development and Another v Zealand (387/06) [2007] ZASCA 92; 2007 (2) SACR 401 (SCA) (20 June 2007)

Minister of Law and Order v Kader (275/89) [1990] ZASCA 111; 1991 (1) SA 41 (AD); [1991] 1 All SA 256 (A) (27 September 1990)

Minister of Police v Dhali (CA327/2017) [2019] ZAECGHC 16 (26 February 2019)

Minister of Police v Ndaba and Others (A553/2014) [2016] ZAGPPHC 277 (6 May 2016)

Minister of Safety and Security v Sekhoto and Another [2011] (1) SACR 315 (SCA); [2011] 2 All SA 157 (SCA); 2011 (5) SA 367 (SCA)) [2010] ZASCA 141; 131/10 (19 November 2010)

Minister of Safety and Security v Tyokwana, (827/13) [2014] ZASCA 130 (23 September 2014)

Minister of Safety and Security v Van Niekerk (CCT74/06) [2007] ZACC 15; 2007 (10) BCLR 1102 (CC); 2008 (1) SACR 56 (CC) (8 June 2007)

Mkolo and Others v Jacobs and Another (1831/2015) [2017] ZAECGHC 46 (11 April 2017)

S v Mpetha 1981 (3) SA 803 (C)

Mphohoni v National Police Commissioner and Another (608/2011) [2014] ZALMPHC 7 (9 September 2014)

Mofokeng v S (A212/2021) [2021] ZAGPPHC 522; 2022 (2) SACR 184 (GP) (12 August 2021)

Molefe v S (A129/18) [2018] ZAGPPHC 271 (18 April 2018)

Mokoena v S (200/2018) [2019] ZASCA 74 (30 May 2019)

Motsi v S (A37/22) [2022] ZAWCHC 151; 2023 (1) SACR 218 (WCC) (15 August 2022)

Mququ v S (CA&R78/2019) [2019] ZAECGHC 55; 2019 (2) SACR 207 (ECG) (14 May 2019)

S v Mthembu (379/07) [2008] ZASCA 51; [2008] 3 All SA 159 (SCA); [2008] 4 All SA 517 (SCA); 2008 (2) SACR 407 (SCA) (10 April 2008)

Mthimkhulu v Minister of Law and Order 1993 (3) SA 432 (E)

Munsamy v S (A34/2022) [2023] ZAGPJHC 972 (29 August 2023)

Mvambi v S (A113/2021) [2022] ZAGPJHC 157 (4 February 2022)

Mvu v Minister of Safety and Security and Another (07/20296) [2009] ZAGPJHC 5; 2009 (2) SACR 291 (GSJ); 2009 (6) SA 82 (GSJ) (31 March 2009)

Mwelase v Minister of Social Development and Others (CA74/16) [2018] ZAECMHC 16 (22 March 2018)

N

Naidoo and Others v National Director of Public Prosecutions and Others (06/2004) [2005] ZASCA 23(29 March 2005)

Naidoo v Minister of Police (20431/2014) [2015] ZASCA 152; [2015] 4 All SA 609 (SCA); 2016 (1) SACR 468 (SCA) (2 October 2015)

S v Naidoo (A 293/2011) [2011] ZAWCHC 448; 2012 (2) SACR 126 (WWC) (6 December 2011)

Naidoo v Regional Magistrate for Durban Magistrates' Court, Mr M Maharaj and Another

(AR769/14) [2017] ZAKZPHC 19; 2017 (2) SACR 244 (KZP) (23 May 2017)

Namlela and Another v S (Bail Appeal) (CA&R 16/2024) [2024] ZAECGHC 25 (7 March 2024)

National Commissioner of Police v Coetzee (649/11) [2012] ZASCA 161 (16 November 2012)

National Director of Public Prosecutions v King (86/09) [2010] ZASCA 8; 2010 (2) SACR 146 (SCA); 2010 (7) BCLR 656 (SCA); [2010] 3 All SA 304 (SCA) (8 March 2010)

S v Ndibe (14/544/2010) [2012] ZAWCHC 245 (14 December 2012)

Nel and Others v S (A508/2017) [2017] ZAGPJHC 296; 1018 (1) SACR 576 (GJ) (17 October 2017)

S v Ngete (25/2023) [2023] ZAWCHC 116 (19 May 2023)

S v Nkogatse 2002 (2) SACR 369 (TPD)

Nkuna v S (A324/2022) [2023] ZAGPPHC 55 (26 January 2023)

Nkwentsha v Minister of Law and Order, RSA & another (554/86) 1988 ZASCA 33; [1988] 2 All SA 420 (A) (30 March 1988)

Nwabunwanne v S (CA&R114/2016) [2017] ZANCHC 9; 2017 (2) SACR 124 (NCK) (31 January 2017)

O

Omotoso and Others v S (CC 15/2018) [2018] ZAECPEHC 81 (30 October 2018)

Omotoso v S (CC15/2018) [2020] ZAECPEHC 43 (4 November 2020)

P

S v Packham (CC50/2018) [2018] ZAWCHC 183 (20 December 2018) *Panayiotou v S and Others* (CC26/2016) [2016] ZAECPEHC 50; 2017 (1) SACR 354 (ECP) (20 September 2016)

Pataka v S (A337/2017) [2018] ZAGPJHC 73, 2018 (2) SACR 135 (GJ) (23 April 2018)

S v Permall (171172) [2017] ZAWCHC 143; 2018 (2) SACR 206 (WCC) (8 December 2017)

S v Petersen (A717/07) [2008] ZAWCHC 11; [2008] 3 All SA 301 (C); 2008 (2) SACR 355 (C) (27 February 2008)

Phadi and Another v S (A1/2024) [2024] ZAFSHC 169 (3 June 2024)

Pharmaceutical Manufacturers Association of South Africa and Another: In re Ex Parte President of the Republic of South Africa and Others (CCT31/99) [2000] ZACC 1; 2000 (2) SA 674; 2000 (3) BCLR 241 (25 February 2000)

Phaswane v Minister of Police (735/2014) [2018] ZALMPPHC 48 (6 September 2018)

Porritt v S (SS40/2006) [2018] ZAGPJHC 45 (2 March 2018)

S v Porritt [full bench] (A202/2018) [2018] ZAGPJHC 698 (10 December 2018)

S v Porta 2004 (2) SACR 242 (WCD)

S v Porthern and Others (A736/2003) [2003] ZAWCHC 36 (21 August 2003)

Pretorius v S (CC91/2003) [2011] ZAGPPHC 65 (29 April 2011)

Prokureur-generaal van die Witwatersrandse Plaaslike Afdeling v CJ van Heerden en Andere 1994 (2) SACR 469 (W)

R

S v Rabele (76/2014) [2016] ZAFSHC 178 (29 September 2016)

S v Rademeyer (A186/17) [2017] ZAGPPHC 175 (12 April 2017)

Raduvha v Minister of Safety and Security and Another (CCT151/15) [2016] ZACC 24; 2016 (10) BCLR 1326 (CC); 2016 (2) SACR 540 (CC) (11 August 2016)

Ramabele v S; Msimango v S (CCT 232/17; CCT 207/18) [2020] ZACC 22; 2020 (11) BCLR 1312 (CC); 2020 (2) SACR 604 (CC) (16 September 2020)

Ramasia v S (A24/2012) [2012] ZAFSHC 88 (3 May 2012)

Ramonyathi v S (A470/2014) [2014] ZAGPPHC 915 (23 October 2014)

Ranana v S (CA&R15/ 2017) [2017] ZAECPEHC 48 (10 October 2017)

Republikeinse Publikasies (Edms) Bpk v Afrikaanse Pers Publikasies (Edms) Bpk 1972 (1) SA 773 (A)

Rodrigues v National Director of Public Prosecutions and Others (1186/2019) [2021] ZASCA 87; [2021] 3 All SA 775 (SCA); 2021 (2) SACR 333 (SCA) (21 June 2021)

Rudolph v S (484/2009) [2009] ZASCA 133; 2010 (1) SACR (SCA); [2010] 2 All SA 178
(SCA) (30 September 2009)

S

S v S K (Reasons: Cancellation of Bail) (CC21/2023) [2024] ZANWHC 152 (3 June 2024)

Sanderson v Attorney-General, Eastern Cape (CCT10/97) [1997] ZACC 18; 1997 (12) BCLR 1675; 1998 (2) SA 38 (2 December 1997)

Savannah Country Estate Homeowners Association v Zero Plus Trading 194 (Pty) Ltd and Others (773/2022) [2024] ZASCA 40 (4 April 2024)

Savoi v S (722/11) [2011] ZASCA 335; 2012 (1) SACR 438 (SCA) (1 December 2011)

Sedi v S (A35/2024) [2024] ZAFSHC 90 (15 April 2024)

Seleko v Minister of Police (931/2011) [2014] ZANWHC 47 (30 October 2014)

Sesing v S (A11/2019) [2019] ZAFSHC 9 (25 January 2019)

Setlhapelo v Minister of Police and Another (45031/2012) [2015] ZAGPPHC 363 (20 May

2015)

Setwaba and Others v De Souza NO and Others (M90/16) [2016] ZANWHC 30 (3 March 2016)

Shabalala v Attorney-General of the Transvaal and Another (CCT23/94) [1995] ZACC 12; 1995 (12) BCLR 1593; 1996 (1) SA 725 (29 November 1995)

Shabangu v S (A727/2014) [2014] ZAGPPHC 832 (17 October 2014)

S v Shaik and Others (CCT 86/06) [2007] ZACC 19; 2008 (2) SA 208 (CC); 2007 (12) BCLR 1360 (CC); 2008 (1) SACR 1 (CC) (2 October 2007)

Sibeko v S (BA17/2020) ZAMPMHC 13 (30 May 2020)

Sikwe v SA Mutual Fire & General Insurance 1977 (3) SA 438 (W)

Sinqu v S (CA&R31/2016) [2016] ZAECBHC 14 (21 December 2016)

Sithole and Others v S (25/2016) [2017] ZAFSHC 160 (12 September 2017)

S v Sithole and Others (7032/11) [2011] ZAKZDHC 36;2012 (1) SACR 586 (KZD) (19 August 2011)

Skhosana v S (BA16/2020) [2020] ZAMPMHC 10 (27 May 2020)

S v Smith and Another 1969 (4) SA 175 (N)

Songono v Minister of Law and Order 1996 (4) SA 384 (E)

R v Stinchcombe [1991] 3 SCR 326; 18 CRR (2d) 210; 68 CCC (3d) 1 (SCC)

Sulani v Mathiya and Another (9246/2016) [2018] ZAECPEHC 2; 2018 (2) SACR 157 (ECP) (2 February 2018)

T

Tafeni v S (A282/2015) ZAWCHC 150; 2016 (2) SACR 720 (WCC) (16 October 2015)

Terblanche v S (CA&R 05/2022) [2022] ZAECQBHC 36 (4 October 2022)

Terry v Botes and Another (1868/2002) ZAWCHC 22; [2002] 3 All SA 798 (C); 2003 (1) SACR 206 (C) (30 April 2002)

Thandani v Minister of Law and Order 1991 (1) SA 702 (E)

S v Tong (1287) [2012] ZAWCHC 169; 2013 (1) SACR 346 (WCC) (7 September 2012)

S v Tseko (04/2022) ZANWHC 195; 208 (NWM) (25 October 2023)

Tsose v Minister of Justice 1951 (3) SA 10 (A)

V

Van As v Additional Magistrate Cape Town and Others (18052/2022) [2023] ZAWCHC 170; [2023] 4 All SA 231 (WCC) (24 July 2023)

Van Der Walt and Another v Director of Public Prosecutions and Another (1281/2019) [2021] ZAE- CGHC 64; [2021] 4 All SA 251 (ECG); 2022 (1) SACR 320 (ECG) (13

July 2021)

Van der Westhuizen v S (CC 11 of 2018) [2018] NAHCMD (28 September 2018)

Van Deventer v National Director of Public Prosecutions NO (64268/2013) [2015] ZAGPPHC 550 (7 August 2015)

S v Vanqa 2000 (2) SACR 371 (TkHC)

Van Wyk v S, Galela v S (20273/2014, 20448/2014) [2014] ZASCA 152; [2014] 4 All SA 708 (SCA); 2015 (1) SACR 584 (SCA) (29 September 2014)

S v Vermaas 1996 (1) SACR 528 (T)

S v Viljoen (286/2002) [2002] ZASCA 81; [2002] 4 All SA 10 (SCA); 2002 (2) SACR 550 (SCA) (27 August 2002)

S v Visagie 2009 (2) SACR 70 (W)

W

W.S.L and Another v The Minister of Police and Others (6467-2020) [2024] ZAGPJHC 181;2024 (1) SACR 546 (GJ) (19 February 2024)

Y

S v Yanta (CC44/2021) [2023] ZAWCHC 23 (1 March 2023)

Yuma v S (A09 / 2022) [2022] ZAMPMBHC 7 (3 February 2022)

Z

S v Z G (70/W 3389548) [2019] ZAWCHC 45; 2019 (2) SACR 162 (WCC) (27 February 2019)

Zondi v S (SS15/2017) ZAGPJHC 82; 2020 (2) SACR 436 (GJ) (8 April 2020)

Zwakala v S (CA&R10/23) [2023] ZANCHC 20 (14 April 2023)

LEGISLATION

Adjustments of Fines Act 101 of 1991

Child Justice Act 75 of 2008

Child Justice Amendment Act 28 of 2019

Criminal and Related Matters Amendment Act 12 of 2021

Judicial Matters Amendment Act 15 of 2023

Criminal Procedure Act 51 of 1977

Constitution of the Republic of South Africa, 1996

Prevention of and Treatment of Substance Abuse Act 70 of 2008

Probation Services Act 116 of 1991

Promotion of Administrative Justice Act 3 of 2000

South African Police Service Act 68 of 1995

Superior Courts Act 10 of 2013

INTERNATIONAL CONVENTIONS

United Nations Convention against Torture and Other Cruel, Inhuman or Degrading Treatment or Punishment Assembly resolution 39/46 of 10 December 1984

GOVERNMENT NOTICES

Code of Conduct for all Legal Practitioners, Candidate Legal Practitioners and Juristic Entities GN 162 in GG 42337 on 29 March 2019

Determination of Amounts for Purposes of Certain Provisions of the Criminal Procedure Act, 1977 GN R62 in GG 36111 of 30 January 2013

COURT RULES

Magistrates' Court Rules of 2010

Uniform Rules of Court: Rules Regulating the Conduct of the Proceedings of the Provincial and Local Divisions of the High Court of South Africa

Supreme Court of Appeal Rules

COURT DIRECTIVES AND MEMORANDA

Criminal Practice Directives for the Regional Court of South Africa 2023

Gauteng Provincial Division [Pretoria] Practice Directives

KwaZulu-Natal Provincial Division [Pietermaritzburg] Practice Directives

Limpopo Provincial Division [Polokwane] Practice Directives

Norms and Standard Directive of the Chief Justice, 28 February 2014

Supreme Court of Appeal Practice Directive 2014

The Memorandum to Practitioners regarding Procedure in the Pretoria Urgent Motion Court Roll

NPA POLICIES

Child Justice Act (75/2008): Directives in terms of Section 97 (4), No. R. 252 (31 March 2010)

National Prosecuting Authority Policy Directives Issued by NDPP 01 June 2014

National Prosecuting Authority's Prosecuting Policy, Revised in June 2013

SAPS STANDING ORDERS AND NATIONAL INSTRUCTIONS

Circular 1/1/4/1 Dated 2019/11/19 Instructions Relating to Arrest and Detention of Suspects

National Instruction 2 of 2010 Children in Conflict with the Law

National Instruction 6 of 2014: The Prevention and Combating of Torture of Persons

National Instruction 8 of 2016: Medical Treatment and Hospitalization of a Person in Custody

National Instruction 11 of 2019: Arrest, Treatment and Transportation of an Arrested Person

National Instruction 13 of 2019: Management of Persons in Custody of the South African Police Service, para 21 (3)

Standing Order (G) 361 *Handling of Persons in the Custody of the Service from Arrival at the Police Station*

Standing Order (G) 341 *Arrest and the Treatment of an Arrested Person until such Person is Handed Over to the Community Service Centre Commander*

★

DEPARTMENT OF JUSTICE GUIDELINES

A Practical Guide: Court and Case Flow Management for the Regional and District Criminal Courts in South African Lower Court Division

INDEX

Numerical

A

B

C

D

E

F

H

I

J

L

S

T

U

W

Y

www.ingramcontent.com/pod-product-compliance
Lightning Source LLC
LaVergne TN
LVHW060034210926
848481LV00013B/3859